The Makii Social Policy ii.

THIRD EDITION

From the Poor Law to New Labour

KATHLEEN JONES

continuum
LONDON • NEW YORK

Continuum

The Tower Building   15 East 26th Street
11 York Road   New York
London   NY 10010
SE1 7NX

First published in 2000
Reprinted 2005

British Library Cataloguing in Publication Data
*A catalogue record for this book is available
from the British Library*

ISBN 13: 978-0-8264-8062-0

Library of Congress Cataloging in Publication Data
*A catalog record for this book is available from
the Library of Congress*

Distributed in The United States, Canada and South America by
Transaction Publishers
390 Campus Drive
Somerset, New Jersey 08873

Contents

Figures

Tables

Introduction

When the first edition of this study was published in 1989, the Thatcher Government, which set out with the intention of demolishing the 'welfare state', was still in power. Mrs Thatcher's resignation took place when the book was in press. A decade later, the mechanisms of that policy are much clearer. The present edition includes a longer and more informed account of the Thatcher years, an assessment of the social policy of the Major Governments, and a preliminary analysis of the first three years of the Blair administration, bringing the study up to the eve of the Millennium. Some of the early material on the Poor Laws has been condensed to make room for the additional chapters.

If it was a fairly rash exercise to try to condense 160 years of social policy into a single introductory text, it is still more rash to add another ten years – particularly ten years in which welfare principles have been again challenged and reformulated. A. J. P. Taylor reflected that 'history gets thicker all the time, because there are more people, more events, and more is written about them'. This last period is particularly thick as we move into the age of the Internet and information overload.

Why attempt such a difficult task? Why not stop with the events of 1990, and leave other writers to tackle the 1990s? There are several reasons. Students have found the book useful. The publisher asked for a new edition; and the study of Social Policy is open-ended: social policy analysts do not draw a line between 'the past' and 'the present day' as historians do. Each generation brings fresh questions and new insights, and the ideas and events of the 1990s offer some remarkable changes and challenges in policy formation; but the most important reason is that we are living in a society where the very idea of learning from history is being discounted. Some Post-Modernists maintain that anything that happened before globalization and information technology is simply irrelevant, and talk of 'the end of history'. This rather glib proposition needs to be challenged. If the past is irrelevant, and the present is 'post-modern', where do we go from there? Claims to be 'modern' or 'post-modern' tend to look distinctly shabby when society has moved on to the next phase. What will Post-Modernism look like in another ten, fifty or a hundred years, and what can the next new movement possibly be called? Meanwhile, are we to go on re-inventing the wheel because we no longer look at what we can learn from past efforts?

People do not change as fast as machines, and many of the problems of Social Policy are endemic. Wealth creation may possibly end Want if we achieve a more just distribution of income; but Beveridge's other four giants – Disease, Ignorance, Squalor and Idleness – are not so easily tackled. Since Beveridge, we have come to recognize other problems – notably those of social discrimination in terms of social class, gender, ethnicity, age and disability. By now, attempts to secure social justice for all these groups also have their history.

Finally, the last quarter of this story is my own story. I was a child in the early 1930s. I can remember the dole queues of shivering men in thin jackets, and the smell of poverty and the smell of fear. In 1942, as a student, I queued at His Majesty's Stationery Office in London to buy the Beveridge Report. 'Social Security from the cradle to the grave' said the tabloids. It seemed possible, then. When the 'welfare state' machinery was being set up, I was lecturing for the WEA, trying to make the changes comprehensible to groups ranging from naval officers to the Women's Co-op. In the 1960s, I was given the job of founding a Department of Social Administration in one of the new 'plateglass' universities. We changed its name to the Department of Social Policy when it became apparent that our subject was not about running a bureaucratic state machine, but about formulating responses to diverse and changing social problems. In the 1970s, we ran courses for senior Social Work and NHS staff, to help them cope with the new administrative frameworks introduced in the period of expansion. In the 1980s, we worked hard to maintain Social Policy research and teaching against a Government which distrusted anything with 'social' in the title; and in the 1990s, we have shared in the general upheaval as less abrasive governments have struggled to reformulate the problems and the solutions in a fast-changing world.

So this is a time to look back – not in anger, and not with sentimentality, but in an attempt to clarify and understand. The making of Social Policy is sometimes obscure and sometimes surprising, but it is always interesting.

Kathleen Jones
York

Acknowledgements
Professor Jonathan Bradshaw and Professor John Ditch of the University of York have been helpful in offering comments and criticisms on the final chapters. Dr John Lockhart helped in the drafting of Chapter 14, and we had some long and interesting discussions which were of great assistance in evaluating recent changes. I am very grateful to all three, and I should like to make it clear that they are not responsible for the views expressed, or for any errors in the text.

CHAPTER ONE

The Poor and the Poor Law

Between 1832 and 1834, the Whigs set out to bring a new humanity and a new efficiency to government. They introduced factory reform, prison reform, the abolition of slavery and the foundation of local government in the towns; and while these enlightened measures were going through Parliament, they set about reforming the Poor Laws. One of the basic questions of Social Policy is why their Poor Law reforms turned out to be illiberal and inefficient.

Earlier governments had tried to reform an antiquated system. The Younger Pitt had tried in 1797, and failed. A Select Committee of the House of Commons had considered the matter in 1816, but had been defeated by the complexity of the issues. So in 1832, the consolidating Poor Law Act of 1601 (43 Eliz. c.2) was still in force. It provided a set of arrangements – hardly a system – for a predominantly rural society, based on some 15,000 separate parish authorities.[1] Overseers carried out the work of poor relief under the jurisdiction of the local magistrates: some were humane, some were harsh; some were efficient, some were muddled; some were honest, some corrupt.

From the 1660s, when population movement from the rural areas to the towns threatened to overwhelm the town parishes, the law required that paupers should be given relief only in their parish of settlement – usually the parish in which they were born. The vagrancy laws were an older method of controlling movement from place to place, designed to deal with such undesirables as tramps, poachers and gypsies, who might be consigned to the local gaol for the crime of 'wandering without visible means of support'. The days when they were tied to the back of a cart and whipped through the streets were over, but in the early nineteenth century, people who were genuinely seeking work might find themselves confined to the local Bridewell, forced to work for a month, often on the tread-mill, to cover the cost of their transport, and then sent back where they came from. Though there was a need for labour in the new manufacturing areas – Birmingham, Leeds, Manchester, Liverpool -the risks of moving to find work were consequently high. When economic hardship forced whole families to move in from the country, there was near-panic in the city vestries. Harassed overseers spent much of their time in arguing about which parish was responsible for particular paupers, and moving them about the country.

Probably most parishes were more lax in their treatment of paupers in times of prosperity, when the better-off could afford to pay the poor rate and there were fewer claimants. In times of economic depression, when the need was greatest, they had less to give, and more needy people to provide for. By the time the Whig Government turned its attention to the subject, the traditional patterns of village organization were no longer adequate to cope with the problems. The Enclosure Movement, by which wealthy and powerful landowners took over common land and devoted it to the profitable practice of sheep-farming, had destroyed many village communities. Sheep required only a shepherd, while mixed farming or corn-growing were labour-intensive. The villagers lost their jobs and their grazing rights simultaneously. Between 1761 and 1844, nearly 4,000 pri-vate Acts were passed, enclosing some six million acres of land.[2] The Agricultural Revolution of the first half of the eighteenth century increased the problem, for new techniques of farming and new crops decreased the need for labour even where the farms survived. The drift to the newly industrializing areas intensified, and the massive disruption of the Industrial Revolution completed the change from quiet rural poverty to the bitter and more visible squalor of the crowded towns.

The population was rising rapidly: in 1801, the first national census listed the population of England and Wales as 8,893 thousand; by 1851, it had more than doubled. Vagrancy and destitution were not new factors: what was new was the sheer volume of distress, and the total inadequacy of traditional methods to meet it. People desperately seeking a means of livelihood were flocking to the towns, in spite of the Vagrancy Laws and the Acts of Settlement.

'The men, women, country and houses are *all black*' marvelled the future Queen Victoria when she toured the Midlands in 1832 at the age of thirteen.[3] They lived in hovels or cellars among the belching fumes of the

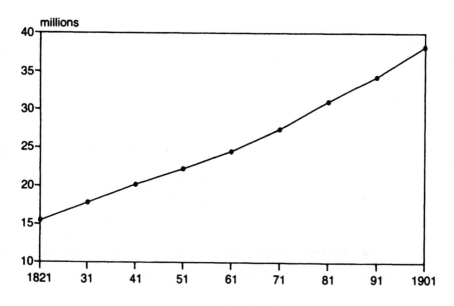

Figure I Population, United Kingdom, 1821–1901
Source: Annual Abstract of Statistics, 1935, table 6.

factories, filthy and hungry and disease-ridden, helpless in the face of a new industrial system which exploited their labour. And they died young.

Even after the Reform Act, the Whigs had little understanding of the new industrial middle classes or their labour force. 'Blackguardly manu-facturers' said Lord Melbourne – not objecting to the way they treated their workforces, but merely indicating that they were not gentlemen. The main problems as the Whig Government of 1832 saw them were chronic under-employment in the rural areas, and the effects of bad harvests. British corn-growers were protected by the Corn Laws, which prohibited the import of foreign corn when the price of corn was low; but bread was the staple diet of the poor, and a bad harvest could mean a winter of near-starvation.

In the late eighteenth century, different parishes had tried a number of expedients to deal with the problems. None of them worked well. There was the 'labour rate', or 'rate in aid of wages', by which employers were encouraged to take men on for less than a living wage, and a supplement was paid from Poor Law funds; but though this increased the number of jobs available, it depressed wages, and the poor rates soared. There was the Roundsman system, which involved collecting all the able-bodied paupers together, and marching them round from farm to farm or from factory to factory, to hire them out at low wages. This led to frequent conflict: the labourers often reacted angrily to the orders of the overseers and the demand that they work for less than they and their families could live on, and the farmers resisted taking on gangs of sullen and angry men. There was parish labour, which meant that the able-bodied paupers were set to work on the roads or in the gravel-pits in their own parishes, and that was no more popular. Some overseers found it less intimidating to introduce schemes of 'relief without labour', enclosing the resentful and humiliated paupers in a stockade during the hours of daylight, or making them walk long distances to claim their relief, or summoning them to frequent and arbitrary roll-calls to prove that they were available for work. There were attempts to introduce a fairly primitive cost of living index, of which the best-known is that introduced by the magistrates of Speenhamland in 1795. This involved tying the level of relief to the price of a gallon loaf, and the size of the family.

The theme of 'setting the poor to work' had been debated again and again in Parliament ever since Tudor times, for it seemed that this surplus labour ought to be capable of being turned to profit. The term 'workhouse' has acquired strong connotations of a different kind since 1834; but before that time, it was a place where able-bodied male paupers were set to work for their families, not a place for the 'impotent poor' – those who were unable to work. A permissive Workhouse Test Act of 1722 allowed any Poor Law authority to set up a workhouse; but many parishes were too small, and their administration was haphazard, so it was not until Gilbert's Act of 1783, which enabled parishes to form Unions with a common policy for poor relief, that the movement spread. But the Labour Rate Acts, the Workhouse Test Act and Gilbert's Act were all permissive measures, adopted in one area and ignored in the next. Expedients were tried and abandoned. The problems seemed insoluble. The numbers of paupers rose, the cost of relief rose, and the frustration and anger rose through the long years of Tory repression. When a Whig government took power in 1830, there was pressure for a radical solution. The new science of Economics was invoked to provide scientific and rational answers to old problems.

The Liberal Economists

Progressive economic thinking of the period was based on Adam Smith's doctrine of *laissez-faire* and the untrammelled operation of market forces.[4] The confused expedients of Poor Law policy were held to be mistaken not because they failed to solve the problem of poverty, but because they involved intervention in the market. The future prosperity of rich and poor alike depended on a free market in labour. The laws of supply and demand would operate to fix wages at their natural level.

Professor Nassau Senior, the Oxford economist who was to head the Poor Law Commission, thought the suggestion that labourers were entitled to a living age was 'monstrous and anarchic'. A proper wage depended on what the employer was ready to pay, not on the needs of the labourer and his family.[5] This bracing doctrine was reinforced by the theories of an Oxford lecturer in Mathematics, the Rev. T. R. Malthus. His *Essay on the Principles of Population*[6] was a curious combination of the new science of economics, the old science of mathematics and the even older art of theology. Malthus was concerned by the lack of congruence between food supply and a rising population. Food was necessary for human existence, and 'the passion between the sexes' showed no sign of diminishing, which meant that there were ever more mouths to feed:

> Population, when unchecked, increases in a geometrical ratio. Subsistence increases only in an arithmetical ratio. A slight acquaintance with numbers will show the immensity of the first power in comparison with the second.

Arithmetical ratio, as Malthus explained, proceeds by addition (i.e. $2 + 2 = 4$, $4 + 2 = 6$, $6 + 2 = 8$ . . .). Geometrical ratio proceeds by multiplication (i.e. $2 \times 2 = 4$, $4 \times 2 = 8$, $8 \times 2 = 16$ . . .). It was inevitable that many children must be born who could not possibly be fed. 'These,' he noted, 'are the unhappy persons who, in the great lottery of life, have drawn a blank.' Vice, epidemics and pestilence would 'advance in terrific array, and sweep off thousands and thousands', and 'gigantic, inevitable famine stalks in the rear, and with one mighty blow, levels the population with the food of the world'. His conclusion was that the poor were to blame for breeding irresponsibly, and that poor relief only encouraged them in irresponsibility.

When Malthus wrote, population was outstripping food supply. Before the days of modern contraception and intensive farming methods, population did outstrip food supply. To that extent, he was right. Any attempt to relieve the condition of the poor would result in the birth of more children, who, in his view, must inevitably die as the grim agents of population control took their toll. Malthus worked closely with David Ricardo, an economist and member of Parliament, who translated his ideas into economic terms in the form of the Iron Law of Wages: labour, like other commodities, was subject to the laws of supply and demand. If the supply of labour was less than the demand, wages would go up. If the supply of labour exceeded demand, wages would go down. But the supply of labour was dependent on the numbers of children reared to working age. If the labourer starved, his family would starve with him, and the children would not live long enough to join the labour force. The supply of labour would drop, wages would increase; but on increased wages, more children would survive. In time, the labour force would be increased, wages would be depressed, and the labourer and his family would be back to starvation level.[7]

Such were the ramifications of what Ricardo called 'the fair and free operation of the market'. These mechanistic ideas were not particularly new in the early 1830s; but they were given a new prominence by the thinking of Jeremy Bentham, the founder of Utilitarianism. Bentham devoted his life to the search for rational principles to replace the 'hotbed of uncertainty' which he found in English government and administration. He looked for a new guiding principle. He was 'in a mizmaze' until he discovered the doctrine of 'the greatest happiness of the greatest number'.

This doctrine needs careful interpretation: it is ironic that the scholar who wanted to reorganize the entire system of law and government in England could not organize his own work. His vast and unmanageable corpus of writing contains many fragments, endlessly revised and annotated, difficult to identify and date; but his biographer, Mary Mack, makes it clear that in his more considered versions of the doctrine, he was not advocating the greatest sum total of pleasure, regardless of the numbers of people involved, nor did he look for the greatest happiness of a simple majority of the people. He meant 'the greatest pleasure and the least pain of all the people involved'.[8] Towards the end of his life, he moved (characteristically, in a footnote) to the view that 'the greatest happiness of *all*, not of the greatest number only, would in the end be aimed at'.[9]

But the damage had been done. The 'greatest happiness' principle was taken to mean that the poor must suffer for the rest of society; and Bentham's exposition of the pleasure–pain principle, or 'hedonistic calculus', was used to provide the means. Bentham observed that human beings sought pleasure and avoided pain. The best and least interventionist form of government therefore involved the utilization of 'the logic of the will' – framing laws and organizing government so that good actions were pleasurable to the individual, and evil or anti-social actions were painful. By this means, social problems could be not merely tackled, but virtually eliminated. It could be argued that to make poor relief painful was good for the poor, since it would lead them to be self-supporting. They would no longer be parasites. They would be given back their dignity.

In his plans for the new Milbank Penitentiary, Bentham developed an ingenious architectural device for dealing with that small proportion of the population who were unable or unwilling to follow 'the logic of the will' and to take responsibility for their own lives. This was the Panopticon – a circular building like a wheel where the inmates were distributed along the spokes and the staff concentrated at the hub. The inmates were thus under continuous surveillance, and unable to take joint action, while a small staff could supervise and quell any disturbances. The Penitentiary, a number of prisons and some asylums followed this design. Some of the prisons are still in use.

The main application of the 'Panopticon' concept was much wider than a design for buildings: it was an administrative design for the government of England. The concept of central government as the all-seeing eye, controlling and setting standards for local authorities, was fundamental to his view of constitutional order. The device of a powerful central government agency with an inspectorate to oversee local bodies was repeatedly employed in legislation in the 1830s and the 1840s. The country squires and magistrates who had been left very much to their own devices in the days of poorer roads and slower travel did not like it; but as the great nineteenth-century engineers built the roads, the bridges, and later the railways, central control became possible.

The New Poor Law

The problem was how the new ideas were to be translated into law. One of the major puzzles of social history in this period is why a political party (soon to be renamed the Liberal Party) which stood for all that was enlightened and progressive at the time introduced a Poor Law system which has become a byword for inhumanity. Some explanations can be found in the economic and constitutional ideas described above. The arguments of the economic theorists were forcefully put, and appeared irresistible; but another set of explanations lies in the continuing fear of revolution and the breakdown of public order. In 1832, when the Poor Law Commission was appointed, England was in a turmoil of civil unrest. Strikes, riots and machine-breaking occurred in at least eighty different parts of the country in that single year.

In the cities, there were marches and demonstrations, and the banners often bore the slogan 'Bread or Blood'.[10] The trade unions, then regarded as subversive organizations, were rumoured to be drilling their men in preparation for the revolution. In the rural areas, hay ricks blazed, land agents were manhandled and the clergy, traditional supporters of the landed gentry, were threatened. Derby gaol was broken into, Nottingham castle was destroyed, and the Bishop's palace at Bristol went up in flames. There was panic in the London clubs and drawing-rooms. William Cobbett, who was to become one of the leaders of the anti-Corn Law and anti-Poor Law movements, travelled the country on horseback, and observed in the North of England 'just the state of things that existed in France on the eve of the Revolution'.[11] The riots were a threatening background to the work of the newly appointed Poor Law Commissioners.

The main work of the Commission was organized by two men: Nassau Senior and Edwin Chadwick, who had been Jeremy Bentham's secretary. Chadwick, a Manchester lawyer of comparatively humble birth, organized the first major social survey in England. Carefully constructed questionnaires were sent out to a sample of some 10 per cent of the 15,000 parish authorities. The Assistant Commissioners carried out follow-up visits, asking supplementary questions of those magistrates, clergy and overseers who had replied, and securing returns from those who had not. They compiled exhaustive reports on their findings.[12] Nassau Senior concentrated on the analysis of the existing system, and Chadwick on the recommendations, which were inevitably on Benthamite lines. They were precise and far-reaching:

Centralization: there would be a Central Board of Control in London, with Assistant Commissioners to act as its inspectors. Local administration would be carried out by paid overseers under their direction.

The Workhouse Test: able-bodied paupers would receive only 'the offer of the house'. Outdoor relief (money payments to paupers living in their own homes) would be abolished, so that entry to the workhouse would be the only alternative to self-maintenance.

Uniformity: the Laws of Settlement would be abolished, to establish a free labour market. Conditions in all workhouses would be the same, so that the pauper would gain no advantage in moving from one parish to another unless in search of work.

Less eligibility: the condition of the labourer in the workhouse would be 'in no case so eligible as the conditions of persons of the lowest class subsisting on the fruits of their own industry'. There would be no incentive to idleness.

Classification: general mixed workhouses would be replaced by well regulated and classified workhouses.

The whole scheme bears the impress of Jeremy Bentham's relentless logic; but the Poor Law Act of 1834 was to be implemented by harsher minds than Bentham's.

Changing the Poor Law

The analysis was accepted by Lord Melbourne's government. It displeased the Tories by its radical nature, and it equally displeased Radicals like Cobbett, who were aware that the problems of the industrial north had been totally ignored in this recipe for the agricultural south. Melbourne himself was not enthusiastic about the Poor Law Bill. He was 'repelled by the idea of dragooning the poor into thrift and industry ... the consequence was that he defended [the Bill] in lukewarm tones, and was heard swearing in a loud angry undertone as he gave his vote for it'.[13]

The Bill became law because the situation was desperate. Only a few months earlier, Melbourne, as Home Secretary, had been responsible for confirming the sentences of transportation on the Dorchester labourers, or Tolpuddle Martyrs: men who had dared to band together to ask for a small increase in their wages. Some 30,000 trade unionists had marched on London in their support. The new economic philosophy seemed to offer a way out of a crisis situation. The investigation had been exhaustive, running to sixteen volumes of evidence. The conclusions were closely argued, and seemed inescapable. Though many reservations were expressed in heated debate in the House of Commons, the Bill passed into law because it was the only solution available.

The Poor Law Amendment Act of 1834 followed all the main points of the Commission's regulations, but it was not implemented as Nassau Senior and Chadwick had planned. Nassau Senior had no desire to be appointed as one of the executive Commissioners himself, but he assumed that Chadwick would be in a position to carry out the new policy. In the event, three prominent men were appointed to the lucrative posts of Commissioner: Thomas Frankland Lewis, a Tory member of Parliament who had been a member of a previous Poor Law enquiry; George Nicholls, manager of the Birmingham branch of the Bank of England, and J. G. Shaw-Lefevre, a personal protégé of Lord Althorp, the Chancellor of the Exchequer. Chadwick's modest social status told against him, and he was merely appointed secretary to the Commission. From the first, the other three, who became known as 'the Uncrowned Kings of Somerset House' went their own way, and ignored their secretary's advice. The real obstacle was Frankland Lewis, who had been appointed to save the Whigs from charges of political bias. He was determined that 'less eligibility' should be translated into whole-hearted deterrence, enforced against all the poor, including the sick, the old and the children.

Differences of purpose and an impossible administrative situation soon led to open conflict. Frankland Lewis attempted to dismiss Chadwick – only to find that, by the terms of his office, he was irremovable. He retaliated by barring Chadwick from the Commissioners' policy meetings.[14]

In the early days of the Commission's work, the Commissioners' interests centred less on the relief of poverty than on the bureaucratic tasks of creating Unions and setting up Boards of Governors to administer them. Within two years, they had combined 7,915 parishes with a total of 6,221,940 inhabitants into 365 Unions. Chadwick's intention had been to utilize the existing parish poorhouses and workhouses for different groups of people in need, rather than housing all a Union's paupers under one roof. He was a Benthamite, not a Malthusian, and a decentralized system with separate accommodation for children, sick people, old people and the able-bodied might have been relatively humane; but some of the existing poorhouses dated from Tudor times, and substantial rebuilding was necessary. Frankland Lewis determined that the whole workhouse system should be replaced, and soon the Commissioners rejoiced that 'the same low, brown homely buildings were going up all over England'.

This decision had three main consequences: the new Union workhouses were more amenable to central control than a scattered system of small establishments; because they were large, their management was formal and bureaucratic; and they were run very cheaply, because the capital expense of rebuilding could only be justified by low running costs.

Classification by need was not possible, but classification by age and sex was rigidly enforced. Men and women were separated, children over the age of seven were separated from their mothers, and the aged from their younger relatives. If families were allowed to remain as units, they would continue to breed, and that had to be avoided at all costs.

Minimal diets were drawn up in great detail in Somerset House. The Commissioners boasted that they knew what every pauper in England had for breakfast; and the provision of meagre and unpalatable food was accompanied by other measures to reinforce the lesson of 'less eligibility'. Paupers had to wear workhouse dress, a badge of shame. Until 1842, silence was enforced at meals. Most bitter of all were the conditions of a pauper funeral: the plain deal coffin, the ban on tolling the church bell. The workhouse became not only the 'uninviting place of wholesome restraint' which Chadwick had envisaged for the idle able-bodied, but an object of dread to every working-class family.

Opposition to the New Poor Law

The new policy was widely opposed and widely hated. Even Tories were appalled by it. The *Metropolitan Conservative Journal* exhorted the poor: 'Peasants of England! Be not trodden under like Russian serfs or African slaves!' and even Lord Eldon, a former Lord Chancellor of extreme Tory views, thought it 'the most execrable law that ever was enacted in any Christian country'. But a writer with no less indignation and more literary skill personalized the activities of the Boards of Guardians in the story of a small hungry boy who asked for a second helping. Charles Dickens's first instalment of *Oliver Twist*, published in Bentley's *Miscellany* in February 1837, gave a savage description of the 'parish boy's progress'. Oliver, born in the workhouse of an unmarried mother who died at his birth, challenged the whole structure of the New Poor Law.

Both the radical Press and the Tory Press fought against the Poor Law Commissioners. While Dickens was writing his fictionalized account at white heat for the weeklies, the daily newspapers were reporting real cruelty and inhumanity. John Walter II, editor of *The Times* and a Tory of Tories, called the Act 'an insult to our common sense', and thundered against the power of the centralizers. The *Bradford Argus* – a radical paper in an area where there was much unemployment and poverty – described the Poor Law Act as 'That Act which separated those whom God had joined together, gave a premium to murder, made poverty a crime, starved the poor man, and tried to prove whether he could not live on bread and water.'[15] In the north of England, the radical leaders Oastler and Cobbett addressed huge protest meetings in violent and denunciatory terms, such as Cobbett's description of the Act as 'the damnable, the devilish, the anti-God New Poor Law', 'infernal, anti-Christian, the catechism of hell . . . the devil's own book.'

The workhouse system, designed for unemployed labourers in the rural areas, was no answer to the problems of the manufacturing towns, where the closure of mills and factories brought mass unemployment. The worst problems were in the smaller cotton and wool towns – Huddersfield, Todmorden, Bradford, Bury, Keighley, Preston, Oldham – where there was no possibility of alternative employment. Attempts to impose the workhouse test brought great hardship, and the workhouses overflowed. The Assistant Poor Law Commissioners (charged with the duty of enforcing the workhouse test and banning outdoor relief in the north) went literally in fear of their lives.[16] Chadwick wrote to Lord John Russell in 1838 that one had been 'pursued by wild persons intent on assassinating him', another 'had been shot at, a third manhandled, while others had been driven out of the towns by threats'. The policy of banning outdoor relief in the north was never fully implemented.

In Parliament, criticism of the New Poor Law was vocal; and in 1837, a Select Committee of the House of Commons was set up to study the situation. Its report records faithfully the cruelties, the public unrest and the political struggles at Somerset House; but in spite of the public outcry, the Commissioners remained in power until 1848. The scandal in 1846, when hungry paupers in the Andover workhouse were found to be eating the gristle and sucking the marrow from bones they had been given for sorting,[17] was the high point of public revulsion, and led to their removal from office. The three Commissioners were replaced by a Poor Law Board whose President was a member of the Government, and thus directly answerable to Parliament. The extreme rigours of 'less eligibility' were dropped, and some local diversity developed; but the mark of the New Poor Law, the shame and privation of pauperism, continued to sear the public memory.

It is possible to view the work of the Commissioners from a variety of perspectives: as the vain attempt of politicians with an eighteenth-century cast of mind to deal with nineteenth-century problems; as the failure of economic dogma to solve the problems of human distress; as a tragedy of

Benthamism distorted to purposes Bentham would never have countenanced; as the story of Chadwick defeated by snobbery and jobbery; as a study in class conflict and social control; as the resurgence of a puritan and punitive streak in the English character; as the inevitable result of major social change too long delayed and then too harshly implemented; or as a case study in social policy, illustrating the twists and turns which can occur between the recognition of a problem and the impact of a proposed solution. The story will bear all these interpretations; but the truth is that the issues were very complicated – much more complicated than the solutions – and the situation was unprecedented. There was no experience to draw on. In the last resort, the inhumanities of the New Poor Law may have been due more to stupidity than to malevolence.

The Whigs of the 1830s got some things right: they initiated social survey methods, they recognized the need for bold innovation, they realized that new communications implied new administrative patterns; but in the last resort, the basic principles of the Poor Law system they introduced remained untouched for many decades simply because no one could think of anything better.

CHAPTER TWO

Dirt, Disease and Danger

Initially, Chadwick appears to have attached little importance to sickness as a cause of poverty. His formidable mind was engaged with the application of Benthamite principles to the problem of able-bodied paupers, who had to be made to work; but by 1838, after four years of frustration at Somerset House, his interest was caught by the views of three medical colleagues on the Poor Law Commission: that much poverty and misery was caused by sickness, and that much of the sickness could be prevented.

Dr James Kay (later Sir James Kay-Shuttleworth and better known as an educational reformer), was an Assistant Poor Law Commissioner who had been a physician in a poor area of Manchester – Ardwick and Ancoats. His work on *The Moral and Physical Condition of the Working Classes* was already well known.[1] Dr Neil Arnott had worked with Kay on the incidence and causes of fever in London.[2] Dr Southwood Smith was physician to the London Fever Hospital and, like Chadwick, had worked closely with Jeremy Bentham, and absorbed many of his ideas and principles. Southwood Smith delivered the funeral oration over Bentham's body before it was handed, as Bentham directed, to the anatomists. (Bentham's skeleton, dressed in his clothes and installed in his sedan chair, sits in the entrance hall of University College, London, and is regularly carried in procession by the students of that Utilitarian institution.)

All three doctors were concerned at the toll which cholera, typhus, tuberculosis and other diseases took of the population in the poorer districts of the crowded towns. Britain had been a safer place to live in when the population was spread thinly over the country, but the move to the towns had brought new dangers. Between 1821 and 1831, West Bromwich increased its population by 60 per cent, Manchester and Salford by 47 per cent, Bradford by 78 per cent, Glasgow by 37 per cent;[3] and as the poor congregated and multiplied, so endemic, epidemic and contagious disease spread.

In 1834, although bubonic plague had not returned, outbreaks of cholera, typhus, typhoid and 'consumption' created spasmodic attacks of public panic reminiscent of the terrible plague year of 1665, when the death carts had toured the London streets with the cry, 'Bring out your dead'. Cholera first occurred in Britain in 1831–2. There were recurrences in 1848, 1849, 1854 and 1867. Cholera attacked all social classes. It 'struck swiftly and sharply, raising local death rates dramatically, if ephemerally. Cholera frightened people.'[4]

Typhus and typhoid fever were largely diseases of the poor. There were epidemic outbreaks in 1826–7, 1831–2, 1837 and 1846–7, and these coincided, as Dr Southwood Smith had noted,[5] with periods of economic recession and high unemployment. Both were endemic – that is, the incidence rate was high even in the periods between epidemics; and many doctors had reported that it was highest in the poorest quarters of the towns, where people lived in overcrowded conditions in insanitary hovels surrounded by mounds of rubbish.

'Consumption' was also a disease of the poor. In most cases, it was probably tuberculosis, but this now-discarded diagnosis may also have included other wasting diseases, undulant fevers, anaemia and severe malnutrition. In 1796, according to the London Bills of Mortality, it accounted for nearly one-third of all deaths in the Metropolis.

Here was a set of problems which seized Chadwick's attention while he brooded over his exclusion from the decisions of the Poor Law Commission. While the Poor Law Report had concentrated on the problems of the able-bodied poor, he seems to have been increasingly convinced by his medical colleagues that sickness and the early death of the breadwinner were major causes of poverty. He was tough-minded, and often high-handed, but he respected evidence, and he was capable of shifting his position if the evidence warranted it. He became convinced that there were new skills available which could be utilized to provide remedies.

There was a new science of 'vital statistics'. The British Association was founded in 1831. Three years later, its President deprecated the application of statistics to social problems on the grounds that statistical enquiries would 'touch on the mainsprings of feeling and passion'.[6] There was a sense in which he was right, for few subjects were to raise so much feeling and passion in the next two decades. The Statistical Society of London was formed as a breakaway movement from the British Association, and Chadwick became a member and a regular attender.

Through the Statistical Society, he was already in contact with a number of these enquiries, and had exerted some influence on the framing of the Registration of Births, Deaths and Marriages Act of 1836. The initial purpose of this Act was not to collect social statistics, but to end the monopoly of registration held by the clergy of the Church of England, who charged fees for registering marriages and funerals. Local registrars were appointed, and returns were made to the General Register Office in London.

Chadwick was not responsible for the main provisions of the Act, though the general public blamed him for the new bureaucratic procedures, and the notification process was commonly referred to as 'being Chadwicked'.[7] His main interest was in the use which might be made of the returns. He was quick to see the potential for providing information about the causes of death for different age-groups and in different areas. On his suggestion, a clause was included to ensure that when a death was notified, it was accompanied by a medical certificate stating the cause. The returns provided a wealth of information about disease.

Chadwick had a fruitful partnership with Dr William Farr, who was appointed Compiler of Abstracts in the new office of the Registrar-General in 1837. There was a sense in which they were two of a kind. Both were technically civil servants. They shared a sense of outrage at the waste of human life involved in urban squalor; and both were prepared to appeal to anyone who would help their cause – ministers of state, members of the nobility, bishops, academics – over the heads of their immediate superiors. Farr's Annual Reports from the General Register Office were vehement by modern Civil Service standards. For instance, his tenth report states:

> This disease-mist, arising from the breaths of two millions of people, from open sewers and cess-pools, graves and slaughterhouses, is continually kept up and undergoing changes. In one season, it is pervaded by cholera; in another, by influenza; at one time, it bears smallpox, scarlatina and whooping-cough among our children. Like an Angel of Death, it has hovered for centuries over London. But it may be driven away by legislation.[8]

Another new development which offered a promise of improvement was the developing science of civil engineering. Sewers in the big cities were commonly fed from open drains. With the huge increase in population, they were becoming choked, and there were engineers with new ideas on how new drains might be constructed and kept clean. Chadwick's chief adviser on this subject was John Roe, engineer to the Holborn and Finsbury Commission of Sewers. Roe's technical advice was that drains should be in closed pipes, not open; and sewers should be capable of being easily flushed with water, so that they did not silt up. This would involve a major reconstruction of the metropolitan sewage system: sewers would be built to curve rather than having right-angled bends; they would have steep gradients down which the water might run; and they would be 'egg-shaped' with 'a pinched-in base' through which the water would flow with a stronger pressure.[9]

Though Chadwick's public image was that of an aloof and bureaucratic official, he was at the centre of the new Utilitarian movement, with many fellow workers who shared and contributed to his innovatory ideas. If he was cold and abrasive in his relationships with the Poor Law Commissioners, he could show warmth to people who shared his furious distaste for squalor and muddle and incompetence, and who were prepared to match him in industry. Fired with the new ideas of Farr and Roe and their supporters, he turned all his considerable energies to this fresh cause.

The first step was to systematize the evidence. The opportunity came when London suffered an epidemic of influenza and typhoid fever in 1837–8. In the following year, on a motion from the bishop of London, the House of Lords instituted an enquiry into the Sanitary Condition of the Labouring Population of Great Britain. Technically, the enquiry was under the auspices of the Poor Law Commission. Chadwick, Kay, Arnott and Southwood Smith were relieved from their Poor Law duties, and given a fresh sphere of operation, unhampered by the tensions and frustrations of daily battles with the Commissioners.

The Sanitary Report

Chadwick, in charge at last, organized the field. He used the Poor Law machinery to obtain evidence and written reports from Assistant Commissioners, Poor Law Guardians, Relieving Officers and Medical Officers, and approached a wide variety of other individuals with knowledge of the problems of squalor and disease in the towns. In all, he approached over 2,000 possible informants, and most of them replied with detailed evidence. There was 'a flood of written evidence'[10] which he ploughed through with characteristic thoroughness. He read widely, studying reports from other European countries, and paying particular attention to the work of Quetelet, a Belgian statistician who had published a pioneer study comparing population statistics for countries in western Europe in 1827. Chadwick used statistical evidence from countries as far apart as Mexico and Egypt, though he may have been somewhat optimistic about the accuracy of the figures.[11]

Despite all this labour, he was not office-bound. He visited Manchester, Leeds, Macclesfield, Leicester, Edinburgh and Glasgow to see for himself, and proved to have a stronger stomach than some of his companions. At one point he noted:

> My vacation has been absorbed in visiting with Mr Smith and Dr Playfair some of the worst parts of the worst towns. Dr Playfair has been knocked up by it, and has been seriously ill. Mr Smith has had a little dysentery. Sir Henry de la Beche was obliged at Bristol to stand at the end of alleys and vomit while Dr Playfair was investigating overflowing privies. Sir Henry was obliged to give it up.[12]

When Chadwick sent the draft of his report to John Stuart Mill, the acknowledged leader of the Benthamites, he received devastating criticism in return. Mill wrote back acidly to point out 'defects of arrangement', 'numerous typographical errors' and 'occasional ungrammatical sentences'. Chadwick evidently had the humility to profit from this critique, and the self-discipline to revise his work. The final version is cogent, lucid and impressive, and Mill expressed his satisfaction with it.[13]

The report, published in 1842, consists of three volumes – one written by Chadwick, and two consisting of an edited version of the detailed reports on which his conclusions were based. Chadwick starts with an analysis of the deaths in one year, 1838. Two points stand out: there were 56,461 deaths from epidemic, endemic and contagious diseases, 'the great proportion of which are proved to be preventible [*sic*]'. This was equivalent to the entire population of the county of Westmorland (now the southern half of Cumbria). It was as if the entire population of one such county were wiped out annually. Further, the 'annual slaughter' in England and Wales from typhus alone, 'which attacks persons in the vigour of life', was twice that of the Allied casualties in the Battle of Waterloo.

Chadwick goes on to give a catalogue of the problems, drawn from the detailed reports of his many correspondents. It is an unpleasant record, but Chadwick was prepared to make the public face facts without euphemism or evasion. He recorded in blunt terms the problems of 'human refuse' (few houses had water-closets, and some lacked even earth privies); the accumulation of rubbish, which rotted and stank in heaps; the blockage of drains, silted up with excrement; the filthy, fly-infested slaughter-houses; the pale and sickly people, living their short lives surrounded by disease and death before they too succumbed; the young widows, left without a breadwinner, and the abandoned orphans. He estimates that 'nearly 27,000 cases of premature widowhood and more than 100,000 cases of orphanage may be ascribed to removable causes'.[14]

In Wigan, the Poor Law medical officer reported on 'the filthy condition of the town':

> Many of the streets are unpaved, and almost covered with stagnant water, which lodges in numerous large holes which exist upon their surface, and into which the inhabitants throw all kinds of rejected animal and vegetable matters which then undergo decay and emit the most poisonous exhalations.[15]

A number of correspondents reported on poor families living in 'damp, dark cellars'. A medical officer from West Derby wrote of 'a family of thirteen, twelve of whom had typhus fever', lying on the floor without even straw or wood shavings (common substitutes for bedding). In the Axbridge Union in Somerset (which might have been thought to be relatively healthy), the Poor Law Medical Officer described circumstances in which 'filth and poverty go hand in hand without any restriction or control'. In Windsor, under the shadow of the young Queen Victoria's castle, 'a double line of deep, open, black and stagnant ditches' scored the poorer areas of the town, and 'an intolerable stench is perpetually arising, and produces fever of a severe character . . . cases of typhus fever are frequent in the neighbourhood'. The Prince Consort was to die prematurely of typhoid, and the drains of Windsor Castle were blamed for his death.

In Macclesfield 'in a part of the town called The Orchard', one of Chadwick's informants found:

> a most foul and putrid mass, disgusting to the sight and offensive to the smell: the fumes of contagion . . . produces different types of fever and disorders of the stomach and bowels. The people inhabiting these abodes are pale and unhealthy.[16]

He described the 'filthy, putrid gutters' of Carlisle; the insanitary habits of the population of Gateshead, where chamber pots were still emptied out of the window; the condition of the poor of Edinburgh – 'worse off than wild animals'; the agonizing cold and damp in winter, causing rheumatism and chest infections, and the more dreaded heat of summer, when the stench became overpowering, and disease multiplied.

A largely neglected section of the report deals with 'Comparative Chances of Life in Different Classes of the Community'. Chadwick was struggling with imperfect statistics and a lack of statistical technique, and he realized this, complaining of the 'very dangerous errors' which could arise from crude statistical returns. But he initiated the first analysis of mortality by social class, and he provided some disturbing statistics on death-rates, comparing those for urban areas with those for rural areas. These showed that the average age of death for mechanics, labourers and their families in Manchester was 17. In Leeds, it was 19, in Bethnal Green, 16, in Liverpool, 15, but in rural Rutland, it was 38. Though infant mortality statistics had not yet been evolved, Chadwick recognized that the figures for infant deaths pulled down the average. The techniques were rudimentary, but the case for action was proved.

Chadwick ended his report with an argument for state intervention. He was aware that many members of the Whig Government were supporters of a *laissez-faire* philosophy; but he was at pains to demonstrate that both Benthamite theory and practical experience supported the case for state action. He argued that 'the physical evils by which the health, strength and morals of the labouring classes are depressed' could not be remedied by 'private and voluntary exertions'. He pointed out that Parliament had already sanctioned 'legislative interference' for factory reform, reform of conditions in the mines, and the relief of the 'climbing boys', or young chimney-sweeps (all issues which his ally Lord Ashley, later the seventh Earl of Shaftesbury, had brought before the House of Commons).

Chadwick was prepared to be unashamedly interventionist. Efficient drainage, sewerage and town cleansing were matters for government action, and came 'within the acknowledged province of the legislature'.[17] The summary was made with relative brevity and unanswerable logic. Epidemic and endemic diseases in the towns were spread by four factors: refuse, damp, dirt and bad housing. 'These adverse circumstances tend to produce an adult population short-lived, improvident, reckless and intemperate, and with habitual avidity for sensual gratifications.'[18] This passage has been much quoted and misunderstood. Chadwick writes of 'pestilence and moral disorder' made 'fearfully manifest', but on the whole he shows a remarkable avoidance of moral condemnation for his time. He takes the view that the environment degrades the poor, and understands that they snatch the few pleasures they can get: 'Discomfort comes before intemperance . . . workpeople are generally found to have few or no rival pleasures to wean them from intemperance.'[19] He was not judging the poor. He was making an intellectual point on population growth. Malthus had assumed that disease and early death would level the indigent population; but it seemed that the poor bred faster than they died. Chadwick had already noted that, though the poorest districts had the highest death-rates, they also had the highest birth-rates; and he cited the city of Alexandria, 'a seat of pestilence', where, despite a horrific death-rate, the population had more than doubled in twenty-five years.

The conclusions of the report were both clear and coherent. The answer lay in water supply. Pure water could clean the people, the houses and the streets, and flush the sewers. Nor was this all; for sewage suspended in water might be 'most cheaply and innoxiously conveyed to any distance out of towns' and used for liquid manure on the land.

Here was the perfect Benthamite solution – the perfect self-eliminating mechanism. The effluvia of the towns would increase the productivity of the rural areas. The result would be an improvement in the moral condition of the population, a decrease in sickness and suffering, and a remarkable saving in public expenditure. No longer would it be necessary for rubbish to be shovelled up and taken away in stinking carts, for sewers to be scoured by hand. Water would do the task, once the drains and sewers were properly constructed.

The scope of the project was awesome. Reservoirs would have to be constructed to hold the huge quantities of water necessary. It would be necessary to tunnel under every street in every town, laying mile upon mile of pipes; and every house would eventually be connected to them. For this massive undertaking, legislative action was necessary, and all new public works should be 'devised and conducted by responsible officers qualified by the possession of the science and skill of civil engineers'.[20]

The Health of Towns Movement

Chadwick's vision of a more hygienic England impressed the House of Lords, and in 1844, a Health of Towns Commission was set up under the chairmanship of the Duke of Buccleuch. Since all the members were peers, Chadwick was officially only a witness, but he drafted most of the report, and spelled out the legislative implications of the proposals in the Sanitary Report, devising an administrative framework for a new Public Health service. David Roberts notes that this was basically the same Benthamite device which he and Nassau Senior had employed for the Poor Law Amendment Act: a central board in London with inspectors who would supervise the work of consolidated local bodies.[21]

Sir Robert Peel's government was not enthusiastic about the scheme. It had other preoccupations. The Irish Famine occurred in 1844–85, the Corn Laws were finally repealed, and the Conservative Party irretrievably split in 1846. A slogan burned with a hot iron into the wood of a door opposite the Chapter House in Christ Church, Oxford, the last ditch of Tory resistance to the Peelites, remains to this day: it reads 'No Peel', and testifies to the violence of extreme right-wing reaction. It is hardly surprising that Chadwick's ambitious scheme was not a priority in this time of violent political upheaval. Parliamentary passions were roused in the mid-1840s, but not by the prospects of civil engineering. So the Government took no action, apart from framing two minor and largely ineffective pieces of legislation in 1846 – the Nuisances Removal and Diseases Prevention Act, and the Baths and Wash-houses Act. Both were permissive Acts. Many local authorities ignored them. Chadwick wanted a firm national framework and mandatory legislation. The next step was a public campaign.

Chadwick was not officially a member of the Health of Towns Association, founded in 1844. As a public servant, and one with a professional interest in the reforms the Association existed to promote, he preferred not to be directly identified with it. However, Southwood Smith was a member, and Chadwick worked behind the scenes, suggesting courses of action, providing information and writing many of its reports. More than that, as the Association grew, he acquired a new and astonishing popularity. S. E. Finer notes that 'the Public Health movement was approaching its flood-tide, and Chadwick was its hero'.[22] Health of Towns Associations sprang up in most of the cities – London, Birmingham, Manchester, Liverpool and elsewhere. Speaker after speaker quoted Chadwick's analysis. He was supported, not only by his Benthamite colleagues, the public health doctors and the civil engineers, but by many influential figures in the metropolis and the provinces.

In 1847, the City of Liverpool secured a private Act of Parliament, and appointed the first Medical Officer of Health, Dr Duncan. In 1848, the

City of London followed suit, and appointed Dr John Simon (pronounced 'Simone', with the accent on the second syllable). In the same year, Lord John Russell's governrnent brought forward the Public Health Bill to set up the system which Chadwick had designed.

The Public Health Act 1848

A central authority, the General Board of Health, was instituted, with three Commissioners and a secretariat. Municipal corporations were empowered to set up local boards of health to consolidate and extend public health work. They were to appoint staff: a surveyor, an Inspector of Nuisances, a Treasurer, a Clerk and a Medical Officer of Health, this last appointment to be subject to the approval of the General Board of Health in London.

Local boards were given wide powers to deal with sewage and drainage; to ensure that the streets were swept, cleansed, watered, flagged and repaired; to erect public conveniences; to register slaughter-houses and common lodging-houses; to regulate offensive trades such as butchering in slaughter-houses and dangerous chemical trades; to clean and purify 'unwholesome houses'. All new houses constructed after the passing of the Act were to have a water-closet, an ash-pit and drains.

The implementation of the Act must have looked fairly straight-forward. It was clear and unambiguous. It introduced much-needed measures which would benefit all members of the public. It had a wave of public support behind it. The three members appointed to the General Board of Health were Lord Morpeth, later the Earl of Carlisle, Lord Ashley (who became the Earl of Shaftesbury in 1851) and Chadwick, who was at last given full public recognition. Their enthusiasm and commitment were beyond question. It was a moment of triumph. Yet five years later, the Commissioners were summarily dismissed from office. What went wrong?

Action and Opposition

The records read like a Greek tragedy. Everything went wrong. To begin with, the Act itself was defective. It was a permissive Act, which meant that it had to be formally adopted in each area in turn; and while some local authorities, like those for Liverpool and the City of London, saw the necessity only too clearly, there were many vested interests to hold the measure back in others. An element of compulsion was introduced by the ingenious provision that the General Board of Health could enforce action in either of two sets of circumstances: if it received a petition signed by one-tenth of the ratepayers for a particular area, or if the death rate exceeded 23 per thousand population.

David Roberts takes the view that the Public Health Act 'demanded an exact definition of the relations of central and local government', and that the lack of this exactitude was a major feature in its failure. His analysis of the early Victorian opposition to centralization and national inspectorates forms a valuable background to understanding the opposition which the Act aroused. 'Centralisation?' says Mr Podsnap in Dickens's *Our Mutual Friend*, 'No, never in my life-time. Not English.'[23]

A newspaper protest was less dismissive but more vehement: 'How much further are we to go with centralising?' it asked. 'Is it to come to the supply of raiment and food? Is there to be cobbling and baking boards at Whitehall?' Local susceptibilities were offended. The local authorities felt that the new measures were an infringement of their powers. The hatred which the centralized Poor Law had raised was easily transferred to this new centralized body which proposed to regulate English streets, English homes and English sewers.

In fact, the General Board of Health had too little power rather than too much. It could only intervene in an area in response to a public petition or a high mortality rate. It did not even have a permanent inspectorate, and it was poorly funded. There were constant battles with the Treasury over even minor items of expenditure. The Board thus combined the maximum threat with very limited efficacy.[24]

Despite the financial and administrative problems, Chadwick recruited an enthusiastic team of young civil engineers as temporary inspectors. They toured the country, investigating, advising, recommending, and brought some 200 areas under the operation of the Act. There was a massive investigation into water supply in the metropolis, where sewage, discharged into the Thames, was held up at Teddington Lock, and flowed back again. There were battles to be fought with the water companies, which resisted the introduction of a public service. There were more battles to be fought with the vestries and the private cemetery owners. Chadwick had deliberately left the subject of interment out of the Sanitary Report, but he had completed a separate and supplementary report on the subject[25] which described in much detail the grisly conditions to be found in many of the cemeteries of the metropolis. An Interment Act of 1850 gave the General Board of Health power to construct and manage public cemeteries, but there was furious opposition, and not enough money.

All this activity commenced during the period of a cholera epidemic. Cholera came from Asia across Europe and flared up in all the big cities – often in the same places as in the previous epidemic of 1831–2. In the heat of summer in 1849, it hit London. Out of a population of 2.2 million, 14,601 people died before the epidemic waned. In England and Wales as a whole, the total deaths from this epidemic were 72,180. The inspectors toured indefatigably. Chadwick and his colleagues were grossly over-worked. Early in 1849, Chadwick told Lord John Russell that one of his colleagues was 'knocked up', another 'overdone with work' one inspector had the first signs of cholera and another had fever. He commented 'Lord Carlisle [Morpeth] excepted, it may be said the Board of Health is very unwell.'[26]

A stream of memoranda went out from the Board's headquarters in London to the municipal authorities, but these were often counter-productive, since they served only to increase local resistance. In many areas, there were divided authorities – Poor Law Guardians, Cleansing Boards, Sewage Commissioners, all insisting on their own rights, and failing to work together.

The *Lancet* was quick to point out the anomalies of the situation to the medical profession. Here was a General Board of Health managed by two noblemen and a lawyer, prescribing treatment for an epidemic. Civil engineers spent their time analysing mortality statistics; and the only doctor in the team spent his time in organizing street cleansing and the emptying of privies.[27]

To some extent, medical opposition may have been a matter of profes-sional conflict – the traditional healers of the sick resenting the power and prestige of the sanitary engineers. Chadwick had never concealed his thorough contempt for curative medicine, though he was able to work with members of the medical profession like Southwood Smith and William Farr. The medical establishment, represented by the Royal College of Physicians, was firmly devoted to curative medicine. It was in relation to curative medicine that Chadwick made his much-quoted remark, 'I always doubt the success of mere medicine.'[28] What made it 'mere' in his eyes was the unwillingness of the medical profession to take any steps which would eliminate the causes of disease.

There was a substantive issue at stake – the causation of the major epidemic diseases. The Sanitary Report provides ample evidence that Chadwick and his colleagues believed that bad smells were the cause of disease – there are repeated references to 'noxious effluvia', 'poisonous vapours', 'obnoxious atmospheres', 'miasma' and 'stench'. His medical supporters shared this belief.

Farr had referred to a 'disease-mist' over London, and Southwood Smith described the process in precise terms:

> Wherever human beings live together in communities, these large masses of animal and vegetable substances, the refuse of food and other matters essential to human existence, must be always decomposing. If provision is not made for the immediate removal of these poisons, they are carried by the air inspired to the air-cells of the lungs, the thin, delicate membranes of which they pierce, and thus pass directly into the current of the circulation. It has been shown that by the natural and ordinary flow of this current, three distinct and fresh portions of these poisons must be transmitted to every nook and corner of the system every eight minutes of time.[29]

Chadwick put it more briefly: 'All smell is, if it be intense, immediate acute disease.' As Finer comments, he often acted as though the reverse were true: all disease is smell.[30]

This 'miasmatic theory' was basic to the formulation of the new preventive ideas. Southwood Smith adhered to it so thoroughly that he took his granddaughter with him through the wards of his fever hospital, convinced that if patients were clean they could not transmit disease.[31]

> They were not even aware that cholera was a specific infection, as distinct in its nature from plague and typhus as the elephant from the giraffe and camel . . . Cholera was no more than a virulent form of those familiar crowd diseases which killed thousands every year in the slums of the great towns.[32]

In the early 1850s, the bacilli of disease had not yet been isolated, though many doctors believed that they existed. The Royal College of Physicians held to the 'germ theory' or 'theory of specific contagion', concluding that dirt and smells were harmless, and rejecting what they regarded as the unscientific views of the sanitary reformers. With hindsight, we can see that both were right. Bacilli do exist, but they breed faster in dirty conditions. At this time, neither theory could be proved, and each appeared to exclude the other.

The opposition to the General Board of Health piled up: the doctors, the municipal authorities, the local office-holders, the private water companies and their shareholders, the private cemetery companies and their shareholders, the Mr Podsnaps: to these powerful groups could be added others who had their own reasons for desiring the failure of the General Board of Health: the tenement landlords who were alarmed at the prospect of having to make costly improvements to their property; the builders, resistant to building working-class houses with water-closets and piped water supply because working people would not be able to afford them; the factory owners engaged in dangerous trades; the butchers and other shop owners; the older engineers, not trained in the new methods; the ratepayers (since someone had to pay for all the improvements and Chadwick's financial calculations were distinctly sketchy); and finally the Press and Parliament.

A number of newspapers carried out campaigns against the General Board of Health. They included *The Economist*, *John Bull*, the *Standard*, and the *Morning Chronicle*; but the Board's most powerful opponent was John Walter III, editor of *The Times*, who carried out a campaign of extraordinary vindictiveness. He continued his father's earlier campaign against Chadwick's centralizing policy, commenting that if the government had considered that Chadwick was the most efficient representative of all the issues which arose, 'the proper course would have been at once to invest him with a sanitary dictatorship. This, however, was not done, and the results have been what we now witness.'[33] His attacks culminated in the statement that 'We prefer to take our chance of cholera rather than being bullied into health.'

Chadwick was essentially a believer in the power of the senior civil servant. Though he was adept at inducing members of both the House of Commons and the House of Lords to promote his policies, he never really understood the parliamentary system. He had little time for politicians, whose interest in his schemes was relatively superficial. Finer quotes him as saying 'By all means have a Minister – but only as the defender of the chief permanent officers.'[34]

By 1851, both his fellow Commissioners on the General Board of Health were in the House of Lords, having succeeded to family titles. Lord Ashley became the Earl of Shaftesbury and Lord Morpeth the Earl of Carlisle. Chadwick had few defenders in the Commons, and a number of powerful adversaries: Sir Benjamin Hall, champion of the select vestries – the old authorities which Chadwick's new local boards of health were supplanting; John Walter III of *The Times*; Thomas Wakley, the editor of the *Lancet*.

In spite of all the sources of opposition, the Board might have survived into a second term (its initial term of office was five years from its formation in 1849) had it not been for one critical occurrence. In 1853, there was a new cholera epidemic which started in Croydon soon after a local board of health had been set up, and new pipes installed. The suspicion arose that *the cholera was water-borne*. The more water was used in cleansing, the more the cholera spread, and the new sanitation was blamed directly on the activities of the General Board of Health. The matter appeared to be settled by the celebrated affair of the Broad Street Pump.

Dr John Snow had already written a treatise in 1849 entitled *On the Mode of Communication of Cholera*. In the epidemic of 1853, he obtained a list from the General Register Office of deaths from cholera in particular districts of London. He found that there had been 89 deaths in a single week from the area served by one pump in the Broad Street area of central London. He called late one night on the vestrymen of St James's, who were responsible for the area, and advised them to remove the pump handle. When they did so, the deaths from cholera stopped.[35] The miasmatic theory was utterly discredited, and so was the ill-fated General Board of Health.

Chadwick and his colleagues were dismissed. Chadwick, as the salaried member, was given a pension of £1,000 a year. He was then 54 years old, and he lived to the age of 90. Though he continued to investigate a variety of social conditions and to write voluminous reports, he never again achieved public eminence. Finer encapsulates nearly forty years of his subject's life in obscurity in a nine-page chapter headed 'The Spent Prophet'. In Chadwick's old age, a member of the Political Economy Club commented that he babbled 'not of green fields, but of sewage'.[36]

Perhaps the most bitter aspect of his downfall was the constitution of the new General Board of Health: his replacement was Sir Benjamin Hall; but the Board was too generally unpopular for even this administrative somersault to make it palatable. In 1858, it was abolished, and replaced by a Medical Department of the Privy Council under the direction of John Simon. While that body carried on the work of vital statistics, it never attempted the kind of centralized direction which led to the destruction of the General Board of Health.

The Sanitary Act of 1866 provided an appropriate epilogue to the story of the Board's activities. This Act placed all the responsibilities which had been laid down in the 1848 Act, plus some others, such as dealing with overcrowding, smoke abatement and infection, squarely on the municipal authorities. It was mandatory, and not permissive. There was no central control, and no inspectorate.

There was no public outcry this time. The medical profession, given an enhanced status under the Medical Qualifications Act of 1858, was possibly more secure, and less threatened by the sanitary engineers. It could afford to admit the value of prevention in public health, and to make preventive medicine a specialism. The municipal authorities were given both the powers and the duties of public health work to exercise without interference; and there was a greater public awareness of public health hazards than in the early 1850s. Local control had achieved what centralization had failed to do.

CHAPTER THREE

Voluntary Action

While Members of Parliament and civil servants were struggling with the legislation and the apparatus of government necessary for social reform, many other groups and individuals were trying to tackle the worst evils on a voluntary basis. William Beveridge, looking back in 1948 in a survey of voluntary social service, defined three distinct movements: Philanthropy, Mutual Aid and what he called 'Personal Thrift'.[1] Philanthropy was a movement between the social classes, from the haves to the have-nots. Mutual aid was the attempt of working men to support each other against the predictable crises in their lives: unemployment, sickness, disability, old age, and to protect their dependants in the event of their early death. Personal Thrift was a matter of making what provision was possible for oneself.

Philanthropy

Victorian philanthropy is a highly controversial subject. In its own day, and for decades after, it was much admired. Every school history book carried stories of the great pioneers who dedicated their lives to the poor and unfortunate, and fought against great odds. Hospital wards and school houses were named after them, voluntary societies perpetuated their memory. By the middle of the twentieth century, a reaction had set in. There was more awareness of the humiliation often involved for the recipients in being offered (and perhaps having no alternative but to accept) 'charity'; of the way in which psalm-singing and Bible-reading were forced on people with empty stomachs by the well-fed; of the social climbing which often went with charity dinners, charity balls and royal patronage. Derek Fraser expresses this view in a mild but dismissive way:

> The Victorian response to the powerlessness (or, as it was often conceived, the moral weakness) of the individual was an over-liberal dose of charity . . . it was small wonder that self-congratulation was so common a theme in contemporary surveys of Victorian philanthropy. So many good causes were catered for – stray dogs, stray children, fallen women and drunken men: there was apparently no subject which could not arouse the philanthropic urge of the Victorian public.[2]

Yet neither cynicism nor hero-worship will fit the complexities of philanthropic activity in the Victorian period. We should not read back our own current debates about individualism and collectivism into so different a context, and any generalization is likely to be superficial. 'Victorian philanthropy' is an umbrella term for many different activities which took place at many different levels and in almost every community, carried out by thousands, possibly tens of thousands, of people with a variety of motives; and the motives, like most human motives, were very often mixed. Those who are attracted by the altruistic element in philanthropy cannot assume that it was always conducted on a high spiritual plane, or that it was always efficient in meeting the needs of the recipients. Those who are repelled by snobbery and moral coercion cannot dismiss it all on that account. To conclude that all philanthropists were virtuous and self-sacrificing, or that all philanthropists were gratifying their own egos, is to do less than justice to a very complex subject.

The Victorian period lasted over six decades, at a time of rapid and disrupting social change; and philanthropy also changed, both in methods and scope, during that period. There were at least four different, though overlapping phases: small-scale voluntary giving of the kind common in the eighteenth century: a landowner might look after his cottagers, a merchant might bequeath a sum of money for the relief of apprentices or indigent seamen or the aged poor of the parish; pioneer work by outstanding individuals like Florence Nightingale, Lord Shaftesbury, Dr Barnardo, General Booth of the Salvation Army, or Octavia Hill, the housing reformer, who brought particular social evils to the public notice; the work of major national societies and associations, often set up by the pioneers, but sometimes developing out of more widely supported local philanthropic effort; and the activities of the Charity Organisation Society, founded in 1869. The COS attempted to place a mass of unregulated charitable activity on a more constructive basis, but earned a reputation for rigidity and harshness in its approach to poor people. Much of the criticism directed against philanthropy relates to the operations of this organization in the late Victorian period. If any group gave charity a bad name, it was the COS.

Philanthropy could be patronizing, and humiliating to the recipient; but the quotation which is frequently used to demonstrate the class-ridden nature of Victorian philanthropy is highly misleading. The popular version is:

> The rich man in his castle,
> The poor man at the gate,
> God made them high or lowly,
> And ordered their estate.

This verse from the hymn 'All things bright and beautiful' was written by Mrs C. F. Alexander, wife of the Bishop of Derry, in the 1850s. She was a Greek scholar, and a philanthropist in her own right. What she actually wrote was 'God made them, high or lowly'. The comma changes the sense: this was a statement of social equality (rich and poor are both God's creation), not an acceptance of the existing social order.[3]

Who were the pioneers, and what motivated them? As Lord Beveridge points out, many of them were neither rich nor aristocratic, though they all had time to spare from the daily grind of earning a living. Many of them were women. F. K. Prochaska, setting out to fill 'one or two gaps' in the history of philanthropy, found that he was writing a contribution to the history of the emancipation of women as well.[4] Denied many kinds of self-expression – in education, in employment, in politics – leisured Victorian women could find an outlet for their talents in charitable work. Their leisure was, of course, bought at the expense of a much larger number of women who worked as domestic servants for very low wages, and freed them from household responsibilities; but they often used that leisure positively and courageously. They were active in fund-raising – all the way from bazaars and sales of work to the kind of social influence which produced large donations from the masculine empires of industry and commerce. They visited the poor in their homes, in workhouses and hospitals and asylums and prisons. They became acquainted with poverty and sickness and dirt and violence. They learned not merely to manipulate the men who held the power and the purse-strings, but to challenge them openly. They learned to work on committees, to organize, to write minutes and manifestos, to run meetings, and to speak in public. Prochaska quotes in estimate of 1893 that well over half a million women were then working 'continuously and semi-professionally' in philanthropy, while a further 20,000 were 'paid officials' in charitable societies and tens of thousands more worked part-time. He comes to the conclusion that 'the charitable experience of women was a lever which they used to open the doors closed to them in other spheres'[5] and gave them both the experience and the confidence to move on to female suffrage.

Many philanthropists were people of religious conviction. Kathleen Heasman's *Evangelicals in Action*[6] gives a full account of the many philanthropic works undertaken by the Protestant denominations in the nineteenth century: the missions, the relief committees, the ragged schools, the temperance societies, the settlements. The Quaker contribution, characterized by such families as the Frys, Tukes, Cadburys and Rowntrees, was particularly innovative. Roman Catholic, Anglo-Catholic and Jewish groups were to develop their own organizations for social care later, in the second half of the century, but the Evangelicals led the way.

Were the philanthropists sincere, or were they merely paying lip-service to a dominant ideology? We can only answer this by asking – if they were not sincere, what drove them? For driven they were. They worked tirelessly. They went into appalling slums, risked physical attack and disease, and faced lice, bugs and the contempt of their peers for doing so.

Victorian philanthropy was not summed up in the practice of taking soup and calves' foot jelly to the poor – though that kind of gentle, leisured activity survived in country districts, it bore no relationship to the many socially valuable movements which developed in the towns. Philanthropy may not have been well organized, but it was certainly organized.

Voluntary societies developed from the middle of the eighteenth century on; and as communications improved, local movements became national movements. The Annual Register for successive years shows a lengthy and growing list of societies for the Promotion of This or the Abolition of That which were skilled in what we would now call pressure-group activities. Philanthropy involved public meetings, committees, speeches, memoranda, subscriptions, people who could rival Chadwick in their tireless industry and their ability to influence politicians and members of the cabinet. They lobbied ceaselessly, and without mercy.

Philanthropists have often been charged with using the movements which they founded as a means of social control. Many of them certainly preached respectable middle-class values – cleanliness, sobriety, self-improvement and responsibility; and some at least did not realize the inadequacy of these prescriptions for people who lived in disease-ridden squalor on the edge of starvation; but they protected frightened women from violent and drunken men, sheltered neglected and abandoned children, provided schools, cared for social outcasts, and improved housing, providing the evidence and the experience on which the statutory services could later build.

It has been argued that philanthropy was a way of taking the edge off social revolt, and that the real driving force was fear of the mob.[7] This may well have been one motive up to 1848, when the Chartists marched on Westminster; but when Paris, Milan, Naples, Prague, Vienna, Berlin and Budapest were in the hands of revolutionaries, the English Chartists took cabs across Westminster Bridge to present their petition to Parliament in the politest possible manner.[8] The aims of the Chartist movement were mainly achieved in the Parliamentary Reform Acts of 1867 and 1884. There was no danger of revolt after 1848. Social reform turned to more peaceful means of expression, but the philanthropic movement continued to grow in strength.

The best of the philanthropists were neither sentimentalists nor political die-hards. The mild and self-controlled Lord Shaftesbury exploded into anger when he met a lady who objected to the climbing boys going to school in the afternoons, and called her 'a woman who could cut up a child for dog's meat, or for making manure'.[9] When one of Florence Nightingale's shipboard companions gushed 'Oh, let us get straight to nursing the poor fellows', her reply was 'The strongest will be wanted at the washtub.'[10]

It is an over-generalization to say that 'the whole concept of charity was one that tended to degrade rather than uplift the recipient'.[11] There was nothing very uplifting about starving in a garret or dying in a military hospital. At a time when the only statutory service was the dreaded Poor Law, there was no alternative to philanthropic action; but philanthropy did not provide a sufficient structure for meeting need. By the late 1880s, the amount of money involved was very large – voluntary societies in London alone were handling between £5.5 million and £7 million a year;[12] but these huge sums of money were often not being properly accounted for, or directed where they would do most good. The Charity Organisation Society (originally the Society for the Organisation of Charitable Relief and the Repression of Mendicity) argued that charities should co-operate, that individual claims for assistance should be investigated in depth, and that aid should be constructive rather than merely palliative.

This basic argument was sound enough. Modern international charities like Oxfam and War on Want take a similar view; but the COS propounded its views in a manner which was punitive, moralistic and highly offensive to other charities. The foundation of the COS coincided with an important policy statement from the Gladstone Government, known as the Goschen Minute.[13] George Goschen, then President of the Poor Law Board, was concerned to tighten up the Poor Law, which had become comparatively generous (or in his view, lax) in its administration. Local Boards of Guardians had achieved a considerable measure of independence from central control in the preceding twenty years, and some were again giving outdoor relief on a considerable scale. The Goschen Minute was basically a restatement of the Poor Law principles of 1834, but with the concession that, in view of the rapid growth of voluntary charity, a distinction should be drawn between the 'deserving' and the 'undeserving'. The 'deserving' might be helped back to independence by charitable organizations; the 'undeserving' would go to the workhouse.

It is not clear whether this statement was actually inspired by members of the COS, or whether the statement of Government policy inspired them,[14] but it formed the basis of their activities. Many members of the COS were also members of their local Boards of Guardians. They applied themselves with energy to working on both sides of the newly erected fence, apparently experiencing little difficulty in applying their simple binary division. 'Deserving' people were clean, sober, polite and grateful. They had fallen on hard times, but might be assisted back to independence. 'Undeserving' people were dirty, drunken and frequently abusive, lacking a respect for their betters.

The COS never achieved the national status it claimed, and its abrasive methods were widely resented. COS enquiries into individual cases were detailed, severe and highly judgemental, based on the conviction that poverty was a personal failing, and that the poor needed to be forced back into self-sufficiency. They took the view that the poor were being demoralized – turned into beggars of coal tickets, clothes tickets and cash handed out in a manner which encouraged shiftless and irresponsible attitudes.

The COS came into conflict with Dr Barnardo, claiming that his medical qualifications were false, and that he was misappropriating funds.

It was true that Dr Barnardo's original qualifications were somewhat suspect (though he had covered them with a licence from the Royal College of Surgeons by the time the investigation took place), and that he was handling some £30,000 a year without proper accounts, but there was no evidence of malpractice. The COS opposed the Salvation Army with particular bitterness, claiming that its work actually created homelessness.[15] Their approach, both with their clients and with more compassionate relief organizations, was so abrasive that it earned much of the opprobrium which has since been directed against philanthropy in general. Their diagnosis of the problems of large-scale Victorian philanthropy was sound enough; but their proposed cure gave the whole movement a bad name.

Mutual Aid

Mutual aid started spontaneously on a local level. It became the custom for groups of men to meet in the local inn for a drink on pay-day, and to contribute a few pence a week for some common purpose. Dissenters, who did not drink beer, met in the chapel. Such groups served a variety of purposes: good fellowship, exchanging information about available work, providing sickness and burial funds for their members. From these simple beginnings, friendly societies, trade unions, housing associations, people's banks and co-operatives were all to develop.

Some of these groups were trade clubs, having their origins in the craft societies of the Middle Ages. A union of a number of trade clubs was called a 'trade union'. In the eighteenth century, many trade unions were declared illegal because they defended wage rates. As poverty grew and wages were cut, some of the trade unions showed signs of militancy, and in the years after the French Revolution, employers and magistrates saw them as centres of conspiracy and civil unrest.

Rose's Act of 1793 effectively separated the militants from the non-militants by requiring friendly societies to register, and laying down rules for their operation. A friendly society was defined as 'a society of good fellowship for the purpose of raising from time to time by voluntary contributions, a stock or fund for the mutual relief and maintenance of all and every the members thereof, in old age, sickness and infirmity, or the relief of widows and children of deceased members'.

The Act made provision for a register of such societies, and laid down rules for their operation. From that time on, registered friendly societies confined their activities to protecting working men against the predictable dangers of interruption of earnings. Their numbers ran into thousands, and they were never fully counted and classified, though a number of official bodies attempted the task.[16] The Old Amicable Society of Grantham spent five shillings a month on ale, but prudently ruled that the business should be completed before the ale was consumed. The Manchester Unity of Oddfellows was organized by the landlord of the Ropemakers' Arms in Salford. (Jeremy Bentham commented that to run a friendly society in a public house was like 'choosing a brothel for a school of continence' and preferred the concept of 'frugality banks'.)

The provision made by friendly societies varied. Some were primarily burial societies, protecting the working classes against the ever-present fear of a pauper funeral. Some provided for widows and children, or for sick or aged members. Some were 'collecting' societies, precursors of the People's Banks. Some were 'dividing' societies, which had a 'share-out' from time to time, often at Christmas. It was almost exclusively a men's movement, though there were three 'female clubs' in the villages of Cheddar, Wrington and Shipham in the 1790s, which may have owed something to the work of the Somerset bluestocking, Hannah More.

Many of them had curious names, and some had their own rituals and ceremonies. There were Rechabites, Foresters, Oddfellows and Hearts of Oak. There were the Total Abstinence Sons of the Phoenix Society, and the Yorkshire Delight Lodge, and the Halifax Order of the Peaceful Dove. None of them was radical. Radicalism developed in the trade union movement, which had a different and more stormy history.

Trade unions were outlawed altogether by the Combination Acts of 1799 and 1800. Any man found joining with another to demand an increase in wages was liable to a prison sentence of three months, or two months' hard labour. Though the Combination Acts were repealed in 1824, the legal position remained obscure, and any trade union activity – like that of the six Dorchester labourers or 'Tolpuddle Martyrs' – was liable to be treated as a criminal conspiracy in times of unrest. In the more peaceful period of the 1850s and 1860s, the trade union movement spread, mainly in the skilled and relatively well-paid trades. These often developed their own insurance schemes for members, independently of the older friendly societies.

The first housing society was founded in Birmingham in 1781 for the purpose of 'raising by small periodical subscriptions a fund to assist the members thereof in obtaining a small leasehold or freehold property'. By 1874, there were some 2,000. There is an interesting example of a society in Swansea which operated a tontine: members subscribed for five years to buy five houses to let. When only ten members remained alive, they were to have the option of selling or keeping the houses. If they opted to keep them, the tontine would continue until only five were left alive, when they were to be allotted one house each.[17]

Housing societies developed into two rather different kinds of organizations: housing associations, which had a philanthropic element, and built for the working classes; and building societies, which were mainly a means of investment for the middle classes. Many subscribers made quarterly payments – they were not weekly wage earners, who were usually 'spent up' by pay-day. Building societies were not friendly societies, and their legal position was obscure until the passing of the Building Societies Act of 1836.

By the 1820s, few building societies were actually concerned with building houses. Their main activity was in lending money to others at interest. As the Royal Commission of 1872 reported 'Building societies do not build they simply make advances on building.'[18] Cole and Postgate argue that building societies were not a mutual aid movement. They exacted high rates of interest, and if housing prices fell, the house-buyers had to stand the loss. Further, they were a force against social change, because people with a mortgage were afraid of social and economic instability.[19]

People's Banks grew naturally out of the collecting societies. As wages improved for some classes of skilled workers, they needed a safe place to keep their limited reserves. The working man was to become 'his own capitalist'.[20] By the second half of the nineteenth century, there were village banks and municipal banks among many other forms of savings institutions. The Post Office Savings Bank dates from 1861 – an innovation by Sir Rowland Hill, who introduced the penny post.

The co-operative movement had its origins in short-lived workers' co-operatives set up in the eighteenth century, and in the pioneer work of Robert Owen, who bought the New Lanark cotton mills in 1800, and set out to prove that capitalism need not mean exploitation. Owen was a model employer who failed to convince other factory owners of his day that it would pay them to look after their workers. When his attempts to secure factory reform failed, he moved steadily towards Socialism with a scheme to set up 'Villages of Co-operation' where the unemployed would be set to work. Jeremy Bentham was one of many influential people interested in his plans. But Owen parted company with many of his supporters when, long before Marx, he developed a system whereby the currency was based on the human labour employed in production, not on demand and supply. The Owenite villages, including New Harmony, his North American settlement, had a relatively short life; but the idea of linking labour directly to the sale of goods without the intervention of the capitalist class survived. In 1844, a group of flannel weavers in Rochdale set up a shop in a warehouse in Toad Lane to sell their own produce. They were 'followers of Mr Owen', but they dealt in money. The new factor was that they sold at market prices, but gave members of their society a dividend on their purchases which could be reinvested. This encouraged 'moral buying as well as moral selling'.[21] Though the local shopkeepers tried to put them out of business by undercutting their prices, the 'divi' proved a powerful incentive.

In the event, co-operative production did not last for more than a few decades, but co-operative retailing flourished. In the long term, the Co-operative movement did not overturn capitalism, but it became a wide-spread working-class movement with political influence and many services to offer to its members, including adult education and investment.

From 1854, when the Prudential was set up as a joint stock company, mutual aid insurance schemes began to be overtaken by the commercial insurance companies. By 1872, the 'Pru' had more than a million policyholders. A Royal Commission in 1871–4 found that there were some social dangers in this new movement: less scrupulous companies were urging parents to insure sickly children (the infant mortality rate was very high) and to 'have sixpence on grandmother'.[22] Acts of 1875, 1896 and 1909 led to successive restriction of the right to insure the lives of others.

All these developments showed a sturdy independence among the more prosperous and regularly employed working classes, who wanted to distance themselves from the hopelessness and helplessness of poverty. Only the trade unions and the co-operative movement kept their original radical stance. The other mutual aid movements tended to draw the working man into small-scale capitalism.

Self-Help

In *Voluntary Action*, Beveridge avoids the term 'self-help', preferring 'personal thrift'. It is possible that he wanted to keep the subject of individual saving clear of the views of Samuel Smiles, whose book *Self-Help* enjoyed a remarkable success in the late Victorian period. Smiles' views were looking very dated by the time *Voluntary Action* was published in 1948.

'Heaven helps those who help themselves', Smiles announced at the beginning of *Self-Help*, published in 1859. An example of his own philosophy, he was apprenticed to a group of medical practitioners at the age of fourteen (his father died of cholera) and he studied in his spare time, gaining a medical diploma at the University of Edinburgh. He abandoned medicine, first for journalism and then for the exciting new world of the developing railway system. After some years of being secretary to the Board of Management for Leeds Central Station, he moved to London to manage the South-Eastern Railway in 1854; and throughout his career, he wrote and lectured on his main theme, which was the importance of encouraging providence and industry. 'The spirit of self-help is the root of all genuine growth in the individual', he told his public, ' . . . help from without is often enfeebling, but help from within invariably invigorates.'[23]

Bad luck or lack of opportunity was no excuse. 'There is . . . a Russian proverb which says that Misfortune is next door to Stupidity.' Men who lamented their luck were merely 'reaping the consequences of their own neglect, mismanagement, improvidence or want of application'.[24] There were splendid examples in the developing industrial economy of men who had started from humble beginnings, and achieved wealth and fame: Isaac Newton, James Watt, inventor of the Spinning Jenny, Robert Stephenson, inventor of the steam engine, Isambard Kingdom Brunel, the great engineer – the list was long; and Smiles dealt sharply with the argument that the achievement of such pioneers was chiefly due to talent, quoting Voltaire and Beccaria to the effect that talent was much less important than industry, diligence and continuous application. Given continuous application, almost anyone could become a great musician or a great artist. Michelangelo, for example, completed the ceiling of the Sistine Chapel through continuous application.

Shakespeare is dealt with in a chapter on 'Great Men of Business'. Smiles praises his industry in managing the Globe Theatre; ignores the literary value of the plays entirely, and then compliments the playwright on having 'prospered in his business and realised sufficient to enable him to retire upon a competency to his native town of Stratford-upon-Avon'.

This remarkable work was rejected by one publisher, but taken on rather doubtfully by another, who found that he had a bestseller on his hands. Books did not sell in millions in Victorian times, but *Self-Help* had unprecedented sales which ran into tens of thousands. It was translated into French, Dutch, German, Danish, Swedish, Spanish, Italian, Turkish, Arabic, Japanese and 'the native tongues of India', and widely circulated in the United States.[25] Queen Victoria recorded that she wept when she read it, because it was so beautiful.

Smiles (that was his real name) preached a gospel of social optimism. *Self-Help* was followed by a series of other books with similarly promising titles: *Character* (1871), *Thrift* (1875) and *Duty* (1880). These never achieved the overwhelming success of *Self-Help*, and over the years the message became somewhat repetitive; but it had made its mark.

Thrift was a particularly sharp attack on those who asked for help:

> We often hear the cry raised, 'Will nobody help us?' It is a spiritless, hopeless cry. It is sometimes a cry of revolting meanness, especially when it issues from those who, with a little self-denial, sobriety and thrift, might easily help themselves.[26]

Thrift and industry enabled 'the poorest man to achieve honour, if not distinction. The greatest names in the history of art, literature and science are those of labouring men.' Thrift and industry were the essence of civilization: for 'the savage is the greatest of spendthrifts . . . he has no forethought, no tomorrow'. Anyone – anyone at all – could rise from the depths. 'The Parthenon began with a mud-hut.'

Smiles writes much about the qualities of a True Gentleman: he was, after his fashion, an egalitarian, for these were qualities of character, not of birth and social advantage. He is the apostle of social mobility. 'Truthfulness, integrity and goodness . . . form the essence of the manly character.' Little is said about the female half of the population, though any women readers could take hope from the improving story of the Helpful Wife. When this woman was married, she stipulated to her husband-to-be that she must have threepence, the price of a pint of ale, every day. Though puzzled, he agreed. The time came a year later when (having indulged heavily in drink himself) he was short of money. His wife then triumphantly brought out of her stocking three hundred and sixty-five threepences, for she had saved the money instead of drinking it away. 'The wife's little capital was the nucleus of frugal investments that ultimately swelled out into a shop, a factory, a warehouse, a country-seat, and perhaps a Liverpool mayor.'[27] In a rapidly expanding economy, all things seemed possible.

Despite his strictures on Shakespeare and Michelangelo, Smiles was not entirely a Philistine. He wanted to better the conditions of working-class life, and advocated free public libraries, free education and museums. The poor could appreciate the beauties of nature, and bring flowers into their homes. Pictures, prints or engravings that represented 'a noble thought . . . a heroic act' might be bought for pennies.

Smiles articulated an important strand in Victorian experience. There were some grains of truth in his insistence that the age of the common man had arrived, and that those who were born poor need not despair. He did provide some sense of worth and dignity for the industrious working man. His work is also of some value because of the biographical studies he undertook on the new men of the industrial age: he wrote a life of George Stephenson, and his three-volume work on *The Lives of the Engineers* (1861–2) became a classic. All the same, his frequently repeated theme about the value of self-help and the undesirable effects of philanthropy provided the well-to-do with a defence against compassion. When social misery was so apparent, and social despair so prevalent, it was profoundly comforting for his huge public to be told that individuals were responsible for their own condition, and that any attempt to help the unfortunate was 'enfeebling'. The poor need trouble their consciences and their purses no longer.

Contrasting Philosophies

In the Victorian context, philanthropy, mutual aid and self-help were contrasting and often competing philosophies. Philanthropy was tender-minded, stressing the extent of social misery. At worst, it was patronizing and snobbish, but at best, it had the merit of reaching the poorest and most disadvantaged classes in a divided society, and developing a public conscience about conditions which no civilized society could tolerate. Mutual aid was an intensely practical movement for the better-off and more regularly employed members of the working classes. It was not a way out of poverty, but it was a means for supporting and protecting members of societies against sudden financial disaster. Self-help was tough-minded, of greatest use to the individualistic and hardworking who were prepared to overcome obstacles of any kind in order to further their own ambitions. For such people, the developing capitalist system, the opening up of roads, railways and international trade, offered many opportunities of advancement. But however crass its expression, the self-help movement did mirror the breakdown of the traditional class barriers, and offer self-respect and hopes of a better future to those who were prepared to work for them.

CHAPTER FOUR

Darkest England and the Poverty Surveys

The need for information about changing social conditions was well recognized before the end of the eighteenth century, but much of the early work was anecdotal and impressionistic. Investigators who attempted to convey factual information could only list what they had found, relying on the accumulation of material to prove their case, because they lacked the techniques for processing and analysing data.

The introduction of the National Census in 1801 and the Registration of Births, Deaths and Marriages Act of 1836 led to a new framework of investigation in which it was possible to obtain statistical information about the whole population for the first time, and statistical techniques began to be developed and refined. The Statistical Society of London was paralleled in other major cities, and the study of patterns of sickness and mortality developed comparatively rapidly. These were a matter of hard data: people were born, married, had children, and died from carefully classified causes; but despite the pioneer work of Chadwick and his colleagues, the development of social statistics, involving softer data about living standards and the meaning of poverty took longer. The Social Science Association, founded in 1857, created a new focus for social analysis, but much of the early work was localized, and the techniques were comparatively shaky.

The 'African Parallel'

The popularity of Henry Mayhew's *London Labour and the London Poor* (1851) indicates how far the field of social investigation was lagging behind that of medical investigation at the mid-century. Mayhew was a journalist, and he conducted his own colourful investigations of low life, concentrating on street traders and the criminal classes. His stereotyped sketches of such categories as 'Bawds', 'Procuresses, Pimps and Panders', 'Fancymen', 'Sneaks or Common Thieves', 'Magsmen or Sharpers', 'Beggars and Cheats' provided lively reading for his public, but scarcely added to the sum of knowledge about poverty. The general impression was that the poor were artful and amusing, and their way of life foreign to his respectable readers.

British imperialism had entered its expansionist phase, and many remote areas of Asia and Africa were being explored. As information filtered back about the lives and customs of 'primitive' tribes (some of which were later found to have very complex social systems) it was inevitable that comparisons would be drawn between their condition and that of the poorer classes in Britain. Mayhew used such reflections to support the somewhat startling theory that the London poor were *not English*: 'Each civilised or settled tribe has generally some wandering horde intermingled with, and in a measure preying upon it.' The Fingoes (literally beggars or outcasts) preyed upon the Kaffirs of southern Africa, the Lapps preyed upon the Finns, the Bedouin on the Fellahin of North Africa and Egypt. His conclusion was that 'there are two distinct races of men':

> We, like the Kafirs [*sic*], Fellahs and Finns, are surrounded by wandering hordes – paupers, beggars and outcasts, possessing nothing but what they acquire by depredation from the industrious, provident and civilised portion of the community.[1]

The identity of this nomad race could be ascertained by the shape of their heads (low-browed and small-skulled), by their unintelligible language – 'greatly advantageous in the concealment of their designs' – and by their deplorable personal habits:

> The nomad, then is distinguished from the civilized man by his repugnance to regular and continuous labour – by his want of providence in laying up a store for the future – by his inability to perceive consequences . . . by his passion . . . for intoxicating fermented liquors . . . by his comparative insensibility to pain – by his immoderate love of gaming . . . by an immoderate love of libidinous dances – by the pleasure he experiences in witnessing the sufferings of sentient creatures . . .

by the looseness of his notions as to property – by the absence of chastity among his women.[2]

Many of these strictures might equally well have applied to wealthy young men about town; but the theory that the poor were not only embarrassing and a nuisance, but foreigners as well, evidently appealed to his readers.

General William Booth of the Salvation Army also saw the 'African Parallel', but came to very different conclusions. *In Darkest England, or The Way Out* (1890) is a passionate plea for social reform. Booth drew on the exploration of Henry Stanley in the Congo. Stanley's dramatic rescue of David Livingstone in 1871 in an expedition funded by the *New York Herald* had excited much public interest, and his subsequent accounts of the life of the forest pygmies were eagerly received. As General Booth said, they presented 'a terrible picture':

> But while brooding over the awful presentation of life as it exists in the vast African forest, it seemed to me only too vivid a picture of many parts of our own land. As there is a darkest Africa, is there not also a darkest England? Civilisation, which can breed its own barbarians, does it not also breed its own pygmies? May we not find a parallel at our own doors, and discover within a stone's throw of our cathedrals and palaces similar horrors to those . . . existing in the great Equatorial forest?[3]

He wrote 'not in despondency, but in hope'. In England at least, the problems were soluble. For 'Darkest England' was only a fraction of 'Greater England', and there was wealth enough to rescue the 'submerged tenth' of the population.

This last phrase caught the public imagination in a way Booth cannot have expected. In the ensuing years, efforts were made to breed out the 'submerged tenth'. The science of Eugenics was in its infancy and its principal exponent was Francis Galton, a cousin of Charles Darwin. Galton's *Hereditary Genius* (1869) argued that mental ability, aptitudes and qualities of character, like such physical characteristics as hair colour and eye colour, were directly transmissible from one generation to the next: mathematicians tended to have mathematical children, musicians begat musicians. Conversely, criminal tendencies, mental illness, mental handicap and fecklessness ran in families.

Mayhew regarded the poor as alien and predatory, William Booth saw them as lost and helpless, the eugenicists argued that their condition was hereditary; but none of these lines of approach added what would now be regarded as scientific data to the debates about poverty.

Charles Booth and the Development of Quantitative Techniques

The work of the Social Science Association had been complemented in the second half of the nineteenth century by that of a number of provincial organizations, notably the Manchester Statistical Society; but the definition of poverty, and the extent of poverty, though much discussed, eluded the investigators. Charles Booth (a Liverpool businessman and a staunch Conservative, not related to the Salvation Army leader) embarked on a major survey after coming to the conclusion that the extent of poverty was being grossly exaggerated by such groups as the Marxist Social Democratic Federation. The secretary of the S.D.F. was F. D. Hyndman, who had been Karl Marx's pupil, and Marx's daughter Eleanor ('Tussie') was a member. Hyndman is vague about dates and methods, but some time before 1883, the S.D.F. carried out a survey in working-class areas of London, and came to the conclusion that some 25 per cent of the working population was living in poverty. The publication is not listed among Hyndman's works, and it appears to have drawn a good deal of criticism, as Hyndman writes 'Of course we Socialists were denounced as deliberate falsifiers of facts and exaggerators of the poverty of the mass of the people'.[4]

When Booth looked for accurate data to disprove the figure of 25 per cent, he found none. In 1883, he read a paper to the Royal Statistical Society in which he complained that many of the official figures were meaningless: the basic work of enumeration was poorly performed, and the categories in which information was collected varied from decade to decade.[5] He called on Hyndman, and informed him that he intended to investigate the matter himself. Hyndman later wrote, 'Mr Booth even [went] so far as to denounce me in a quiet way for putting such erroneous, and as he termed them, 'incendiary' statements, before the people'.[6]

Booth used the new organizational and statistical techniques of the business world to which he belonged in what was to be the first major social survey. He financed all his own work. One of his voluntary assistants in this enterprise was his cousin Beatrice Potter (later Mrs Sidney Webb), who wrote a vivid description of 'Cousin Charlie' in her autobiography: tall, abnormally thin, ascetic, looking like a university professor or a priest, or 'with another change of attire . . . an artist in the Quartier Latin'.[7] He was not at all like a great captain of industry.

The framework of Booth's investigation resembled a major military operation. His headquarters were at Toynbee Hall, the first of the great university settlements in London. There was a Poverty Map, with flags indicating the areas under investigation. He organized a two-tier exercise: most of the information was collected from School Board Officers, appointed under Lowe's Education Act of 1870 to investigate the reason for children's non-attendance at school. The central team received and cross-checked the information.

Booth's major findings were published in 1889. What he had discovered was that Hyndman's 25 per cent was not an overestimate but an underestimate. His own classification of the London populalion[8] showed 30.7 per cent of the population in poverty.

Table 4.1   *Charles Booth's classification of the distribution of poverty*

Category	A	Loafers, drunkards and semi-criminals	0.9 per cent
	B	Casual hand-to-mouth earnings	7.5 per cent
	C D	Seasonal or small regular wages	22.3 per cent
	E F	Regularly and fairly well-paid	51.5 per cent
	G H	Lower middle class Upper middle class	17.8 per cent

Most of those in categories A to D were people who had a precarious existence through no fault of their own. Low wages and the precarious nature of seasonal and casual work were the major causes of poverty.

Booth's first volume was published at top speed – written in his spare time. Since he continued to run his shipping business in Liverpool, made frequent trips to the New York office to oversee the work of his brother, and lived the life of a country gentleman at Gracedieu Manor in Leicestershire, most of it must have been written on trains and ships. The demand was pressing – papers to London societies had aroused interest, and the first printing was quickly sold out. Most reviewers were adulatory – though the writer for the *Athenaeum* sniffed 'The book is entirely without literary merit, but contains information useful for philanthropists.'

Booth had discovered his life-work. In all, he was to publish seventeen volumes, piling fact on fact. The Poverty Enquiry ran to four volumes, and was followed by the Trades (Industry) Enquiry, volumes on Religious Influences and a final volume on Social Influences, published in 1903; and nearly all of it is unreadable.

Booth was aware of this himself. He wrote with difficulty, running to many drafts. He lived with working-class families, slept in doss-houses, and experienced the life of poor people at first hand. He 'walked in faith' that somehow the piling up of information would 'make the path more clear', but further enquiries only 'enlarged the wilderness of figures'. In the Trades Enquiry, he retained his belief in the efficacy of the capitalist system, but hoped to find some way of relating employment conditions to social conditions. He was disappointed, and his wife related that the study 'fell flat' on publication. His study of Religious Influences took him round the churches and chapels, the Gospel Halls and the Salvation Army Citadels in a ceaseless search for information. He developed a map with symbols – 'scarlet for places of worship, black for houses licensed to sell intoxicating drinks, and a lovely blue for the schools of the Board'; but though Professor Alfred Marshall from Cambridge found his report 'An angelic book, holy and beautiful outside and in', there was bitter criticism from the churches.

Booth's final volume was short. He was sure that the enquiries he had carried out were worthwhile (they had cost him some £33,000 of his own money) and that his methods of investigation were sound; but he could not see where they led. He was acutely aware of the limitations of his own work. 'The dry bones [of the argument] lie scattered over the long valley,' he wrote. 'May some great soul, master of a subtler and nobler alchemy than mine, disentangle the confused issues . . . and make these dry bones live, so that the streets of our Jerusalem may sing with joy.'[9]

From a modern viewpoint, Booth's work has marked limitations. The scope of his surveys was not clearly delineated: the first volume related only to East London, and though he subsequently extended the work to other districts of the metropolis, he certainly did not cover the whole of London. He talked about a 'Poverty line', and suggested that this might be drawn at an income of twenty-one shillings a week for a 'moderate family', noting that it would vary with circumstances; but he did not investigate either the size or the age of the family members. His biographer, Professor T. S. Simey, explores his definitions of poverty, and finds them 'imprecise'.[10]

Despite the concern which led Booth to devote much of his life and much of his fortune to the study of poverty, he could be judgemental – he wrote that drunkards, criminals and prostitutes ought to suffer 'all the natural consequences, short of actually perishing from cold and hunger'; but he was overwhelmingly convinced by the evidence that poverty was not a personal failing, but a failure of social organization. He modified his adherence to capitalism sufficiently to advocate a doctrine of 'limited socialism' for the poor: services should be provided for the underprivileged, to bring them up to the level where they could hold their own in a capitalist society.

Booth lacked the capacity to develop conceptual frameworks; but his contribution to the development of social policy and methods of social investigation was greater than he knew. He was the first person to ask 'Who are the poor?' and to replace stereotypes and prejudice with factual answers. He used quantitative methods of investigation. He pioneered the technique of the large-scale social survey in Britain. He made an early contribution to the categorization of social class. He made out a case for minimum standards of social provision – even if he did not wholly believe it himself. If he provided only the 'dry bones' of the argument, there were others who could bring them to life.

Seebohm Rowntree and the York Studies

One of the many people impressed by Charles Booth's work was Seebohm Rowntree, a young industrialist working in the family firm at York. At the end of the nineteenth century, Rowntree's was rapidly developing chocolate production, and employed some two thousand workers. The Rowntree family were Quakers, with a strong tradition of social concern. Seebohm Rowntree had visited slums in Newcastle, and studied food chemistry at Owen's College, Manchester (now the centre of the University of Manchester, and at that time surrounded by slum property). He had corresponded with Charles Booth, and determined to carry out a similar survey in his own city of York, to establish whether Booth's findings were particular to the London area, or whether the problems were equally to be found in provincial cities.

Seebohm Rowntree was somewhat disingenuous in claiming that York was a 'representative' provincial city. It was his own city, and he was determined to work there. Though York had a mixed industrial pattern, and a fair spread of wage levels it was already a well-known tourist centre. York Minster and the Roman and Danish heritage were major attractions; but if the tourist trade lessened the city's claim to be typical, it also ensured that the findings of the survey would receive attention from people who were attracted to the city.

Work on the survey began in 1899. Seebohm Rowntree was 28 years old, and had been relieved from his more pressing duties in the Rowntree Works by the appointment of a second industrial chemist. Like Charles Booth, he was determined that the most up-to-date quantitative methods would be employed. Unlike Booth, he had a discrete area to work in. York was a reasonable size – some 15,000 houses, a population of 75,812. Rowntree excluded the 'upper class', including Booth's Class H, who kept at least one servant, and reduced his population to 46,754.

He was not happy with Booth's two-tier survey method. The information provided by School Board Officers and other informants had proved to be of variable quality. He had only two paid investigators, but he determined on a first-hand investigation, with a questionnaire of his own design. Since sampling had not yet been invented, that meant knocking on every door. The investigators knocked on every door; and when Rowntree discovered that one of them was producing unreliable results, he had the visits repeated. The work was meticulous. It also had the advantage that Rowntree had studied Booth's work in detail, and so could be more precise about his objectives, The survey, *Poverty – A Study of Town Life*, was completed within two years, and published in 1901.

Rowntree took Booth's description of the poverty line and elaborated it. He developed two concepts of poverty – *Primary Poverty* and *Secondary Poverty*. These were carefully defined. Families were in primary poverty when their income was insufficient to provide the basic necessities for biological efficiency: food, fuel, shelter and clothing, even if every penny were spent on these our items. People were in secondary poverty when their income would have been sufficient to cover the four basic necessities, but where some of the money was diverted to other purposes. It is important to note that this second category did not imply a moral judgement that the money was misspent. Rowntree recognized that in some cases, the cause might be drinking or gambling; but he was at pains to point out that the money might be spent on other essentials – necessary household replacements, trade union dues, fares to work, or helping some less fortunate member of the family. He also made the point that living effectively on a minimum income required almost superhuman powers of energy and intelligence, which did not come easily to people living on the breadline.

Booth had noted that the poverty line would move, depending on the circumstances of the family. Rowntree worked it out in detail. As a nutritional chemist, he knew what people should eat to keep fit, and how much a minimum diet cost. In the end, to prove his point, he selected a diet given to him by the Local Government Board, which was less generous than that available at the time for able-bodied paupers. He checked his prices in the back streets of York. He checked local rents, and the cost of clothing in the cheaper shops, and the price of fuel. He took into account the size of the family and the age of the children.

His conclusion was that the wages paid for unskilled labour in York were insufficient to 'maintain a family of moderate size in a state of bare physical efficiency'. According to his calculations, 9.91 per cent of the working-class population of York were living in primary poverty, and 17.93 per cent in secondary poverty. Though his figures were not directly comparable with Booth's, because both the base and the definitions differed, the total of 27.84 per cent was sufficiently close to Booth's figures to make a public impact.

Rowntree's second conceptual breakthrough was in the formulation of the *Poverty Cycle*. Working-class families went through predictable periods of relative poverty and prosperity. A couple would be living in or near poverty while their children were young; rise to comparative affluence as the children began to work and bring in wages to the household; sink back into poverty when the children left home to start their own families, and the man was no longer able to work in old age. Meanwhile, the children would have started on their own poverty cycle in their families of marriage, beginning in poverty, rising to comparative comfort, and returning to poverty again as they too became old. Here was the basic analysis which was to lead in time to contributory old-age pensions and family allowances.

Rowntree's findings on family incomes strongly supported Booth's. He estimated that a man, wife and three children of given ages needed 21s 8d a week to keep them out of primary poverty. Booth's estimate had been

21s. The average weekly wage in York at that time was between 18s and 21s. Like Booth, he found that the major cause of poverty was not individual weakness of character, but 'the adverse conditions under which too many of the working class live'. He reinforced Booth's findings about the consequences of seasonal or casual labour, which made it impossible for a family to budget, since their earnings were so uncertain. These were the economic causes of poverty. The social causes were poor health services, poor housing and a lack of education for living; and state intervention was needed. Though 'the dark shadow of Malthusian philosophy' had passed away, he insisted that 'No civilisation can be sound or stable which has as its base this mass of stunted human life.'[11] Rowntree's single volume, written with a dispassionate clarity, showed that the situation Booth had described was not only a metropolitan problem – it existed in York, and almost certainly in other cities throughout the country.

The Critics

Charles Booth was a Conservative, and a member of the new aristocracy of the industrial age. Many of his own social circle privately thought his ideas socialistic, but criticism was relatively muted. Rowntree was a Liberal, a Quaker and a provincial, and his work had a sharper cutting edge. The criticism was consequently more vocal.

Much of the initial opposition to his ideas came from the Charity Organisation Society. The COS secretary, Charles Loch, was scathing about Rowntree's 'generalisations cloaked in numerical phraseology' and accused him of recommending the creation of 'a recognised servile class – paupers, old age pensioners and State-dependent wage-earners'. Rowntree pointed out in his sober way that the problems of poverty were often submerged – wives and children went without in order to keep the wage earner healthy enough to earn; and that poverty had long-term consequences – 'the high death rate among the poor, the terribly high infant mortality, the stunted stature and the dulled intelligence'.[12]

His findings were to have a considerable influence on the Liberal Government which took power in 1906, and formed the background to their social reforms. Rowntree would have been the first to admit that his work was dependent on Charles Booth's – but then, Booth's work was dependent on Hyndman's. Marxist, Conservative and Liberal formed an odd chain in the development of survey methods.

More recently, Rowntree's work has come under strong attack from social policy analysts on the grounds that poverty is relative (in relation to the standard of living of other people in the same society) rather than absolute (a measure of bare physical subsistence). Peter Townsend finds Rowntree's scales too arbitrary and too harsh, pointing out that the diet he used was one designed for American convicts, and harsher than that used at the time by the Local Government Board for workhouses.[13] Rowntree's Human Needs Diet was certainly barely eatable. Miss Trudi Schultz of the Oxford University Institute of Statistics was still reworking it annually in the late 1960s. At that time, it cost just under £1 a week per head, and consisted largely of porridge, oatmeal, pulses and herrings – items which do not figure largely in working-class diets.

Robert Holman echoes Townsend's criticisms and concludes that Rowntree 'ignored social, cultural and psychological needs'; [14] but both Holman and Townsend miss the point. Rowntree was not arguing that the working classes should be able to live at this stringent level. Asa Briggs, Rowntree's biographer, emphasizes that Rowntree deliberately chose the starkest of theoretical measures in order to demonstrate to his fellow industrialists that workers could not possibly maintain their biological efficiency on current wage levels. In their own interests, if they wanted a fit workforce, they must provide a better standard of living for the workers. He quotes Rowntree's own explanation to prove that the concept of absolute poverty was a theoretical tool: he was not advocating this minimum standard in real life:

A family living upon the scale allowed for in this estimate must never spend a penny on railway fare or omnibus. They must never go into the country unless they walk. They must never purchase a halfpenny newspaper . . . They must write no letters to absent children, for they cannot afford to pay the postage . . . They cannot save, nor can they join a sick club or Trade Union, because they cannot pay the necessary subscriptions. The children must have no pocket money for dolls, marbles or sweets. The father must smoke no tobacco, and must drink no beer. The mother must never buy any pretty clothes for herself or her children . . . Should a child fall ill, it must be attended by the parish doctor . . . should it die, it must be buried by the parish. Finally, the wage-earner must never be absent from his work for a single day.[15]

Rowntree was pointing out how impossible it would be to live at this level of deprivation, hoping (unsuccessfully, as it turned out) to pre-empt the inevitable criticism from the COS. He said 'I chose this criterion because I didn't want people to say that 'Rowntree's crying for the moon'.'[16] John Veit-Wilson has listed a number of leading writers in social policy who have maintained 'persistent misconceptions' about Rowntree's work, failing to appreciate the distinction between his theoretical definition of absolute poverty, and the empirical criteria he employed in his survey. In 1901, absolute poverty was still a stark reality, but Rowntree's work on secondary poverty shows that he regarded it as only part of the problem. As Veit-Wilson notes, it is important to distinguish the methodological issues of establishing a poverty line (a technical activity which should not involve political considerations) from the 'quite different activity of taking political decisions' about the relief of poverty,[17] and modern commentators have frequently not appreciated the distinction.

CHAPTER FIVE

Bypassing the Poor Law

By the 1860s, both the Poor Law and the Public Health services had moved away from controversy and into a phase of consolidation. After the horrors of the Andover scandal, the Poor Law Board became directly responsible to Parliament, since its President was a minister, and Parliament could question, debate and investigate. The administration became less centralized, less doctrinaire, and to some extent less harsh. Inspectors turned to advising on workhouse management rather than applying blindly deterrent policies. Boards of Guardians had more freedom to respond to local conditions, and outdoor relief, never entirely abolished, was given more frequently. Diets improved, and interest revived in constructive forms of classification -- schools for the children, transition to work for young people, separate wards for the sick, and a non-deterrent regime for the old people.

Even so, the problems were enormous, partly because of the size of the pauper population. In 1865, Florence Nightingale sent her 'best and dearest' pupil, Agnes Jones, to be Matron of the Brownlow Hill Institution in Liverpool. She took with her twelve Nightingale-trained nurses. Within a month, she had dismissed 35 of the untrained pauper nurses for drunkenness. The number of pauper patients varied from 1,350 to 1,500, and the conditions reminded Miss Nightingale of the military hospital at Scutari.[1]

When Louisa Twining, the pioneer of workhouse visiting, visited an old lady of her acquaintance who had moved into a workhouse, she discovered that the master and the matron were the only staff – responsible for 500 inmates. Here was a new field for voluntary action. Local groups, mainly of women, were formed to visit the workhouses, read to the old people, take flowers to the sick wards – and keep a sharp eye open for abuses. They believed in 'working quietly' rather than in conflict; but they soon discovered 'the power of red-tape' – the Guardians who refused them admission, the staff who took their requests for admission as criticism of their own work, the endless delays, the perennial excuses. In 1857, Louisa Twining read a paper on the subject to a meeting of the Social Science Association in Birmingham, and the Workhouse Visiting Society was formed, with a prestigious committee. They campaigned for special sick wards and trained nurses, supporting Agnes Jones, who was to die young of typhus probably contracted in her own hospital. They found avenues of employment for young people – usually manual work for the boys, domestic service for the girls. They campaigned for the classification of the inmates and separation of groups with different needs; for the election of 'a superior class of guardian . . . who would be able to discharge their duties in an intelligent and unprejudiced manner'; for the appointment of a higher class of superintendents, with some education and administrative ability.[2]

In many ways, it was a typical Victorian voluntary reform movement, but it had three distinguishing features: first, its publicity was sharply professional: Louisa Twining recounts in her *Recollections of Workhouse Visiting and Management* (1880) how memoranda were drafted for the Poor Law Board and for Members of Parliament, how she wrote articles for newspapers and journals, including the *Guardian*, *The Economist* and *John Bull*, how facts were collated and pressure was maintained. Second, it involved statutory–voluntary co-operation: while most of the voluntary societies ran their own separate services, the Workhouse Visiting Society existed to improve the one basic state service. Third, it was a movement by women with implications for the treatment of women. As Louisa Twining pointed out, there were over 100,000 workhouse inmates in Britain, and more than half of them were women and girls. Yet the overworked matrons (often single-handed) were the only women involved in management:

> No-one who had any knowledge of the work of the society . . . could fail to have observed that the point of *women's work* had all along been urged as of the most vital importance . . . a great part of the evils which had grown up around the system were owing to the fact that it was carried out entirely by men . . . educated women as Guardians, as matrons, as nurses, as inspectors, had been over and over again urged as the one hope of reform and amelioration.[3]

The Society worked on boarding-out schemes for children. A triumph was the appointment of Mrs Nassau John Senior, the daughter-in-law of the economist, as the first woman inspector of the Poor Law Board. Unfortunately she became terminally ill after some two years of work, and had to resign, but a barrier had been overturned.[4]

All this activity improved workhouse conditions and administration. It played a large part in humanizing the 'hell-concocted Poor Law' at a time when the workhouse system continued to grow in size under the impact of population growth and violent fluctuations in the labour market. If the workhouses were not exactly welcoming, they were at least clean and well run, and no longer places of positive and deliberate cruelty.

The Public Health Movement

After the conflicts and crises of the General Board of Health, the public health movement was also settling down to a period of consolidation. The Sanitary Act of 1866 put the control of pollution and epidemic disease firmly in the hands of the local authorities, and in the towns, where the worst problems existed, a new breed of public health doctors went to work to eliminate the worst problems. At central government level, there was a Medical Department of the Privy Council. Its chief medical officer was John Simon, who had been Medical Officer of Health for London, and his assistant was William Farr from the General Register Office. Together, they developed medical statistics, producing a series of brilliantly diagnostic reports on mortality and morbidity -the nature, distribution and effects of epidemic diseases, and the success or failure of different methods of control.

By this time, the theory of specific contagion was generally accepted, and the serious study of bacteriology had begun; but it was also accepted that bacteria flourished most freely in conditions of filth. Chadwick and Sir Benjamin Hall had both been right, and a new generation of doctors devised a system for dealing with epidemics. The pattern which emerged involved a series of steps: research leading to greater precision in diagnosis, specific modes of treatment and techniques of immunization; notification of individual cases, making possible the compilation of medical statistics and the identification of black spots; the elimination of causes (like the Broad Street Pump); the isolation of affected individuals and the cleansing of premises; a system of tracing contacts; public enlightenment

– overcoming secrecy and inducing people to come forward for treatment; and, as further medical research made it possible, the development of immunization.[5]

The evolution of this system, one of the great successes of medicine, involved quite complex patterns of central–local co-operation. Smallpox came under control after the Vaccination Act of 1853; typhus, typhoid and cholera soon followed. The figures fell annually, and with startling effect. By the end of the century, the public health doctors had moved on to deal with the next most serious causes of early death – scarlet fever, diphtheria, tuberculosis; and the elimination of the causes of disease moved from fetid pools and poisoned pumps to the wider issues of pollution, dangerous trades, slum housing and overcrowding.

Though scarlet fever, tuberculosis and diphtheria were not finally to be conquered until the discovery of antibiotics in the 1940s, the pattern of public health care helped to reduce the incidence, and the same principles are applied today in the treatment of venereal disease and AIDS. In the second half of the nineteenth century, every area had its great isolation hospital. In more recent years, these hospitals have stood empty, or have been devoted to other purposes, as improvements in treatment meant that the work could be handled by general practitioners or in hospital out-patient clinics.

An outstanding feature of Simon's work at the Medical Department of the Privy Council was the encouragement of a new generation of local authority public health doctors. Simon expressed the view that Edwin Chadwick – 'a man of very high mark' – had perhaps been in too much of a hurry, and that this had led him into centralizing policies when 'the people and their representative bodies should have made their way in a necessarily gradual process of education'.[6] In the second wave of reform, following the Sanitary Act of 1866 and a very thorough review of the situation by the Sanitary Commission of 1868, the public health service was built up from the local communities, not down from Whitehall, with manifestly better results.

The Local Government Board, 1871

Public health work had started in the Poor Law Commission, with the work of Kay, Arnott and Southwood Smith, and the preparation of Chadwick's *Report on the Sanitary Condition of the Labouring Population.*

Between 1848 and 1871, public health developed separately; but it was evident that the Poor Law Board and the Medical Department of the Privy Council had overlapping responsibilities and a need for liaison.

In 1871, the Local Government Act set up a new form of central administration – the Local Government Board. This combined the work of the Poor Law Board, the Medical Department of the Privy Council and a small Local Government section in the Home Office. What might have been a useful merging of skills and responsibilities was unfortunately frustrated by the structure of the new body. The Sanitary Commission of 1868 had recommended that Poor Law and Public Health should run in tandem, with separate secretariats; but there was one administrative structure – 'virtually continuance of the old Poor Law Office' – and a single secretariat.

'It was as if the Act had ordered that the old Poor Law Board, subject only to such conditions of consultation and reference as itself might impose on itself should be the Central Sanitary Authority for England,' wrote Simon twenty years later. He added temperately enough that the situation was 'not of unclouded promise for sanitary administration.'[7] A highly specialized department had been replaced by an all-purpose one in which public health interests were only one set of issues among many.

> Within the jurisdiction of the Local Government Board are many objects which are only sanitary in a remote instrumental sense, and some which are not sanitary at all; questions of local elections and finance, and boundaries and arbitrations, questions of mere common or commercial convenience in various local matters, questions as to highways and lighting, as to markets and their stalls and weighing machines, as to hackney-carriages and public bathing, as to local steam-whistles and public clocks.[8]

The Poor Law Board and its staff took all the senior positions in the new Board. Simon suffered personally in the reorganization, being reduced from the status of administrative head to that of technical adviser. He stayed on for another six years before retiring, but he thought the new administration was 'grievously wrong'.

The Poor Law was entering on a new period of rigidity and parsimony. Shortly before the dissolution of the Poor Law Board in 1869, the Goschen Minute had outlined only a minimal and deterrent service, any rehabilitative work being left to the voluntary organizations.

In the towns at least, the initiative in public health had passed decisively

to the local authorities. The Public Health Act of 1875 was a great consolidating measure which laid down extended responsibilities for sewage,
drainage, refuse collection, offensive trades, food inspection, infectious diseases, epidemics, hospitals (including isolation hospitals), street cleansing
and housing. All areas were to have a Medical Officer of Health, full-time
or part-time.

The Development of Local Authorities

In 1888, the local government system was at last rationalized. The County
Councils Act set up a comprehensive structure. London was a special case,
administered by the London County Council. Other towns of medium or
large size were designated county boroughs, with their own councils.
County councils took the major responsibility for the rural areas, but
because of the distances involved at a time when communication was still
relatively slow, some responsibilities were left with district and parish
councils. The problems of disease and sanitation and overcrowding were
essentially urban problems, and it was in the growing metropolitan areas
that local government became a strong force for reform. Though the
system led to many boundary disputes between county boroughs and their
surrounding county councils, it endured for nearly a century, until the
county boroughs were absorbed into the county councils in 1975.

Two points are significant: first, a coherent network of locally elected
authorities was set up, replacing a jumble of old municipal authorities and
ad hoc bodies. The general public knew who the members of the authority
were, what powers they held, and how they exercised them. The system
was democratic and accountable. Further, a single local authority in
the towns could appoint its own officers and develop its own expertise in
the light of local knowledge. A career service of local government officers
was beginning to be built up. As local government developed and
strengthened, it became possible for more responsibilities and services to
be delegated from central government.

A major responsibility given to the new local authorities in 1888 was
that for main roads, and 'the new road era began'.[9] Turnpike Trusts, by
which individuals or groups who had developed roads could charge a toll
for their use, were virtually ended in 1895. The development of modern
methods of transport radically changed the lives of people living in rural
areas:

In the 80s the only link between the village and the market town was often the carrier's cart which journeyed between them once or twice a week. Not only had the oldest inhabitant never seen the sea or even visited a town, but the children had to put up with the education which the village could provide.[10]

The railways developed first, then the motor car and the bicycle heralded 'the renaissance of the road, and the intermingling for good or ill of the country and the town'. The Daimler petrol engine, developed in the 1880s, solved the technical problem of the ratio of power to weight (an early 20 hp steam carriage weighed some four tons). In 1896, the Act of 1865 which required all cars to be preceded by a man carrying a red flag was repealed. The bicycle was also becoming a common means of transport – pneumatic tyres were invented in 1889. After 1909, money was raised from petrol duty and motor vehicle licences to develop the roads, and local authorities became very active highway authorities.

Housing responsibilities developed out of public health concerns. The Artisans' and Labourers' Dwellings Improvement Acts of 1875 and 1879 gave local authorities the power to purchase land in slum areas and redevelop it. In 1890, following a Royal Commission on Housing which made detailed recommendations, a consolidating Housing Act gave the new local authorities power to clear whole areas; to repair and improve houses, and to build new houses of better quality. 'The government which in the 1840s had begun to take responsibility for providing drains, became responsible for the quality of the houses.'[11]

An Education Service developed slowly from the time of Althorp's first grant of £20,000 to the voluntary societies in 1833. For much of the nineteenth century, its growth was hampered by the competition between the Established Church and the Dissenters. The only matter on which the two parties agreed was that education was a religious matter, and that state intervention must be fought at all costs. Forster's Education Act of 1870, which is usually celebrated as the major initiative in state education, merely made it possible to fill in the gaps in a very uneven provision, and established the right of every child to education in theory. It was not until 1880 that Mundella's Act specified that the right could be exercised between the ages of five and ten, and not until 1895 or even later that the last remnants of fee-paying (3d a week) were finally abolished. *Ad hoc* School Boards were responsible for the state schools until 1902, when Balfour's Education Act secured uniformity of administration by placing the funding for all schools, statutory and voluntary, in the hands of the local authority.

One of the effects of universal schooling was to present the problems of poverty in a new and acute form. School attendance officers reported that there were children who could not come to school because they had no clothes to wear, or no boots for their feet. Teachers reported that it was impossible to teach hungry children: they simply put their heads on the desks and went to sleep. So some local authorities, like the LCC Education Department, developed schemes in which soup and bread were available at a penny a day for those who could pay, and free for those who could not. The COS bitterly opposed these schemes. 'A PENNY GIVEN AND A CHILD RUINED' was the heading of one COS leaflet published in 1883. 'To feed their children is to debase the moral standard . . . by practically inviting parents . . . to spend in idleness or drink the time and money which should have been given to making provision for their family.'[12] But child poverty and child hunger were becoming visible, and local authorities were moving from a concern with the environment to a concern for individuals.

Maternity and Child Welfare

The Boer War 'crystallized and emphasized' the relatively latent fears of national inefficiency and race degeneration.[13] British forces in South Africa were repeatedly defeated in the early stages of the war and, when conscription was introduced for the first lime, over 35 per cent of the recruits were found to be physically unfit for service. In 1904, the Balfour Government set up an interdepartmental committee to consider the problems.

An inter-departmental committee is a quieter and less publicized procedure than a Royal Commission, and generally works faster. Its members are senior civil servants. They meet as part of their working life, out of the glare of publicity, and as representatives of particular departments of state. They are usually concerned less with debating major issues of principle than with ways and means – how to get things done. The Inter-Departmental Committee on Physical Deterioration had an unmemorable title, but its subject was one of considerable importance, and the findings were wide-ranging and authoritative.

At that time, wars were still fought with men rather than with technology.

The huge and highly disciplined German army was known to be preparing for war: could Britain only muster an 'army of weaklings' to oppose it? This simple image – the well-fed, arrogant German soldier in a spiked helmet and the weedy, under-nourished English youth – drove out the last remnants of Malthusian thinking. Children suddenly became important: they represented the future. And the needs were not only for defence in case of war in Europe. The British Empire had expanded at a remarkable rate in the late Victorian period. Fit young men were needed for India, for Canada, for Australia, for all those areas coloured red on the maps of the world where British jurisdiction ruled.

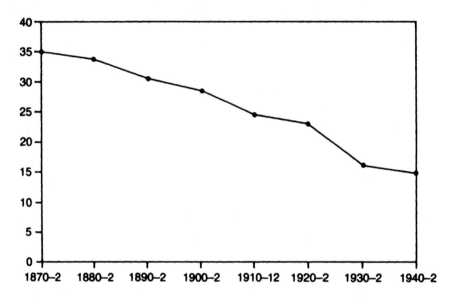

Figure II Live births per thousand population, United Kingdom 1870–1940
Source: Annual Abstract of Statistics, 1989, table 2.16.

It was beginning to be realized that this demand for 'fit young men' depended on the birth and rearing of fit children, and the statistics were alarming: the birth-rate was dropping, the infant mortality rate (i.e. the proportion of babies dying before their first birthday per thousand born) was not. In 1870–2, the crude birth-rate was 35 per thousand population, and the infant mortality rate 150 per thousand births. In 1900–2, the crude birth-rate had dropped to 28.6 per thousand population, and the infant mortality rate had dropped very little, standing at 142 per thousand births. The worst year was 1899, with an infant mortality rate of 163 per thousand: of every hundred children born, sixteen would die before their first birthday. Astonishing medical advances had been made in dealing with epidemic diseases, but the causes of infant mortality were more complex and more personal: they included insanitary home conditions, malnutrition, inhibited attitudes to pregnancy, attendance by ignorant and untrained midwives, poor baby-feeding practices, sheer lack of knowledge and lack of care. Epidemic diarrhoea was the main killer; and many of the children who did survive grew into sickly adults.

The recommendations of the Inter-Departmental Committee covered a variety of issues, and most of them involved extended activity in local authority Health and Housing Departments. The most progressive were already carrying out pioneering work in maternity and child welfare.

Health visiting had been initiated by the Ladies Sanitary Reform Association in Manchester and Salford in 1862, when it was proposed to have 'a lady superintendent for each district, and a health visitor who was a working woman'. Florence Nightingale, who totally lacked class consciousness where nursing was concerned, endorsed it as 'a new work and a new profession for women'. Milk depots, where mothers were encouraged in breast-feeding, and supplied with dried milk if this was not practicable, were the main weapon against epidemic diarrhoea. The depots were developed from the model of a clinic set up in Paris by Dr Pierre Budin, and soon developed into general maternity and child welfare clinics, where mothers were given advice on a variety of child-rearing problems, and the welfare of babies could be monitored.

Obstetric practice was improving. Back in the 1840s Dr Semmelweiss had watched hospital doctors in Vienna go straight from dissecting corpses to delivering babies without washing their hands, and had associated the fact with puerperal fever. The practice of asepsis, or 'Listerism', as it was called, spread slowly. Sir Arthur Newsholme, later Chief Medical Officer of Health to the Local Government Board, could recall his own days as a fourth-year medical student in the late 1870s:

I saw a surgeon pick up a forceps from the floor, and use it again forthwith. The coats in which some surgeons operated were old frock coats, used repeatedly without adequate cleansing . . . . And one saw threaded needles with silken threads hanging down attached to the well-worn coat of the house-surgeon, ready for the surgeon in the later stages of his operation.[14]

Though the hospitals were improving under the twin influences of asepsis and better nursing care, most babies were born at home, and without medical attention. Most villages and city areas had a woman, recognized by her neighbours, who assisted other women in childbirth, and usually laid out the dead as well. The trade was often passed down from mother to daughter. Some of these women were highly competent and some were drunken and sluttish. Gin, which was still very cheap, often provided an anaesthetic for the woman in labour, and a pick-me-up for her attendant. In the last two decades of the nineteenth century, there was a protracted battle over the status of midwives. The medical profession, by that time secure in their own professional status, objected to any formal recognition being accorded to these women. The midwives contended that assisting at a birth was a special skill, not simply a branch of medicine; that the presence of a doctor was usually not necessary and was often undesirable; and that many medical practitioners had no experience in obstetrics.

It was comparatively easy to prescribe training and registration for future midwives; but a particular problem for the parliamentary drafters

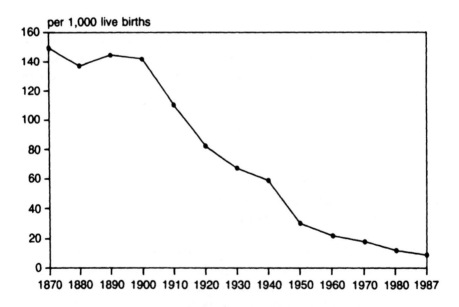

Figure III Infant mortality, England and Wales, 1881–1987
Source: Annual Abstract of Statistics, 1935, table 29, and 1989, table 2.21.

was that of the 'bona fide midwives', the very mixed group of women already in practice. There were obvious objections to giving them all status; yet they could not be forbidden to practise, because there were as yet no trained women to take their place. The Midwives Bill came before a weary Parliament repeatedly for some twenty years. To medical obstructionism and drafting problems were added political problems which delayed and frustrated parliamentary procedure. These were difficult years, when the House of Lords was asserting its powers, and the Irish members, demanding Home Rule, were frustrating many kinds of legislative effort. It was not until 1902 that the Midwives Act reached the Statute Book. The untrained 'bona fide midwives' had finally been 'blanketed in' – that is, given a licence to practise because there was no alternative to their services. For the future, there would be a Central Midwives' Board responsible for proper training in midwifery, and the local authorities would supervise registers of midwives competent to practise.[15]

Maternity and child welfare measures were to have the same effect on infant mortality that the public health measures of the earlier period had had on epidemic diseases: the infant mortality rate fell steadily from the alarming figure of 163 per thousand live births. Today it is below seven per thousand live births, and still falling.

By the early years of the twentieth century, a broadly based system of central and local government agencies had been developed to provide for health and welfare needs: only the Poor Law – aloof, deterrent, uncooperative – remained outside the structure. So what was to be done about the Poor Law?

CHAPTER SIX

Victorian Values or Socialist Visions?

In 1905, in the last few months of the Conservative Balfour Government, a Royal Commission on the Poor Laws was appointed. It was to work for nearly five years, and to provide a classic statement of two opposing views of poverty. The chairman was Lord George Hamilton, a former Under-Secretary of State for India and First Lord of the Admiralty. Lord George, though not a leading Conservative politician, was a respected one. As a free-trader, he had resigned from the Government in 1903 in protest against Austen Chamberlain's protectionist tariff policy. He was a very experienced chairman, and a man of integrity without strong views of his own on the subject of poverty. He must have seemed the ideal chairman for the Poor Law exercise; but the membership of his Commission was to be dominated by two groups who took up irreconcilable positions: the Charity Organisation Society and the Fabians.

The Charity Organisation Society

Three leading members of the COS were appointed to the Commission: Charles Loch, Helen Bosanquet and Octavia Hill. Charles Loch was appointed Secretary of the COS in 1875, when he was only 26 years old. He said on appointment that the task required 'the heart of a Dickens and the will of a Bismarck',[1] and he never lost his iron grip, though the Dickensian heart was seldom in evidence. He was to remain the chief administrator of the COS for nearly forty years, organizing endless committees of investigation into Housing, Unemployment, Vagrancy, the care of blind, deaf and epileptic children, and many other subjects; giving evidence to parliamentary committees, writing indefatigably, founding the Charities Register, the Charities Digest, the Charity Organisation Review. In all this useful and constructive work, he remained strongly opposed to any intervention by the state in the provision of social services, even to schemes for old age pensions, believing that the poor must save for their own old age, and that state grants would pauperize them. He was still opposing old age pensions when he finally retired in 1914.

Under Loch's direction and control, the COS spread. The first district offices were set up in areas in London where the rich and the poor lived closely together – Marylebone, St George's Hanover Square, Paddington, Kensington, Westminster. It proved harder to organize charity in areas like Whitechapel, Shoreditch or Bethnal Green; but by the end of the nineteenth century, the movement had spread to many parts of London and to some of the major provincial cities. These district offices investigated individual cases of poverty in depth, passing on those they considered 'deserving' to other agencies for action. They might ask one society for a donkey for a coster-monger, so that he could ply his trade, and another for a sewing machine for a widow, so that she could make clothes for her children. They were often criticized for arrogance and self-righteousness; but they remained convinced that the only constructive way to meet the problems of poverty was to investigate every case – and that most, on investigation, would be found to be unworthy of help. In his book *Charity Organisation,* Loch wrote his own commentary on Charles Booth's findings, pointing out that 'only' 13.5 per cent of the population of East London were estimated to be in dire poverty, and suggesting that careful and rigorous enquiry would reduce that number to a much lower level.[2]

In spite of its rigorous attitude to poor people and their problems, the COS did develop a degree of expertise which formed the basis for the development of social casework. Early developments in training social workers, in the University of Birmingham from 1908 and in the London School of Economics from 1913, relied heavily on fieldwork experience in COS agencies.

Helen Bosanquet was the wife of Bernard Bosanquet, the Oxford philosopher. Both the Bosanquets shared Loch's perspective. Helen Bosanquet had already made a reputation as a speaker and writer on COS subjects as Helen Dendy before her marriage. In 1893, in a book edited by her husband, she commented that applicants for charity might at first sight seem eminently deserving, but prove on closer examination to be drunkards, spendthrifts or 'quarrelsome and lazy'. She cited the case of a workman who had 'thrown away place after place':

> Of course, the more chances he was given, the more he wanted, and now it has come to this, that his wife and daughter go out to work while he sits home and minds the baby. A little wholesome starvation at the beginning of his career might have taught this man a lesson he would never have forgotten, and enabled him to preserve his manhood.[3]

Octavia Hill, the housing reformer, was also a keen supporter of the COS, but her approach seems to have been less abrasive than that of Loch or Helen Bosanquet. Her slogan was 'not alms, but a friend'. In her early work, she befriended families in tenements in what seems to have been a warm and personal relationship, but she believed that they had to be helped out of a financial muddle of debts and pawn-tickets into managing their resources. She interested John Ruskin in her plans for a contractual relationship between poor tenants and their landlords. The tenants would agree to pay their rent regularly, and not to vandalize the property. They were visited, and helped to budget. In return, the landlord agreed to keep the property clean, and in a good state of repair. Ruskin, who was a philanthropist as well as a writer and a poet, was impressed by these ideas, and bought houses for Octavia Hill to manage. She soon put the enterprise on a business footing, and provided a return on capital of 5 per cent to investors. The Church Commissioners offered her property to manage, and she took over the running of some of their worst properties in the slum areas of London, training her own workers. So began the profession of housing management.[4]

Octavia Hill's interests moved steadily outwards: from individual families paying their rent to blocks of flats, to play streets for children, to town planning and the idea of a Green Belt – the 'green lungs of London'. She was also a founder-member of the National Trust, set up in 1895; but her work with COS arose directly from her relationship with tenant families. She would investigate their budgets, and taught her workers to do the same. If there appeared to be a need for assistance, clients would be sent to the COS.

At least three other members appointed to the Poor Law Commission had extensive COS and Poor Law experience. They formed a formidable and united group: but they faced a formidable opponent.

Beatrice Webb and the Fabians

Since the Commission was appointed by a Conservative Government, and the Liberals were in opposition, no Liberals were appointed to it. Beatrice Webb, formerly Beatrice Potter and Charles Booth's assistant on the great poverty surveys, was the only Fabian Socialist, and her appointment seems to have been a miscalculation: the Prime Minister knew Mrs Webb socially, and understood that she was interested in poverty. His advisers appear not to have realized that a lady who dined with the Prime Minister could possibly be a Socialist.[5]

The Fabian Society, founded in 1884, believed in evolutionary change rather than revolution – it was named after Quintus Fabius Maximus, the Roman general who 'hastened slowly'. They had become the research arm of the Labour movement. Beatrice's marriage to Sidney Webb was the commencement of an outstanding joint career in scholarship and politics.

The Webbs were to be involved in many left-wing enterprises, including the publication of the *New Statesman and Nation* and the foundation of the London School of Economics, where they both taught for many years. Sidney Webb became a professor, and eventually a cabinet minister in a Labour Government in the late 1920s. They became great admirers of Soviet Russia, and their *Soviet Communism* was a classic of the 1930s. The partnership between the Webbs was so close that it is often impossible to distinguish the work of Sidney from that of Beatrice.

In *My Apprenticeship*, Beatrice Webb describes the COS as 'one of the most typical of Victorian offspring', and speaks of its activities with open contempt. She notes 'We fought each other's views to the death.'[6] Beatrice describes herself as temperamentally averse to the rough and tumble of argument (which was a very proper attitude for an Edwardian lady to take, though one suspects that she had a combative streak), but she became the channel through which Fabian ideas, many of them put into draft by her husband, were brought to confront a bewildered and exasperated Commission.

The Fabians believed implicitly in the power of facts. One of their earliest publications, dating from 1888 and regularly updated, was *Facts for Socialists*. As Margaret Cole puts it, they believed that:

> no reasonable person who *knows the facts* can fail to become a Socialist, or at the very least, to be converted to the Socialist policy – that out of their own mouths, or rather out of their published material, the defenders of capitalism can be made to prove that it is inefficient, brutal and idiotic.[7]

This belief is the key to Beatrice's behaviour on the Commission, and also to the curious story of the Hutchinson Bequest, which was commandeered by Sidney Webb to assist in founding the London School of Economics. He was able to argue with perfect integrity to the Hutchinson Trustees that the money would be devoted to strengthening the cause of Socialism in accordance with the terms of the bequest, and to the London Chamber of Commerce that 'the school would not deal with political matters, and nothing of a socialistic tendency would be introduced'.[8] He was convinced that people who honestly looked at the facts would inevitably come to Socialist conclusions.

In *Our Partnership* (1948) Beatrice Webb gives extracts from her diaries which contain a blow-by-blow account of the proceedings, and her changing view of the other participants as the debate went on. She started with great hopes of the chairman, at first describing him as 'this experienced politician and attractive grand seigneur', but later judging him to be 'weak' and 'frightened' under attack by the COS. She seems to have underestimated George Lansbury, the Christian Socialist Member of Parliament from the East End, referred to rather patronizingly in the early days as 'our workingman' [*sic*]. Later, she learned to respect him for his first-hand knowledge of poverty and his strong Socialist and pacifist convictions. She thought Prebendary Russell Wakefield, another Christian Socialist, a very dubious ally, but eventually found that he would support her point of view. She was less fortunate with her cousin Charles Booth, who was 'as delightful as ever' but 'losing his intellectual grip and persistency of purpose. Happily, he is unaware of it.'[9] But her view of the COS members did not change: she regarded them as merely uninformed and prejudiced, and nearly five years of weekly debate did not change her convictions nor mitigate her scorn.

The Commission's Work

There were two acknowledged experts on the Commission – Charles Booth, and a Poor Law historian, Professor William Stuart. There were four senior civil servants – the permanent heads of the Local Government Boards of England, Scotland and Wales, and their Chief Medical Officer. Beatrice Webb called them 'the big officials'. By the second meeting, she had found the procedure a shambles, and was demanding a much more organized way of working. From then on, she and Sidney worked together, drafting memorandum after memorandum, and submitting lists of proposals. 'My little tea-cup of a Royal Commission', she called it; but every meeting was exhausting. She recorded 'the clash of tongues', reproof from the chairman after a particularly bitter comment, and her own resolve to keep to good manners; but Charles Loch, normally the most controlled of men, repeatedly lost his temper and became 'white with rage' when she opposed his views, till Beatrice concluded that he must be seriously ill.[10] Reading between the lines, it seems that she tried to build bridges with most members of the Commission in the hope of converting them to Socialism; but her approach to Loch was a complete failure, and she was equally unable to come to terms with Helen Bosanquet, whom she consistently referred to formally as 'Mrs Bosanquet', describing her contributions to the Commission's debates as 'wonderful' and 'brilliant' in terms which leave no doubt about the sarcasm intended.[11] They were clearly not on each other's visiting lists.

Facts, facts, facts. The Commission's work was extensive, partly because Beatrice Webb drove it on past the collection of opinions to the collection of empirical data. In all, its members visited 400 institutions, attended 160 meetings and interviewed Guardians from 200 Unions. They called for a mass of memoranda and statistical returns from central and local government. They enquired into systems of relief in other countries, including New Zealand and Canada. They collated data on trade depressions, on immigration and emigration, on the growth of trade unions, on the use of female labour.

A report on the operation of Boards of Guardians seems to carry the mark of the COS. They were concerned about the system of election, and the poor quality of those elected. This was partly due to public apathy. Only 28.1 per cent of the population voted in the Guardians' elections in 1906, as against a 78.3 per cent vote for parliamentary elections. People became Guardians for the wrong reasons – often because they had political ambitions. The comment that 'Many men become Guardians as a stepping stone to the Town Council' may have been aimed at George Lansbury, who had begun his own political career as a member of the Board of Guardians for Poplar. In one instance 'A lady was beaten at the elections by a publican who brought twenty-five electors drunk to the poll'. Guardians were 'often totally ignorant of the procedure of a public meeting . . . ignorant and assertive'. Frequently they had no knowledge of the principles of public relief, or of the facts of individual cases. The conclusion was:

It is not a question of the social status of the Guardians, still less of wealth or poverty; but it is a question of choosing, from whatever class of the community, experienced, thoughtful, and above all disinterested men and women, to perform a most important public service. We believe that there are many such men and women quite prepared to give the service, who will not face a popular election carried on under present conditions and will not make the promises of liberal relief which are so potent in an election, and so fatal to good administration.[12]

An exhaustive statistical survey, published as Part II of the Report, was directed by Professor William Smart. It gave a breakdown of the pauper population as at 1 July 1907. There were 868,276 paupers – equivalent to the population of Liverpool. Of these, 27.6 per cent were men, 43.0 per cent were women and 29.4 per cent were children. These figures alone should have been enough to end the persistent myth of the pauper as an able-bodied male. The age breakdown was even more telling: the number of paupers was only 3.3 per thousand in the 15–24 age-group and 6.6 in the 25–34 age-group; but it rose steadily to 163.0 per thousand aged 65–74, 275.9 per thousand aged 75–84, and 353.1 per thousand – more than one in three – of those aged 85 and over. The case for old age pensions could not have been more clearly put; but these figures had no effect in modifying the COS view.

Beatrice Webb set up investigations of her own, which were financed by Fabian sympathizers. At a meeting of the Fabian Executive in July 1907, it was decided to ask 'the richer members the Society' to contribute to the cost, and Beatrice acquired her own research workers and secretariat.[13] An investigation on the effect of outdoor relief on wages elicited the information that there *was* no effect on wages – since hardly any able-bodied men received outdoor relief. This hardly matched the conviction that guardians were handing out liberal relief to undeserving applicants.

Another enquiry was concerned with the effect of a refusal of outdoor relief on families. The report stated that in no case had it led to sustained assistance from relatives; and that no charity had provided more than spasmodic gifts. Unemployed men appeared to be disheartened by a refusal, and did not seem to make greater efforts to obtain work. There was often marked physical deterioration. 'If eventually they are forced to enter the house,' reported the investigator, 'they do so with health gone, home gone, and spirit and courage shattered.'[14]

A report on the 150,000 children on poor relief painted a vivid picture of their condition. They were 'under-nourished, many of them poorly dressed and bare-footed . . . the under-nourished child is easily tired, and usually slow, dull and listless, but he is often not to his knowledge hungry, and will refuse good food'.

The problems of single mothers were described in this report:

They have to take up the position of both parents, be breadwinner and housewife, keep house, often on an impossibly small sum, cook, clean, mend and bake, often when others are asleep. Little wonder that they break down in health and courage, and become ineffective, colourless and whining.[15]

In May 1906, Beatrice Webb could see neither shape nor purpose to the Commission's deliberations. It became clear that she could not hope to convert her fellow members by argument: they had to be confronted head-on. In December of the following year, she submitted to the Commission a closely written document on 'the break-up of the Poor Law' which was 'received in stony silence'. 'The COS were chuckling at the defeat of my scheme . . . by persistent discourtesy, they have absolved me from the obligations of good fellowship.'

This document was to develop into the Minority Report. 'There was coldness towards me', Beatrice notes in October 1908, 'and Lansbury says they are very angry at the length of my report'; and in November:

The poor old Commission – and it is getting more old and weary, if not actually senile, with every week's sitting. It is floundering about in its morass of a report . . . our document stares at them in a fine blue cover . . . there it is, 300 pages of reasoned stuff, with a scheme of reform at the end.[16]

According to Beatrice, when the last meeting came, the final version of the Majority Report was not ready, so the Commissioners who supported the COS view had to sign blank pieces of paper. She implies that some of them may not have been quite clear what they signing. Only three other members joined her in signing the Minority Report – Russell Wakefield, George Lansbury and a trade union member, Francis Chandler. It should be said that this picture of the Commission's final stages is markedly different from that presented by Helen Bosanquet, who totally ignores the Minority Report, and treats the Majority Report as an uncontested triumph for rationality and common sense.[17]

The fact that there are two reports is not apparent from the contents list of the official published version. It is presented as 'The Report of the Royal Commission on the Poor Laws' – with a dissenting minority view listed in small print near the end. All the investigations (including those set up by Beatrice and paid for by the Fabians) are listed as part of the main report. In fact, the two sets of recommendations are of roughly equal length.

Both the Majority and the Minority recognized that the existing Poor Law was obsolete, and wanted to hand its functions over to the county and county borough councils. Beyond that, they diverged.

The Majority Report

The views of the Majority commissioners were that the Poor Law needed reform, but that the principle of the Goschen Minute should be maintained – the public authority should provide only a basic minimum, and voluntary agencies should provide better standards for the 'more deserving'.

The 'leading defects of the Poor Law system' were that the Union areas were too small to meet the growing needs of administration; that the Poor Law system was isolated from other forms of local government, which were developing rapidly; that the Boards of Guardians were unsuitable administrators; and that there was too little central control. They recommended that the central authority (then the Local Government Board) should have a higher status, with a Secretary of State as its head; local administration should be undertaken by a committee of the county or county borough council; the name of the service should be changed from 'Poor Law' to 'Public Assistance'; workhouses should be classified institutions, and their operation should be 'as far as possible curative and restorative'; and outdoor relief (renamed 'Home Assistance') should be handled primarily by voluntary agencies, and conditional on recipients 'living respectable lives in decent houses'.

This final recommendation was an attempt to give a controlling role to the COS, with the state system as the last resort, in the spirit of the Goschen Minute of forty years earlier.

The Minority Report

The Webbs' analysis was of a completely different order. They argued that poverty was not due to personal failing: it was an artificial problem, created by a capitalist society. All the apparatus of voluntary organizations, special administrative machinery and institutions were merely serving capitalist purposes. What was necessary was the total abolition of the concept of 'the poor' as a class and pauperism as a problem, and the total break-up of the Poor Law system.

In its place the Webbs proposed the principle of 'Administrative Functionalism'. This meant that people who were poor would be assisted by organizations framed to meet the different causes of poverty rather than its common effects. Their main recommendation was that the problems of the able-bodied poor and the non-able-bodied poor (this rather clumsy phrase had replaced the 'impotent poor') should be separated.

The non-able-bodied poor should be the responsibility of the local authority, but dealt with by committees with specialist staff: children would be the responsibility of the Education Committee, sick and disabled people the responsibility of the Health Committee, mentally ill and mentally handicapped people the responsibility of the Asylums Committee. These bodies already existed for other purposes. What was new was the proposed allocation to them of responsibility for individuals in need who had previously been classified as 'poor'. The local authority would be empowered to provide institutional or domiciliary care as required, and grants in aid would be provided from Government funds. Each of these local committees would have a clear line of responsibility to a central government department: the Education Committee to the Board of Education; the Health Committee to a Ministry or Board of Health (not the Local Government Board, which was still dominated by the Poor Law ethos); the Asylums Committee to the Lunacy Commissioners. These central government departments would be responsible for administering the grants in aid, and setting down guidelines. Each would have its own inspectorate to ensure the maintenance of standards.

The able-bodied poor would be treated by totally different methods which emphasized the responsibility of the state to provide work rather than the responsibility of the individual to find it. A Ministry of Labour would be set up, with six sections: Labour Exchanges, Trade, Maintenance and Training, Industrial Regulation, Emigration and Immigration, Statistics. A government economic programme would be planned to meet the trade cycle on a ten-year basis: there would be high taxation during the boom years, and lower taxation and encouragement of investment during the years of economic depression. Labour Exchanges would be established in every area. Casual labourers would be woven into two or more trades which might complement each other. There would be a reduction of hours for young workers, so that they had an opportunity for further education, to provide a way out of blind-alley jobs.

The wilfully idle would be sent to a reformatory colony run by the Home Office. It is notable that the Webbs never denied the existence of a small group of people who would not work, and their view was the ortho-dox Marxist one: labour and self-maintenance were duties which the citi-zen owed the state, and those who did not accept those duties had to be taught to do so; but the proper management of the economy and the labour market would ensure that the stigma of idleness was not applied to people who were willing to work.

A bare recital of the main points of the two reports indicates that there was never any real possibility of unanimity, much as Beatrice Webb claims that she hoped for it. Unanimity would only have been possible on her terms. The majority and the minority proceeded from differ-ent views of human psychology, different views of society, different experience, different knowledge-bases.

The Webbs were so incensed by the way in which the reports were officially presented that they published the Minority Report separately at their own expense through the Fabian Society as *Break Up the Poor Law and Abolish the Workhouse*. The Treasury intervened, claiming copyright for what was technically a Government publication. Sidney Webb pointed out that the copyright was properly his, since the document was in his handwriting – final proof of the degree of his involvement in the Commission's work; and the Treasury withdrew its opposition.[18] No one seems to have com-mented on the fact that Sidney was not actually a member of the Commission.

'If we had not taken steps' Beatrice wrote in February 1909, 'we should have been submerged completely.' The Webbs took steps. They embarked on two years of 'raging, tearing propaganda', lecturing or speaking five or six times a week. The National Committee for the Break-up of the Poor Law, soon re-titled the National Committee for the Prevention of Destitu-tion, attracted 16,000 members. The campaign was enough to defeat the Majority proposals, but not enough to carry the country; for while the Commission debated, the Liberals (excluded from its membership) had been in power for three years, and had already embarked on their own programme of social reform. The great Conservative–Socialist debate was on the sidelines of current policy.

The Long View

The recommendations of both majority and minority went on the shelf, and gathered dust for decades. So much heat and anger, so much work, produced so little result; but they were not forgotten. Over twenty years later, the Poor Law Act of 1930 implemented much of the Majority Report, creating Public Assistance Committees of local authorities and a reformed and more specialized Public Assistance Service. By that time, the COS had lost much of its influence, and the recommendations for a distinction between 'deserving' and 'undeserving' and for the enhanced position of voluntary agencies had been dropped. The Society never had the resources nor the organization to undertake such a role, and this fact was recognized in 1930 by a noted jurist, Sir Ivor Jennings:

> Unfortunately, the recommendations of the majority were coloured by the views of certain of the commissioners in favour of organised charity, and are now recognised to be hopelessly impracticable and undesirable.[19]

The Minority Report had a longer time to wait. The Webbs' campaign attracted considerable support, not least among the local authorities, in the few years before 1914. Like many other social movements, it was lost in the stress and muddle of the First World War. It then became part of a Socialist charter, to be implemented when a Socialist government had the power. Nearly forty years after its first publication, the first Labour Government with a clear majority in the House of Commons was to make it the basis for the 'Welfare State' legislation of the late 1940s.

'Hateful friction' wrote Beatrice Webb; but the research and the thinking and even the friction were to be valuable in the long term. Meanwhile in 1909, the Liberals were in office, and already devising their own solutions.

CHAPTER SEVEN

The Liberal Answer

The Liberals took power in 1906 with a parliamentary majority of 356. The pressure for social reform was gathering, and the Government was in a position to enact any measures it considered advisable. Derek Fraser takes the view that reform came slowly, and was mainly due to the small group of Labour MPs who now had a place in the House of Commons. He argues that the Liberals were much more concerned at the time with issues such as free trade, Chinese labour in South Africa, and the battle over denominational schools following Balfour's Act of 1902.[1] Many Liberal MPs were Nonconformists, and religious issues were hotly debated.

A reading of the parliamentary debates for the period does suggest that a great deal of debating time was spent on these issues, and there is no doubt that the Labour members acted as a pressure group; but there is much evidence that the Liberal Government was strongly committed to social reform even during the two years 1907 and 1908 when the cautious and ailing Campbell-Bannerman was Prime Minister. After Asquith became Prime Minister in 1908, with Lloyd George as Chancellor of the Exchequer, the lines of a distinctively Liberal policy were much more clearly delineated, owing little to either Conservative or Socialist thinking. But the record even in the first two years is stronger than Fraser suggests.

The first two measures were admittedly apparently minor ones which seemed to lack the weight of positive Government conviction. The Education (Provision of Meals) Act of 1906 empowered all local authorities to provide school meals in elementary (primary) schools, and to raise a half-penny rate to provide free meals for children who were 'unable by reason of lack of food to take full advantage of the education provided for them'. This was a private member's Bill, and not a government measure. The

Education (Administrative Provisions) Act of 1907 contained among many other clauses an apparently unimportant proposal for medical inspection of schoolchildren. In fact, this measure had very wide implications: it gave wide powers of delegation to the central Board of Education to organize measures for 'the health and physical condition of children educated in public elementary schools'. In time, this led to the setting up of a Medical Department at the Board of Education, close liaison between health services and education services, and a system of school clinics in every area. Since this was the first provision outside the Poor Law for the health. of a whole sector of the population, it was in some sense the beginning of the National Health Service.

By the end of 1908, at least six other measures which had reached the statute-book testify to the Liberal Government's strong concern for social reform: the Workmen's Compensation Act of 1907, and five Acts passed in 1908: the Children Act, the Incest Act, the Probation of Offenders Act, the Labour Exchanges Act and the first Old Age Pensions Act.

The Children Act was primarily a consolidating measure, bringing together provisions spread over 39 different statutes for infant life protection and the prevention of cruelty to children. It also made the first separate provision for juvenile delinquency, setting up special courts with a separate panel of magistrates. The Children Act and the Incest Act had two major policy implications: the recognition that children had rights, and were not simply the property of their parents – a considerable incursion into the closed circle of the Victorian family; and the understanding that there was no sharp line to be drawn between neglected children and delinquent children, since a poor home background might be a contributory cause to either condition.

The Probation of Offenders Act provided the basis for the system whereby some offenders might be allowed to continue to live in the community, with a Probation Officer (usually a worker from a temperance organization in the early days) to 'advise, assist and befriend' them. This was a first step in the development of alternatives to prison, and a major contribution to the development of social work.

The Workmen's Compensation Act of 1907 provided compensation for industrial injuries in dangerous trades, and made it necessary for the employers to insure their workforce. Again, this was a first step in what was to become a national scheme.

The Labour Exchanges measure of 1908 provided a national network of labour exchanges, where those who were seeking work might find out what work was available. The state took over some 61 local labour exchanges already in existence, and run by municipalities. By 1913, there were 430 major labour exchanges, and over a thousand small rural offices. This measure owed much to the work of William Beveridge, who was recommended to Lloyd George by the Webbs.

The major pressure for reform in the period 1906–8 came from Asquith at the Exchequer and Lloyd George at the Board of Trade. They were already thinking about the possibilities of national insurance as a way of lifting the working population out of poverty, and the Workmen's Compensation Act and the Labour Exchanges Act were designed as preliminary steps in the fulfilment of this aim. A further step was the development of the first old-age pension.

The campaign for pensions for old people had by this time a long history of public support. The poverty surveys of Booth and Rowntree had made it clear beyond all doubt that old age was a major cause of poverty. The issues had been long debated and there was agreement in principle; but legislation had been held up by disagreement about the means: should the pension be contributory or non-contributory? How should it be financed? Could the country afford it?

The arguments in favour of a contributory pension were that it would be largely self-financing, and would not immediately affect the budget; and recipients would feel that they had earned their benefits by contributions. The arguments against were that a contributory pension scheme would take years to build up, and that most of the people who needed old-age pensions were women, who were unlikely to have paid contributions, since most women did not then have regular outside employment.

The terms of the Old Age Pensions Act of 1908 may seem timid by later standards, but represented a considerable advance at the time. The Act provided for a non-contributory pension of five shillings a week at the age of seventy for both sexes, subject to a means test and a 'moral' test. The means test involved a full pension for those with up to £21 a year in income, and a sliding scale to £31 10s a year, where the pension dropped to a shilling a week.

The 'moral' test meant that the pension was not to be given to people who were habitually drunken, had served a prison sentence in the previous ten years, were on poor relief or had habitually failed to support themselves. These provisions were to fall into disuse within a few years.

The positive elements were that the pension was non-contributory, and therefore not dependent on proving entitlement. It was paid through the

Post Office, without stigma. Married women received the same pension as men and unmarried women – a proposal that a married couple should receive only 7s 6d joint pension was defeated. The pension had nothing whatever to do with the Poor Law. Five shillings a week was not enough to live on; but for many old people, it was enough, with a little put by, to remove the ever-present fear of the workhouse. Flora Thompson tells in *Lark Rise* how the 'aged cottagers' of her village went to the Post Office with tears of gratitude running down their cheeks, because the pension would allow them to keep their independence; and how they said 'God bless that Lord George' because they thought only a lord could be so kind; and how some brought flowers from their gardens and apples from their trees as presents for the girl behind the Post Office counter who handed them the money.[2] Few government measures can have produced so much simple happiness.

Meanwhile, the main debate about poverty went on. The Royal Commission on the Poor Laws continued to meet weekly. It is revealing to discover that, when the Webbs' Minority Report was in draft and circulating round the Commission, Lloyd George, by that time Chancellor of the Exchequer, asked for a copy, and the chairman refused to let him have one.[3] But before the Commission finally reported in 1909, Campbell-Bannerman had retired, Asquith had become Prime Minister, Lloyd George was Chancellor of the Exchequer, and Winston Churchill took over the Board of Trade.

The many biographers of Winston Churchill do not make much of this period in his life, when he was 'a Radical of Radicals',[4] and he and Lloyd George formed a partnership with common aims and ideals. The Welshman born in a cobbler's cottage in North Wales and the young Churchill shared one quality: a vision of a better Britain. Churchill told an audience at Blackpool that when he read Rowntree's *Poverty: A Study of Town Life*, his hair stood on end.[5] Lady Violet Bonham Carter, who first met him in 1906, when he was 32, wrote:

> The Liberal Government was determined to lay the ugly spectre of poverty, and to spread a net over the abyss. It is to Winston Churchill's signal credit that he embraced these aims, and fought with all his heart and might to realise them.[6]

As the Old Age Pensions Act reached the statute-book, Lloyd George went to Germany to study the scheme of health and unemployment insurance introduced under Bismarck. The tour in August 1908, was an intensive one. Lloyd George and his official entourage visited a number of German cities, including Berlin, where they called at the Imperial Old Age and Invalid Insurance Offices, and dined with the Imperial vice-chancellor. They visited the docks and shipyards at Hamburg, holding discussions with trade union leaders and radical politicians. Though relations between Britain and Germany were deteriorating, Lloyd George seems to have been treated with much courtesy, and to have learned a good deal. On the train on the way back from Southampton to London, he gave a Press interview, and said that he was 'tremendously impressed with the finished character and perfection of the whole machine'.[7] The next step was to devise a broader contributory scheme for England and Wales which could be grafted on to the Old Age Pensions provisions.

The time was hardly propitious. There was a trade recession, a government committed to free trade could not raise money from tariffs, and before Asquith left the Exchequer, he had reduced the duty on imported sugar, which was a popular measure, but left very little provision for social insurance. The cost was estimated at £6 million. The money set aside was only £1.2 million. This disparity was to lead to the controversial 'People's Budget' of 1909, the first openly redistributive budget which proposed a super-tax of 6d in the pound and a tax on land values, and to bitter conflict with the House of Lords in 1911, when the powers of the Lords in relation to Finance Bills were severely curtailed.

In 1909, the Royal Commission on the Poor Laws finally reported. Though the Majority and Minority Reports were fundamentally different in aims and scope, the two sets of Commissioners agreed in refusing to consider national insurance. The Conservative majority were opposed to it on the grounds that it involved state intervention. The Fabian minority were opposed to it on the grounds that workers on low incomes would not be able to afford contributions. According to John Burns, then President of the Local Government Board, Lloyd George was gleeful that he had 'dished the Webbs' and found a non-Socialist solution to the problems of poverty.[8] (Winston Churchill's alleged comment that he would not wish to be locked up in a soup kitchen with Mrs Sidney Webb seems to date from the same period. No doubt Beatrice Webb used all her considerable powers of advocacy).

Once the Liberal Government had determined on an insurance scheme, there were four main decisions to be made. Should it be contributory or non-contributory? If it was to be seen as an extension of the principles of mutual aid to the classes at greatest risk, it was necessary that it should be contributory: workers would pay contributions, and draw benefits in time of need. Should it be financially watertight, like a commercial insurance scheme, or involve an Exchequer contribution? If contributions were to be fixed at a level which workers on low wages could afford to pay, an Exchequer contribution would be necessary, and what proportion could the Exchequer be prepared to meet? Should it be a flat-rate scheme, in which everyone paid the same contributions and was entitled to the same benefits, or should it be wage-related? It was decided, on grounds of social equity and adherence to insurance practice, that it should be flat-rate. Should the scheme work through existing agencies, or should special administrative agencies be set up? Setting up a national network of Government agencies would have been very costly, so it was decided to use the Friendly Societies to administer the scheme. (There was no special machinery for the non-contributory old-age pensions scheme of 1908. That was administered for some reason by the Customs and Excise Department.)

In the budget debate of 30 June 1910, Lloyd George had an answer for those who accused the Liberal Government of making 'reckless promises' to the people. 'What were these reckless promises?' he asked,

> They had made a 'reckless promise' about old age pensions, and there were already between 800,000 and 900,000 people receiving them. They had made another 'reckless promise' that the pensions would be extended to paupers, and on January 1 there would be about 240,000 aged paupers walking to the Post Office for their five shillings a week. They had made another 'reckless promise' about labour exchanges, and these were now in operation, and had provided work for 100,000 people. They had made another 'reckless promise' for next year that they would bring in unemployment insurance.[9]

The National Insurance Act of 1911

In its final form, the Act represented a settlement achieved after long and tortuous negotiations with powerful pressure groups: the friendly societies, the trade unions and the doctors. It had two distinct parts: unemployment insurance and health insurance. The unemployment insurance scheme originally covered only two and a quarter million workers, 90 per cent of them men. The contribution rate was 2d a week for employees, 2d a week for employers, with an Exchequer subsidy equal to one-third of the combined amount. It applied only to workers in fluctuating trades, such as building, shipbuilding and iron founding. Benefit was payable at a basic rate of 7s a week for an adult male (slightly less for women and juveniles), subject to contribution conditions. There were no benefits for dependants, and proposals for widows' and orphans' benefits were dropped. Benefit was payable through the new labour exchanges, which could test the genuineness of claims by making them subject to the availability of suitable employment.

The health scheme had a different and wider basis. It applied to all manual workers between the ages of 16 and 70 earning less than £250 a year (£5 a week was then a good wage) and to non-manual workers earning less than £160 a year. Contributors registered with a friendly society of their choice, and there was a residual scheme, organized through the Post Office, for those refused by the voluntary societies on the grounds that they were poor risks. Contributions were 4d from the employee, 3d from the employer and 2d from the Exchequer – hence the popular election cry of 'Ninepence for fourpence'. The scheme originally provided for sickness benefit (10s a week), disablement benefit (5s a week) and a maternity grant of 30s on the birth of a child, doubled if both husband and wife were insured. If the worker needed medical attention, there was a 'panel system' by which he or she could choose a doctor from a list kept by the local insurance committee.

'I do not pretend,' said Lloyd George, 'that this is a complete remedy; Before you get a complete remedy for these social evils, you will have to cut deeper.'[10] But it was a notable beginning.

The National Insurance Scheme in Practice

National insurance was introduced in 1912. Insured people had a card for unemployment insurance, usually kept by their employers, to which stamps were affixed weekly, thus emphasizing the contributory aspects of the scheme. (Some ladies in Mayfair and Belgravia, appalled at the prospect of having to keep cards for their staff, founded a society which campaigned against 'licking stamps for Lloyd George',[11] but in fact domestic servants were not included in the classes of employees covered). The health insurance scheme, run through the friendly societies, meant a continuation of the existing practice by which agents went from door to door, collecting dues weekly.

For central government, the schemes involved major calculations of risk: the study of economic and demographic trends, estimates of the likely risks of sickness and unemployment. There was no experience of this kind of actuarial work in Whitehall, and it was anticipated that the unemployment scheme would run smoothly, while the health scheme might run into difficulty, because the incidence of sickness was unpredictable.

In the event, the health scheme presented little difficulty. The days of the major epidemic diseases were over, and the scheme was actuarially sound. The big friendly societies made large profits, and ploughed some of them back into additional benefits for their subscribers. The employment scheme started well enough in the two years before the First World War. By 1914, the Fund had a balance of over £3 million, and only £700,000 had been paid out in benefits.

During the war, coverage was extended to munitions workers, who were likely to be thrown out of work when hostilities ended. At the end of 1918, there was a healthy surplus of £15 million. The Government made 'Out of Work Donations' to former munition workers and ex-servicemen, and it seemed that the adjustment to peace-time conditions was proceeding without major problems. Government optimism ran so high in 1920 that the scheme was extended to all manual and non-manual workers earning less than £250 a year apart from agricultural workers and people in per-manent employment, such as railway workers and local authority employees, and plans were made to introduce benefits for dependants – five shillings a week for a wife, and a shilling for a child. At that time, an adult man's contribution was fourpence a week, and the basic benefit twenty shillings. But in 1921, unemployment rose sharply, and the problems began.

CHAPTER EIGHT

The Hungry Thirties

Up to the time of the First World War, the great powers ran their own budgets, and paid relatively little attention to the state of each other's economies. The world after 1918 was to be very different: communications improved, international trade increased, and booms or slumps became impossible for individual countries to control. There were theories about 'the trade cycle', which was thought by some economists to occur at regular intervals on an international scale; but the sudden growth of unemployment in 1921 in the aftermath of war seems to have taken the Liberal Government by surprise.

By the end of 1921, 14 per cent of the insured workforce were unemployed, and the reserves of the Fund had shrunk to £1 million. Two separate Acts had been passed raising contributions and cutting benefit.

Table 8.1 *Unemployment insurance, contributions and benefits 1920–31*

	Worker	Employer	Exchequer	Benefits
Contributions for an adult male worker:				
Nov. 1920	4d	4d	2d	15s
July 1921	7d	8d	3d	15s
Nov. 1921	9d	10d	6d	15s
Jan. 1926	7d	8d	6d	15s
Apr. 1926	7d	8d	6d	17s
Apr. 1929	7d	8d	7½d	17s
Oct. 1931	10d	10d	10d	15s 3d

Source: Royal Commission on Unemployment Insurance, chairman, Judge Holman Gregory, *Final Report*, HMSO, Cmnd. 4185, 1932, pp. 19–20.

That was the beginning of years of frantic juggling with the figures: raising contributions, cutting benefits, setting increasingly stringent conditions before workers were entitled to claim, increasing the waiting period before benefit could be taken up. Table 8.1. indicates the major changes which took place up to 1931.

Table 8.1 tells its own story of the efforts to keep contributions within what a working man could afford to pay, to pass more of the burden on to the employer, to reduce the Exchequer contribution (but then to accept that it must be increased) and the decline of benefits to a level on which a family could barely live.

The 'Geddes Axe' of 1922, the General Strike of 1926, when organized Labour brought the country to a near standstill, and a worsening international economic situation, culminating in the Wall Street crash of 1931 are all reflected in the figures.

The 'Geddes Axe', named after Sir Eric Geddes, Secretary to the Treasury, was a policy by which Government cut public sector employment and state subsidies. It was the beginning of a period of retrenchment based on the economic understanding of the day: that costs had to be cut in order to balance the budget. People in work should accept salary cuts (and the salaries of civil servants and teachers were cut, in some instances by 10 per cent or more). The number of jobs was regarded as fixed, so that people who did not 'need' a job were dismissed, or expected to retire from the job market. Married women were expected to retire from paid employment, and to be dependent on their husbands. It was quite common in the 1930s for young women teachers or civil servants who wanted to continue working to conceal the fact that they were married, to keep their single names, and wear their wedding rings on chains round their necks. Older workers entitled to a minimal retirement pension were expected to give up work 'to make a job for a younger man'. Wages were cut in many trades, and the combined effect of low wages and rapidly rising unemployment inevitably led to industrial conflict.

At that time, coal mining was by far the largest industry in Britain, with over a million workers, and the miners were the pacemakers in terms of industrial relations. By 1925, British mines were running at a loss, due to the import of cheap coal from Germany and Poland The mine owners cut wages, lengthened hours of work, and often ignored safety regulations in an attempt to reduce production costs. Miners had a particular solidarity, born out of the hazardous and gruelling nature of their work, and their resistance to these measures soon developed into acute class conflict. The mine owners threatened a lock-out. The Trades Union Congress backed the miners, and other unions joined the strike.

The General Strike of 1926 lasted only eleven days, but it virtually brought the country to a standstill. The Government tried not to become involved, arguing that this was a private dispute between employers and employees, but was soon sufficiently alarmed to make plans for dealing with civil war. Britain was divided into ten autonomous regions, each with a civil commissioner who could act independently of Whitehall. When the workers on the printing presses came out on strike, and there were no newspapers, Winston Churchill ran an official Government paper which demanded 'unconditional surrender' from the strikers. Churchill's political stance had changed. As A. J. P. Taylor comments, the call to 'unconditional surrender' was to be used to better effect in the Second World War.[1]

There was an appeal for conciliation from King George V, and another from the Archbishop of Canterbury, backed by the leaders of other Churches; but the risk of civil war was never a real one. Organized labour had tried its strength, and it was not strong enough. The trade unions were beaten, their funds depleted. The miners stayed out of the pits for six months before they were 'driven back to work by starvation'. A. J. Cronin's *The Stars Look Down* tells the story of the miners' strike in a powerful novel of the period.

Wal Hannington's *Unemployed Struggles 1919–1936* records the hunger marches organized by the National Unemployed Workers' Movement through those long and desperate years. Hannington was an engineer who became the leader of the NUWM, and took part himself in the marches, which were to become a repeated feature of English life for sixteen years. On the first march: 'Many men took to the road even without overcoats, much less blankets and other necessary kit. There were no food kitchens for the contingents. There were no assurances of food or guarantees of places to sleep. It was an adventure which only men with deep-seated grievances would be prepared to undertake.'[2] The men came from Glasgow, Lancashire, South Wales, Tyneside and the Midlands, often ragged and half starved. They came in their thousands and tens of thousands, walking for weeks, sustained at first only by a sense of common purpose and a sense of injustice. Public sympathy was roused in time: church halls and other buildings were made available to them, local committees arranged food and shelter. The Lord Mayor of London raised a relief fund of over £1 million for the unemployed.

In London, year after year and time after time, the marchers filled Trafalgar Square, and marched through the City and the West End. In Edinburgh on one occasion, 20,000 converged on St Giles' Cathedral, and some 2,000 ended by sleeping in the gutters in Prince's Street. When two miners died on one London march:

> Their bodies were returned to their native soil. In the funeral procession which marched through London, the coffins were covered with the red flag of the workers, and on each stood an unlighted miner's lamp. The silent march to Paddington station was most impressive; thousands on that great station stood hushed in silence as the marchers bore the bodies of their dead comrades to the van of the train.[3]

Probably few of the marchers were Communists, as Hannington was, and even Communist sympathies were with the British workers rather than with Moscow; but successive governments, both Conservative and Labour, saw them as a political danger rather than as citizens asking for help. There were scuffles, and baton charges by the police, and threats of military action. Wal Hannington and his colleagues told the troops that if they were ordered to fire on the unemployed, they should remember their working-class origin, and not shoot their brothers. For this, they were convicted on charges of 'preaching sedition', 'uttering seditious libels' and 'incitement to mutiny amongst H.M. Forces' and sent to prison.

It was a good way to make martyrs. Crowds formed outside, singing 'The Red Flag' and 'The Internationale' in support. Hannington says that there were untrue allegations that the National Unemployed Workers' Movement was supported by 'Bolshevik gold'. The ranks of the marchers were infiltrated by 'spies and *agents provocateurs*', who tried to turn the movement to a violence which would have justified a violent response.[4] But the men (and some women) who marched were not demanding the overthrow of government. They wanted work. Photographs of the period show them as gaunt and hopeless, many of them prematurely old.

George Orwell, in *The Road to Wigan Pier*, gives an unforgettable picture of life in a decaying Lancashire town. He is appalled by the dirt, the squalor, the revolting food, 'the sense of stagnant, meaningless decay . . . the monstrous scenery of slag-heaps, chimneys, piled scrap-iron, foul canals, paths of cindery mud' in a place where people 'go creeping round just like blackbeetles, in an endless muddle of slovened jobs and mean grievances':

For this in part is what industrialisation has done for us. Columbus sailed the Atlantic, the first steam engines tottered into action, the British Squares stood firm under the French guns at Waterloo, the one-eyed scoundrels of the nineteenth century praised God and filled their pockets – and this is where it all led.[5]

Orwell sees all this with great clarity – perhaps the more so because he was not born to it. (He was the son of an Indian High Court judge, and an Old Etonian.) But, like Charles Booth, he knew the smell and the taste of poverty at first hand. He knew the impossibility of living a decent life on unemployment benefit in 'any hole or corner slum, any misery of bugs and rotting floors and cracking walls, any extortion of skinflint landlords and blackmailing agents'.

He estimated the extent of misery: if two million people were registered unemployed, that did not mean that the rest of the population was comparatively well-off. When the destitute, the people who failed to register, the dependent families of unemployed men, the families on starvation wages, the old people unable to earn a little or to get help from their children and 'other nondescripts' were added, he calculated the total at near ten million people.[6]

Two factors mitigated the harshness of the reduced benefits: the introduction of dependants' allowances – at first intended to be only a temporary measure, but incorporated as a permanent part of the scheme; and the introduction of 'uncovenanted benefit', later called 'transitional benefit' for workers who had exhausted their benefit rights. This gave them an extra period of benefit at a lower rate.

Blanesburgh and Holman Gregory

In 1925, when the situation seemed to be improving slightly, the Minister of Labour appointed a Committee to review the unemployment insurance scheme under the chairmanship of Lord Blanesburgh. It sat through the General Strike and the panic measures of 1926, and concluded gloomily 'even actuaries are not prophets'.[7] No one had foreseen the extent of unemployment, and the financial drains on the scheme. Witnesses who gave evidence to the Blanesburgh Committee advocated their own remedies. Some thought that the scheme should become non-contributory, since the needs were so much greater than the workers' capacity to pay contributions. Others thought that it should be abolished altogether, since it had degenerated into 'public charity'. The Committee's conclusion was that the scheme was sound, but that benefit should be paid indefinitely to those out of work without regard to contribution conditions. The main cause of the problem was thought to be the trade cycle, but the Committee took the view that major booms and slumps were predictable enough to be taken into account in actuarial calculations.

'The rather stupid Blanesburgh Committee' wrote Beveridge to Churchill,[8] were recommending the prediction of the unpredictable, and the abolition of the insurance principle which he had fought so hard to establish. In 1930, the Labour Government appointed a higher level investigation, a Royal Commission under the chairmanship of Judge Holman Gregory. But before that Commission could complete its task, a Treasury Committee, the May Committee, reported that the budget must be balanced at all costs, and that Britain must continue to pay off the national debt. Cuts in unemployment benefit were therefore inevitable. The Labour Government fell on the issue. The King asked Ramsay MacDonald to head a National Coalition Government, and the Labour movement never forgave Ramsay MacDonald for doing so. He went to the country. An election was fought largely on the issue of whether the unemployed should receive 17s or 15s 3d a week, and whether they could live on the latter amount. Ramsay MacDonald, returned to power, presided over the cut in unemployment benefit to 15s 3d, and Britain abandoned the gold standard, which was a considerable blow to national morale and to the country's economic standing.

Two years later, the Holman Gregory Commission produced its final report. They had a much clearer policy to offer than Blanesburgh. Insurance was defined as:

> a contract whereby an individual or a group of individuals pays a premium in return for a guaranteed indemnity against a specific loss . . . premiums should be so adjusted as to cover the payment out, together with administrative expenses.[9]

At that time, the unemployment insurance scheme covered 12.5 million workers out of a total workforce of 18 million. In October 1931, 2,726,000 were drawing unemployment benefit, and a further 526,000 were drawing transitional benefit, which could run for up to 100 weeks. If the insurance principle was to be maintained, the scheme should be limited to those whose contributions entitled them to benefit. Those who had exhausted benefit should be funded by a separate mechanism; but the Commission was emphatic that this should not be administered by the Public Assistance Committee:

> The ordinary Poor Law services of the Local Authorities must remain to meet the needs of all who are in distress from causes other than unemployment ... but we desire as far as possible to distinguish for separate treatment those whose distress is due simply to unemployment, *and whose distress is due to no personal or moral defect* (author's italics).[10]

This showed a remarkable shift in opinion from the heyday of the Charity Organization Society. If it was illogical to leave other categories of people in need to the Poor Law, that was not the Commission's concern; but members were quite clear that the Poor Law was not a suitable mechanism for the relief of the unemployed. Some other body was necessary 'to take the dole out of politics'.

The result of these considerations was the Unemployment Act of 1934, which set up the Unemployment Assistance Board. This was seen at the time as a considerable step forward, safeguarding the position of the long-term unemployed and making special provision for them. The UAB developed its own scales of benefit, and its own means test. But the popularity of the new Board soon diminished when it was found that its scales of benefit were actually lower than those given on Public Assistance, and the means test was considerably harsher. This was the Household Means Test, which involved calculations based on the income of the total household, including working children, aged parents and lodgers.

Orwell pointed out that the Household Means Test broke up families. Adult sons or daughters tended to move out rather than have most of their wages deducted as a household contribution. Old age pensioners were no longer welcome in their children's homes if most of the pension was counted against unemployment assistance. When people are living on the breadline, they cannot always afford family feeling. The authorities were constantly on the look-out for 'scroungers', and neighbours would inform on each other:

> The favourite joke in Wigan was about a man who was refused relief on the grounds that he 'had a job carting firewood'. He had to explain that he was not carting firewood, he was doing a moonlight flit. The 'firewood' was his furniture.[11]

The Holman Gregory Commission had noted that unemployment was not a single phenomenon: it took many forms – short-term and long-term, intermittent or continuous, due to a variety of international, national and local factors. Measures to deal with the situation were outside their terms of reference; but though the Commission insisted that the unemployed were 'not a standing army', there were areas of Britain where they were precisely that. In Jarrow, the unemployment rate reached 67 per cent. In Glasgow, the cranes stood idle on the Clyde. In South Wales, the iron foundries stood smokeless. In the coalfields where the pits had been closed, in the mill towns of Lancashire, there was simply no hope of work, and whole communities were near starvation. These areas were widely known as 'Distressed Areas' or 'Depressed Areas'. The Government response was no more than a token one. The Special Areas Act of 1934 provided a more acceptable description, and set up a fund of £2 million to stimulate economic development. As Wal Hannington, was to point out, this was less than half the beet sugar subsidy for the previous year, and less than the beef subsidy for six months.[12]

Liberal and Labour Members of Parliament condemned the scheme as merely palliative. Lloyd George, who had not lost his gift of words, told the House of Commons, 'The age of miracles is past. You cannot feed the multitude with two Commissioners and five sub-Commissioners. The new Commissioners are being sent on their apostolic mission, not without purse and script, but pretty nearly that – just with a little bit of cash, to deal with a problem costing £100,000,000 a year.'[13] The Commissioners were not even given the task of creating jobs. They were to improve the economic development of the area, but they were not allowed to use their meagre funds to supplement any scheme for which a central government grant was payable to a local authority. As Wal Hannington commented, 'if the Ministry of Transport [offered] a local authority a 60 per cent grant towards making a new road, and that authority could not afford to find the remaining 40 per cent, the Commissioners were not permitted to bear any of the local authority's portion, even though the road would lead in their opinion to the economic development of the area'.[14]

The Commissioners had the greatest difficulty in discovering what they might and might not do, and the results of their efforts were not impressive; but by the time they were in full operation, the shadow of long-term unemployment had begun to lift. The mines, the shipyards, the mills and the foundries were busy again, preparing for the war which was only too clearly coming.

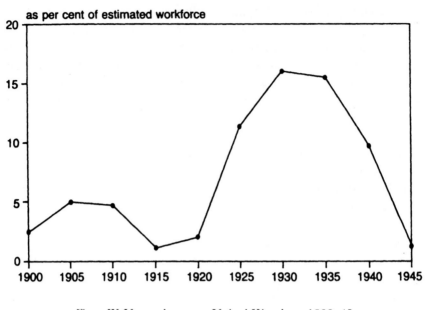

Figure IV Unemployment, United Kingdom, 1900–45
Source: Annual Abstract of Statistics.

Maynard Keynes published his *General Theory of Unemployment, Interest and Money* in 1936, though the ideas were current in left-wing circles some time before that, and had been partially anticipated in the Webbs' Minority Report of 1909. Keynes pointed out that unemployment had a multiplier effect. The unemployed became a charge on the budget, paid no taxes or insurance contributions, bought few consumer goods, and so depressed demand still further. The downward spiral could be reversed by public investment in times of depression, and higher taxation in times of prosperity would provide the resources. This view of economics was unacceptable to the Conservative government of the mid-1930s; but as Fraser points out, the Baldwin Government 'unconsciously proved Keynes right'.[15] By the second half of the 1930s, rearmament provided the public investment. The downward spiral was reversed, but the lessons of the Great Depression were not forgotten.

Better or Worse?

If the 1930s were years of great deprivation and misery for some, there were also signs of development. The very depth of misery in the 'Special Areas' stimulated efforts to improve the health and social services. It is notable, for instance, that in Merthyr Tydfil and some of the towns of south Lancashire, the infant mortality rate actually went down in the 1930s, as doctors and nurses strove to counteract the effects of poverty and malnutrition.

The Poor Law was dying at last. National insurance had lifted whole classes of the population out of its reach. Despite the difficulties of operating the basic sickness and unemployment scheme introduced in 1911, the Widows Orphans and Old Age Pensions Act of 1925 had introduced new contributory schemes to cover the risks of bereavement and old age. Though there were gaps and anomalies in state pension schemes, they guaranteed a minimum income to most working-class people. Improvements in health services, housing and education were all contributing to a better society.

The Local Government Act of 1929 finally transferred the remaining Poor Law functions to committees of the county and county borough councils, ending the rule of the Guardians. They were permitted to have up to one-third co-opted members, allowing for the recruitment of local expertise, and some of the co-opted members were to be women. There were to be sub-committees for various purposes – Finance and General Purposes, Institutions, District Assistance (out-relief) and so on. Institutions were to be regularly inspected.

The complementary Poor Law Act of 1930 at last renamed the service as 'Public Assistance'. Paupers became 'rate-aided persons', and workhouses became 'Public Assistance Institutions'. A Public Assistance Service was set up, with examinations and regular opportunities for promotion, on the lines proposed by the Majority Report of 1909. There was, however, no provision for the voluntary services to take on the 'deserving' cases: the Goschen Minute had had its day, and Public Assistance no longer attempted to distinguish between the 'deserving' and the 'undeserving'.

Though a Public Assistance service was still necessary to deal with residual poverty, successive governments were concerned to decrease its scope. The Unemployment Assistance Act of 1934 made separate provision for the long-term unemployed. The Blind Persons Act of 1938, which made special provision for blind people mandatory, revealingly specified that it should be 'not by way of the Poor Law'. Bernard Wickwar, who published a textbook on the Social Services in 1936, wrote about 'The Rump Poor Law' and looked forward to the demise of the 'two-headed monstrosity' which did not meet the needs either of those fit for work or of those who could not work.[16]

Seebohm Rowntree, by this time over 60, decided to undertake a second study of York:

> In 1935, I determined to repeat the investigation made in 1899, and to find out what changes had occurred in the living conditions of the workers during the thirty-six years which had elapsed since my previous investigation was made . . . in every well-conducted business, a balance-sheet based on a physical stocktaking is prepared periodically: if this were not done, it would be impossible accurately to assess the measure of success which had been obtained.[17]

Again he carried out a house-to-house investigation, covering 16,362 families 'comprising practically every working-class family in York'. He had been told about the technique of random sampling, but was not certain that it would produce accurate results, so he had every family investigated, and then drew samples of one in ten, one in twenty, one in thirty, one in forty and one in fifty from his data to see if the results tallied. His conclusions were that sampling was reasonably accurate if applied to large populations, but that it produced substantial inaccuracies when applied to smaller sub-samples.[18] He employed seven investigators 'on whose work full reliance could be placed', questioned them closely on their returns each week, and instituted check visits to verify their data.

It was extremely difficult to make comparisons over nearly four decades – so much had changed. This time, Rowntree fixed the Poverty Line at 43s 6d a week for a man, wife and three children. He found that 31.1 per cent of his defined 'working class population' lived below this level, and that 14.2 per cent had less than 33s 6d a week. For this latter group, more than half the total income was made up of state benefits – health insurance, unemployment insurance, pensions, Public Assistance. Unemployment accounted for nearly half of the most extreme poverty in the city. The chief causes of poverty were inadequate wages, the unemployment of the chief wage earner, and old age; but there was a paradox in that the increased numbers of old people in poverty actually represented social advance: old people lived longer, and more were able to live alone:

> Today . . . such people can manage to live, though in primary poverty, on their state pensions, often supplemented by a grant from the Public Assistance Committee, and by some additional source of private income. A few, for instance, keep a lodger, others earn a few pence or are paid in kind for rendering small services. To 'mind the baby' for a neighbour while the mother is out, or to wheel a pram on washday and do any necessary errand, will probably mean a square meal or a 'mash of tea' and some coppers, as well as discarded garments, if the neighbour's husband is in good work.[19]

Another and less encouraging reason for the increased numbers of old people in poverty was that, in time of mass unemployment, employers would use the excuse of the pension to dismiss a worker of pensionable age. In 1899, there had been a high demand for workers, and because there was no state pension then, employers had usually allowed those who wanted to continue working to do so.

People were drinking less than in 1899, Rowntree observed, because there were other leisure attractions. 'Cinema, wireless, bicycles . . . excellent roads, free libraries . . . cheap books, parks and public gardens, swimming baths, cheap railway facilities, 5,000 houses with gardens, a first-rate repertory theatre and a music hall, both with seats at low prices, adult educational classes and an educational settlement. It is an amazing list!'[20] He noted, but did not understand, the 'craze for gambling', particularly the football pools. On the whole, he thought that the standard of living was about 30 per cent higher than in 1899, but his rather convoluted statistical exercises do not really provide a firm basis for this estimate. The only figure he was prepared to stand by was his figure for primary poverty. In 1899, this had been 15.46 per cent of his sample. In 1936, it was 6.8 per cent.

In York, the main causes of improvement were a reduction in the size of the average family, an increase in real wages and the growth of social services; but Rowntree still found 'social ills to be diagnosed'. He might have found more if he had conducted his study in one of the 'Special Areas'.

PEP (Political and Economic Planning, one of the leading social research organizations of the day) produced its own national reports on the state of the Social Services and the Health Services in 1937. The Social Services Report described Public Assistance as 'the last resort', accounting for only 12 per cent of total expenditure on public social services. The main recipients were as follows:

Table 8.2 *Persons in receipt of Public Assistance, 1 January 1936*

age	number of persons	per cent of age-group
0–15	460,030	4.6
16–64	640,289	2.3
65 plus	287,401	8.7

Source: PEP *Report on the Social Services,* 1937, p. 144.

Of the 16–64 age group receiving public assistance, slightly over one third were physically or mentally unfit; but in the 65 plus age group, nearly 90 per cent were unfit. There was still a substantial amount of need among old people – and it could hardly be argued that they should stay within the scope of the Poor Law when steps had been taken to provide a less stigmatized service for long-term unemployed and blind people.

PEP concluded that much had been done, but in a pragmatic and incremental way which meant that the principles had not really been examined. There were many anomalies, particularly in the operation of the Unemployment Assistance Board and the local authority Public Assistance Committees. UAB and PAC served the same need, but the UAB's service was available only to an arbitrarily defined sector of the population – able-bodied unemployed who earned less than £250 a year when in employment, and who had been in insurable occupations. The result was that, if a man earning £6 a week became unemployed, he would have to go to the PAC, while his office boy would come within the scope of the UAB.

When families were considered, the anomalies increased; for the UAB was only concerned with workers, not with their wives and children. If a man covered by the insurance scheme was unemployed and ran out of benefit, he could claim from the UAB; but if his wife became ill, the PAC would have to provide for her and the children. What purpose was served by having two poverty services with different scales and different discretionary rules?

The administration was little short of chaotic; for the Public Assistance Service was responsible through the local authorities to the Ministry of

Health (set up in 1919 to replace the old Local Government Board: it had taken nearly fifty years for health interests to defeat Poor Law interests at central government level); but unemployment assistance was administered by a central organization, the UAB, with its own local offices; contributory old age pensions were administered by the Ministry of Health through the Post Office, but the non-contributory pension started in 1908 was still administered by the Department of Customs and Excise.

So there was a mass of provision, but there were too many ill-defined agencies, and many people were not provided for. The next step was rationalization:

> We attach great importance to the emergence of a mature philosophy and a broad strategy of the social services which can take the place of piecemeal political and administrative improvisations.[21]

The Report on the Health Services pointed out that the health insurance scheme created 'wide and irrational divergencies' consequent on the different benefits offered by different friendly societies. Since the scheme did not extend to dependents, it covered 'barely half of the ill-health risk of those contributing to it'; and since only employed people were eligible, the self-employed, such as small shopkeepers and traders, had no cover.

PEP was concerned to study the economics of ill-health:

> Many of the costs of ill-health cannot be measured in money. The subjective element in the endurance of pain and sickness cannot be estimated . . . but the cost of treatment and maintenance of sick persons is susceptible to measurement in money; it would also be possible, if data were available, to put a money value on the work lost through sickness absence from regular employment.[22]

The money value of work lost was estimated, after tentative calculations, at £285 million a year. Expenditure on preventive services came to no more than £117 million a year, and the expenditure on medical research was 'possibly one-fifth of one per cent of the natural expenditure and wastage through ill-health'.[23] What was needed was a health service, which would maintain people fit for work, rather than a sickness service, which dealt with ill-health after it had occurred:

> Millions of pounds are spent in looking after and trying to cure the victims of accidents and illnesses which need never have occurred if a

fraction of this amount of intelligence and money had been devoted to tracing the social and economic causes of the trouble.[24]

War was to be the rationalizer of a confused situation, and the philosophy came from that long-term student of social insurance and the labour market, Sir William Beveridge.

CHAPTER NINE

War, Peace and the Beveridge Plan

The British troops came scrambling back from Dunkirk in 1940, and France fell. Air raid wardens, a new and sometimes authoritarian breed, enforced the black-out and spoke of the 'Red Alert' which would signal a massive German invasion. Much of the adult population was in uniform, and the uniforms of other nations (Free French, Canadians, Norwegians, Danes, the United States and many others) were to he seen on the streets. Life was frequently boring and intermittently frightening, and there were shortages of everything – food, even bread and potatoes, clothes, transport, accommodation; but the problems were not the problems of the 1930s. Unemployment disappeared by 1941, and the 'Special Areas' no longer existed.

The Second World War changed the face of Britain. The Boer War had been comfortably distant. The war of 1914–18 had involved rationing and shortages and price rises, and a few desultory air raids, but most of the action had been in the Flanders trenches; but after the 'phoney war' of 1939–40, in which nothing very much seemed to change, the whole population was virtually on active service. There was conscription – from 1941, for women as well as men. Street signs and road signs disappeared, lest they should guide the invaders, and the country was plunged into darkness. London and other major cities were bombed nightly for long periods. The civilian population grew used to spending its nights in air raid shelters – the Anderson shelter, made of corrugated iron, had to be erected in a hole dug in the garden; the later Morrison shelter, about two feet high, fitted under the dining-room or kitchen table. In London, more old people died as a result of falling down in the black-out than were killed in air raids (one of the reasons for the formation of the National Old People's Welfare

Association, now Age Concern). Children were evacuated from the cities, to live with strangers in unfamiliar environments. Some came back, in spite of the bombs, because family ties were stronger than fear. Hospital beds, particularly those for chronic patients, were hastily emptied, and the Emergency Medical Service took over about half the country's hospital accommodation for war casualties. Exhausted doctors and nurses often worked round the clock. Four million paper coffins were prepared for the victims of air attack – most of them, fortunately, remained unused.

The history of social policy in the Second World War, written in meticulous detail by Richard Titmuss, concentrates on three themes: the evacuation of nearly four million mothers and children, the care of the homeless, and the Emergency Medical Service. Titmuss concluded:

> By the end of the Second World War, Government had, through the agency of newly established or existing services, assumed and developed a measure of direct concern for the health and well-being of the population which, by contrast with the role of Government in the nineteen-thirties, was little short of remarkable . . . it was increasingly regarded as a proper function or even obligation of Government to ward off distress and strain among not only the poor, but almost all classes of society.[1]

This had not happened in any planned or ordered sequence, and was not always the result of deliberate intent; but social values changed, particularly after Dunkirk. 'If dangers were to be shared, then resources should also be shared.' War had unexpectedly turned out to be 'a great engine of social advance'. There was a new altruism, and a new passion for social justice. It is certainly the case that the common experience of privation and danger did much to heal the gap between the social classes; and that from this new sense of 'community' came the demand for a more open and egalitarian society. In the Forces, men and women of very different social backgrounds were brought together, and often shared devastating experiences. Evacuation took children out of the slums – the 'unkempt, ill-clothed, under-nourished and often incontinent children of bombed cities',[2] and prodded the conscience of the well-to-do in the more peaceful rural areas. People accepted an unprecedented degree of government intervention in their lives – conscription, direction of labour, having troops and children billeted in their homes, the compulsory take-over of land and property, Excess Profits Tax – for the sake of winning the war; but it is doubtful whether the wartime experience alone is sufficient to explain the Khaki Election of 1945, when Winston Churchill was summarily swept from power, and a Labour Government with a large majority set about creating a 'Welfare State'.

The demand for a reconstruction policy started early in the war. A Post-War Problems Committee of the Conservative Party, chaired by R. A. Butler, was meeting as early as the summer of 1941, and a minister of state with responsibility for reconstruction was appointed in the same year. The demand and the response came less out of wartime experience, which was then of under two years' duration, than out of the still recent memories of the 1930s. One generation of men had fought a war, and had been promised 'Homes for Heroes'. Those promises had not been kept. There was a grim determination that this should not happen again. Politicians who wanted to mobilize effort for victory could only call on the people to make sacrifices if they demonstrated clearly that new promises would be made, and that this time they would be fulfilled.

The Labour Party, though not officially in power, was in a position to campaign for new and more egalitarian social provision. From May 1940, Churchill headed a Coalition Government in which Labour politicians, including Clement Attlee, Ernest Bevin and Herbert Morrison held office. Attlee was deputy Prime Minister. Though membership of the Coalition had the effect of somewhat stifling criticism of the conduct of the war, it gave the Labour politicians a position from which to begin planning for peace. They had the support of William Temple, Archbishop of York until 1941 and then Archbishop of Canterbury, whose paperback, *Christianity and the Social Order*, was a best-seller.

Temple presided over the Malvern Conference of 1941, which remains a basic statement of the Christian view of social justice. He argued that the private ownership of major resources was a stumbling-block to the development of a truly Christian society.

Professor Arthur Marwick, who has specialized in the impact of two world wars on British life and thought, describes how the centre movements of the 1930s 'sand-blasted by war, began to take on a much harder political edge, eventually going into service on behalf of the Labour Party',[3] but the primary motive which powered the move to Labour was not a love of collectivism. By 1945, most people had had enough of barracks, barbed wire and taking orders, and there was an overwhelming desire for individual freedom and small-scale family life. It was not even a desire for Socialism as such. It was the spirit of 'never again'. Pauline Gregg notes, 'the German war was over. Domestic issues were uppermost in people's minds – the events of 1918–1939 rather than of 1939–45. The Election was a challenge to all the Governments of the past unhappy twenty years.'[4] Fraser comes to a similar conclusion: 'The nation was expressing an opinion not on the previous five years, but on the decade before that.'[5]

Two services which had dominated the social provision of the 1930s had undergone fundamental changes due to war conditions. The Poor Law had disappeared at last. In 1940, the Unemployment Assistance Board, which was no longer needed, gave way to the Assistance Board, which catered for a very different type of client. Among the categories of people who needed emergency help in wartime were such previously unthought-of categories as seaside landladies (put out of business when defence regulations put the coastal areas facing Europe out of bounds to civilians), people who were bombed out, and arrived at the reception centres with no possessions of any kind; and refugees from Europe. When Norway was about to fall to the German advance, the entire fishing fleet from Bergen sailed for England – and arrived unannounced in Blackpool. Wartime needs were sudden and urgent. They had nothing to do with the pre-war debate about the nature of poverty.

In 1940, the Household Means Test, which had aroused so much opposition, was replaced by a personal Means Test. The immediate reason for this was that families were broken up by conscription and the direction of labour, and many people were living in 'scrambled' households. To amalgamate the income of the householder with that of billetees and lodgers would have resulted in obvious injustice.

Similarly the patchy provision of hospital and health services could never be the same again. Private, voluntary and local authority hospitals had been arbitrarily merged in the Emergency Medical Service. Many mental hospitals had been taken over – their most disturbed patients confined to a few wards while the rest of the accommodation was used for military or civilian war casualties. The process of amalgamation swept aside many existing barriers. Former Harley Street specialists were working side by side with colleagues from the Public Assistance Service, psychiatrists with colleagues in general medicine, consultants with general practitioners. If the needs were acute, and the services stretched to the limit, the destruction of the organizational frontiers between different kinds of medical care held promise for the future.

Wartime shortages led to many extensions in social services. School meals and milk were universally provided – no longer a relief measure for low-income families, but a basic social service for all children. There were special services for expectant mothers – orange juice, vitamins, cod liver oil, which led to an unusually healthy crop of babies, but in wartime, babies were scarce, and they and the schoolchildren represented the future of the race. There was a massive expansion in nursery provision, so that mothers could work in factories or on the land – a policy which was fairly rapidly put into reverse when the war was over and the men came home.

If the war accelerated social change, it also distorted it. Wartime social values tend to be primitive: the fighting services come first, the back-up services, such as coal mining, heavy engineering and armaments manufacture second, children (the next generation of the fighting and back-up services) and by extension their mothers third, and the rest of the population nowhere. This set of priorities was exactly reflected in food rationing. The Forces got comparatively large allocations. Miners got an extra cheese ration (for protein); children got the occasional egg, and the first bananas and oranges when the war was over; expectant mothers were given their special supplies. Old people were given only an extra tea ration.

War meant a return to tribal priorities, because all aspects of social life were necessarily subordinated to the war effort. The comforting picture of an England united in community spirit, class barriers swept aside, preparing for the brave new world, may owe more to the efforts of the Ministry of Information than to reality. Certainly the chronic sick, the disabled and the infirm elderly came very low down on the list of priorities. But there was a desire to plan for a better society when the war was over, and the wartime Coalition Government was aware of it. If great sacrifices were called for, it was necessary to demonstrate that this time they would be rewarded.

The Beveridge Report

When Arthur Greenwood, a Labour member of the Cabinet, took over responsibility for 'social reconstruction', the Trades Union Congress pressed him for a review of policies for national insurance, and an inter-departmental committee of civil servants was set up. Sir William Beveridge, Master of University College, Oxford, and former Director of the London School of Economics, who had spent much of his earlier life in the Civil Service working on insurance problems, was appointed as chairman, charged with the apparently innocuous task of rationalizing social insurance provisions. Beveridge saw his opportunity, and took it.

The final Beveridge Report is printed as 'by Sir William Beveridge'. Though much of the background work was done by other individuals, he explained in the Report why he alone took responsibility for it:

> All the members of the Committee other than the Chairman are civil servants. Many of the matters dealt with in the Report raise questions of policy, on which it would be inappropriate for any civil servant to express an opinion except on behalf of the Minister to whom he is responsible; some of these matters are so important as to call for decision by the Government as a whole.[6]

Beveridge was determined to set out a far-reaching plan for post-war social security which went far beyond his terms of reference. Greenwood took the decision to allow Beveridge to put his plan in full – and thereby set the framework for a 'Welfare State'.

The plan was an astonishing mixture of social vision and practical realism. Beveridge started from three guiding principles: first, that any proposals made were to take account of the experience of the past, but to ignore sectional interests. Beveridge could remember the negotiations over the National Insurance Act of 1911, which was very much an affair of pressure groups, and the uneasy compromises with the approved societies and the doctors. 'Now, when war is abolishing landmarks of every kind, is the opportunity for using experience in a clear field.' Second, he saw 'five giants on the road to reconstruction': Want, Disease, Ignorance, Squalor and Idleness. The plan which followed was designed to attack Want and provide income security; but this was to be seen as 'one part only of a comprehensive policy of social progress'. Third, social security should be achieved by co-operation between the state and the individual. The state would provide 'security for service and contribution' but this would be a national minimum, and individuals might secure extra protection for themselves and their families through voluntary contributions. The state plan would provide benefits 'as of right and without means test' so that 'individuals may build freely upon it'.

In this third section, Beveridge was doing three things: he was trying to mark the end of the Victorian view of charity; he was assuring the commercial insurance companies that they would not be put out of business by an extension of state schemes; and he was stating a Liberal principle of freedom of individual choice.

The scheme for the abolition of Want was carefully set out in a form which would make it easy for the public to retain and recall. Numbers helped with the mnemonics. There were six fundamental principles of social security, six classes of the population to be covered, and eight primary causes of need to be remedied.

The Six Fundamental Principles were adequacy of benefit; flat rate of benefit; flat rate of contribution; unification of administrative responsibility; comprehensiveness; and classification.[7] The rate of benefit would be adequate for the ordinary needs of living, and it would be the same for all causes of the interruption of earnings – unemployment, sickness, disability, maternity, widowhood, retirement. The contributions would be on a flat rate, irrespective of income, and not income-related: this preserved the insurance element, and prevented the scheme from becoming 'an income tax assigned to a particular service'. There would be one Social Insurance Fund, with local offices. Individuals would pay a single contribution weekly.

'Comprehensiveness' meant that the scheme should provide for all the basic and predictable needs of the population. 'It should not leave either to National Assistance or to voluntary insurance any risk so general and so uniform that social insurance can be justified.'

'Classification'[8] meant that the scheme should provide for the needs of all sections of the population – employed and self-employed, housewives without paid employment, others of working age, those too young or too old to earn. These made up the six classes of the population. The ways in which they were to be given insurance coverage, and the needs covered, were carefully tabulated. The needs of the different classes would vary – for example, a self-employed person would not be eligible for unemployment benefit, but would need coverage against disability; a full-time housewife would not be covered for disability, but would have cover for 'special needs arising out of marriage', such as childbirth and widowhood.

The Eight Primary Causes of Need and the provision for each[9] are listed in Table 9.1. They were a direct extension from the work of Booth and Rowntree on the causes of poverty. (Seebohm Rowntree was one of Beveridge's advisers.)

The retirement pension would be payable at the age of 60 for women, 65 for men; but the cost of retirement pensions was estimated to be heavy, and those nearing retirement at the time of the introduction of the scheme would not have paid enough in contributions to qualify for the new increased benefits.

Beveridge therefore proposed that there should be a twenty-year period over which benefits would be scaled up to full value. He also introduced an

Table 9.1   *Beveridge's proposals for meeting the Eight Primary Causes of Need*

Need	Provision
Unemployment	unemployment benefit
Disability	disability benefit or industrial pension
Loss of livelihood	training benefit
Retirement	retirement pension
Marriage needs of a woman	marriage grant, maternity grant, maternity allowance, maternity benefit, widow's benefit, guardian benefit
Funeral expenses	funeral grant
Childhood	children's allowances
Illness, disability	medical treatment and rehabilitation

incentive for people of pensionable age to continue in work after their official retirement date. Those who were fit to do so and wanted to go on working would continue to pay contributions, and would receive a higher rate of benefit when they finally retired.

The 'marriage needs of a woman' were carefully thought out. At this time, there were estimated to be 9.3 million 'housewives', and only 1.4 million women of working age in paid employment. There was to be a grant on marriage (presumably for setting up house); a grant for the birth of a child; a maternity allowance for women confined at home;[10] and thirteen weeks of maternity benefit at the full benefit rate for women in paid employment, who could claim in their own right.

Beveridge recognized that widowhood was a severe financial blow to many women, but he wanted to avoid what was widely regarded as a mistaken policy introduced by the Widows, Orphans and Old Age Pensions Act of 1925. That Act introduced a pension of ten shillings a week, payable on the husband's contributions, for any woman who was widowed before she reached her own retirement age. Though the pension could be lost if she remarried or cohabited with another man, there was no lower age limit. Some 'ten-shilling widows', widowed in their twenties or even their teens, were entitled to claim for the rest of their lives. Beveridge's conclusion was that this was inappropriate – the amount was too small, and the period too long. If a woman was young enough and fit enough to work, it would be better for her to re-train and find employment after a period of adjustment. He recommended that widows should receive the full benefit rate for thirteen weeks. After that, there would be guardian benefit for a widow with dependent children at home. Other widows under the age of 55 would be expected to seek employment in their own interest, and if necessary to take a training course (with re-training benefit at the standard rate). Those of 55 and over would be treated as though they had reached the pensionable age of 60.

From his involvement with the approved societies and commercial insurance, Beveridge knew of the importance which many working-class people still attached to a 'proper' funeral, and how many took out a small policy and paid contributions all their lives to avoid being buried 'on the parish'. He thought that this was a predictable need, and one of deep emotional content. Accordingly, he proposed scales which would provide for a decent, plain funeral. This was only to apply to people under the age of 60 at the time the scheme was implemented, to keep the cost down.

The last two categories of need – childhood and illness – brought the subject into the contentious area of Beveridge's *Three Basic Assumptions*.[11] These were children's allowances, a comprehensive Health Service, and full employment.

It is easy to appreciate why Beveridge argued that these provisions were essential to the success of his social insurance scheme. The campaign for family allowances, which arose out of the findings of Booth and Rowntree, had a long history, and is chiefly associated with the name of Eleanor Rathbone.[12] An allowance scheme would ensure some relationship between family size and family income. The Health Service would be both preventive and curative: 'it is a logical corollary to the payment of high benefits in disability that determined efforts should be made by the state to reduce the number of cases for which benefit is needed'. The argument for full employment took a similar line: 'unemployment, both through increasing expenditure on benefit and through reducing the income to bear those costs, is the worst form of waste'. Mass unemployment was demoralizing to the fit; it prevented those with partial disabilities from having 'a happy and useful career'; it gave the sick no encouragement to get well; it wasted national resources in labour; and it placed an impossible strain on any insurance scheme.

Unemployment could not be entirely avoided: there would always be some 'irregularities of work' resulting from trade conditions – what was later termed 'frictional unemployment'; but Beveridge estimated that this should not affect more than 8.5 per cent of the insured workforce at any one time, and that it should be temporary in nature. 'It should be possible to make unemployment of any individual for more than 26 weeks continuously a rare thing.'

The Beveridge Report was published in November 1942 – only weeks after the Battle of El Alamein, which was the turning point in the Desert War in North Africa. Winston Churchill, with his flair for a popular and dramatic act, ordered that all the church bells should be rung to celebrate victory. The significance of this was that church bells all over Britain had been silenced since September 1939 – they were only to be rung to sound the alarm in the event of a German invasion; but now the threat of invasion was past, the bells could be used for their proper purpose, and there was a new mood: victory was possible, the war could be ended, and planning for peace could begin in earnest. Beveridge's report came out at exactly the right time.

The popular Press, coining a phrase, spoke of Social Security 'from the cradle to the grave'. There was immediate recognition that the report was a blueprint for a new and more egalitarian Britain, which could heal the scars of war and the older but enduring scars of the thirties. Beveridge (who can still sometimes be seen in a televised film clip, small and spare, explaining in precise terms the logic and common sense of his plans) became a national hero. From that time on, Beveridge's plans, and Beveridge's assumptions, were firmly written into the political agenda.

The Conservative Party tended to regard the report as unrealistic. Winston Churchill thought that no energy could be spared from the task of winning the war, and was wary of 'false hopes and airy visions of Utopia and El Dorado'.

> I have so far refrained from making promises about the future. We shall all do our best, and we shall do it much better if we are not hampered by a cloud of pledges and promises which arise out of the hopeful and genial side of man's nature, and are not brought into relation with the hard facts of reality.[13]

Though this reaction has been much quoted, it should be said in fairness that Churchill was heavily preoccupied at the time – he was about to leave for Casablanca, and a crucial conference with Roosevelt and Stalin about the conduct of the war. But later, having read the scheme in detail, he concluded that it constituted 'an essential part of any post-war scheme of betterment'.[14]

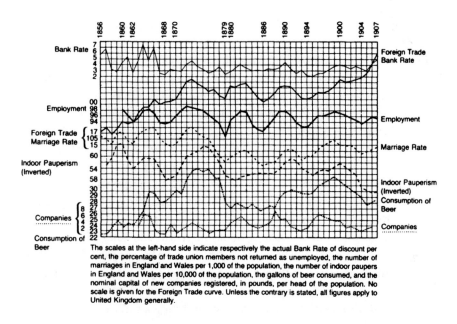

The scales at the left-hand side indicate respectively the actual Bank Rate of discount per cent, the percentage of trade union members not returned as unemployed, the number of marriages in England and Wales per 1,000 of the population, the number of indoor paupers in England and Wales per 10,000 of the population, the gallons of beer consumed, and the nominal capital of new companies registered, in pounds, per head of the population. No scale is given for the Foreign Trade curve. Unless the contrary is stated, all figures apply to United Kingdom generally.

Figure V Beveridge's economic and social indices, 1930

Source: William Beveridge, *Unemployment: a problem of industry*, Longmans Green, revised edition, 1930, p. 44.

Note: Beveridge's intention was to illustrate the correspondence between fluctuations in the unemployment rate and those of other, possibly related, indices.

Could Churchill – could the Conservatives – be trusted? Some alarm was created in the Forces, when the Army Bureau of Current Affairs issued Beveridge's own summary of the Report, and then withdrew it two days later on orders from the War Office.[15] It was three months before the Report was debated by the House of Commons, and then Members of Parliament were invited only to receive and 'welcome' the document. There were no proposals for action, though Labour members moved (and lost) an amendment calling for implementation. The Coalition Government held together for the purpose of winning the war, but was deeply divided on party lines about plans for peace.

Beveridge was to entitle his autobiography *Power and Influence.* His influence was far-reaching, but the power soon passed into other hands. Despite his popularity in the country, and his growing international reputation, he writes that 'While the British people and the free world outside Britain were applauding the Beveridge Report, the Government of Britain, other than the Minister of Information, showed to the report an attitude of marked reserve, and to its author an attitude which developed from ignoring him into boycott.'[16] The one person in Government who supported Beveridge was Brendan Bracken, the Minister of Information, who saw the immense potential of the Report as a weapon in the battle for morale; but when Beveridge asked to see Churchill, the Prime Minister was 'too busy' to see him (again, there were reasons: he was suffering from pneumonia at the time). When a woman Member of Parliament asked Churchill in the House whether Beveridge was being consulted on the implementation of his plans, the reply was brief – 'No, sir.' The question was repeated in an unmistakably feminine voice, and the reply came again – 'No, sir.'[17]

Beveridge went on to write a book on Keynesian lines – *Full Employment in a Free Society* (1944); but the Government refused him official co-operation even from officials he had previously worked with, and succeeded in reducing the impact of this second report by publishing its own version first. Beveridge felt 'like a small boy racing a railway train'.[18] Power had escaped him, though his influence was to endure for many decades and to reach many countries.

Reconstruction: The Public Debate

In the aftermath of the Beveridge Report, government departments began to produce their own plans for reconstruction; but if the original intention had been to take the steam out of the Beveridge proposals, it was soon modified. The plans, in response to public opinion and the logic of the situation, became steadily more progressive. The so-called 'White Paper Chase' of 1943–5[19] included White Papers on the plans for a National Health Service, education, social insurance and assistance, the location of industry, planning for the countryside, land tenure and other policy issues. These will be discussed later in relation to subsequent legislation.

This was open government: the White Papers and explanatory pamphlets were sold on every bookstall, and discussed by groups all over the country, and wherever in the world the Armed Forces were based. In the days before television, and at a time when the radio was used mainly for urgent news broadcasts, the main method of dissemination was through adult education groups. The Army Bureau of Current Affairs, undismayed by its experience over the Beveridge Report, published over fifty pamphlets of its own which were used by Forces education and discussion groups. The Workers' Educational Association had a national network of classes attended by a wide cross-section of people – teachers, doctors, local authority administrators, railway workers, miners, house-wives, factory workers and many others. Each group had its 'book box'. 'Current Affairs' or 'Social Reconstruction' was easily the most popular subject in the last years of the war, and the book boxes contained the Beveridge Report and the White Papers straight from the Stationery Office. University Extra-Mural Departments ran longer and more academic classes on similar subjects.

Never before or since has there been so much committed public debate in Britain about the shape of social policy. Perhaps there was not much else in the way of popular entertainment; but week by week, groups of up to fifty or sixty people met all over Britain in pubs and chapels and school halls, braving the blackout and sometimes the bombs to discuss subjects such as 'Are the Social Insurance proposals fair to widows – to retired people – to the disabled?' 'Flats or Houses?' Will the doctors join a Health Service?' 'Do we want a tripartite Education Service?' 'Can unemploy-ment really be cured?' The Beveridge Report had been the first stage in an irresistible process.

It is important to note that three major social measures – the Education Act of 1944, the Disabled Persons Employment Act of 1944 and the Family Allowances Act of 1945 – were sponsored by the Coalition Government, and passed when there was a Conservative majority in the House of Commons. Some 'Welfare State' legislation was backed by all three major political parties (Beveridge was a Liberal); but the return of a Labour Government in the 'Khaki Election' of 1945, it was believed largely on an overwhelming anti-Conservative Forces vote, ensured that the policies would be whole-heartedly implemented.

This was the first General Election for ten years – the last had put the Baldwin Government into power in 1935. It was a new world.

CHAPTER TEN

Setting Up the 'Welfare State'

In the years 1945–9, Beveridge's 'Five Giants' were systematically tackled by legislation. The Labour Government was convinced, in Hugh Dalton's words, that it was 'walking with Destiny',[1] and despite all the problems of moving from a wartime economy to a peacetime economy, it put the creation of a new and more egalitarian social order at the top of the political agenda.

Many city centres were in ruins. The factories had to turn from heavy engineering to the production of consumer goods. The troops had to be brought home from Europe and the Far East, and demobilized. The task of rebuilding took place at every level, from the international and national levels to the rebuilding of the lives of individual families, as men and women separated by war were reunited, sought jobs and homes, set up house and had their postponed families. The birth-rate soared – and so did the divorce rate, as some hasty wartime marriages failed to survive the transition. Everything was in short supply; but gradually, the basis for post-war England was established on the lines which Beveridge had planned.

Whether those plans would have been carried through with the same vigour if Winston Churchill had remained Prime Minister must be a matter for conjecture. The young Churchill had worked with Lloyd George on health and unemployment insurance, and set William Beveridge to work on labour exchanges in the early years of the century. The older Churchill had seen the need for post-war planning, and had suggested the compiling of a 'book of the transition' for the move to peacetime conditions; but he had insisted that the war must be won first, and he was deeply distrusted by a radical electorate

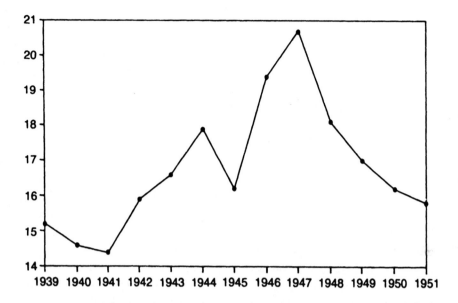

Figure VI Live births per thousand population, United Kingdom 1939–51
Source: Annual Abstract of Statistics, 1952, table 15.

which had bitter memories of the Conservative governments of the 1930s.

His successor, Clement Attlee, was almost tailor-made for the task of bringing a welfare state into being. As a young lawyer, he had given free legal advice to clients at Toynbee Hall. He was secretary to Sidney and Beatrice Webb's National Committee for the Prevention of Destitution, set up in 1909 to campaign for the Minority Report. He had been a Lecturer in Social Science and Administration at the London School of Economics when Beveridge was the Director. This 'sensitive, sincere, shy . . . self-effacing, somewhat chilly little man' according to one American commentator,[2] had very clear ideas on the policy which a Labour Government ought to follow: Our policy was not a reformed capitalism, but progress towards a democratic socialism . . . the war had shown how much could be accomplished when public advantage was put before private vested interest. If that was right in war-time, it was right in peace-time.[3]

So, in the period of Attlee's premiership, the Webbs' principles, Beveridge's plan and Beveridge's assumptions were translated into a statutory framework for defeating the 'Five Giants'.

Want

In 1944, the Ministry of Reconstruction had issued two White Papers on Social Insurance.[4] Both were summarized in a pamphlet, price 3d, which was probably one of the most successful exercises in communication between a government and its people. Graphics and scaled diagrams were used to illustrate a complex scheme in which all would take part, in a way in which all could understand.

The Family Allowances Act, 1945 introduced an allowance of 5s a week for every child under the age of 16 except the first. This limitation was a way of restricting the cost at a time when a great many first babies were being born. It was assumed that a young couple could maintain the first baby, and that the state contribution need not begin until they produced the second. Many organizations were swift to point out that the first child was the expensive one: most working women gave up work before the first baby was born, so the family was dependent on one income rather than two. The pram, the cot and the baby clothes had to be purchased for this baby – they could always be passed on for subsequent children. Family allowances for the first child were not introduced until April 1977.

The National Insurance Act 1946, introduced 'an extended scheme of national insurance providing pecuniary payments by way of unemployment benefit, sickness benefit, maternity benefit, retirement pension, widow's benefit, guardian's allowance and death grant'. All Beveridge's principles were accepted. The only modifications were that the marriage grant was omitted (at a time when the marriage rate was high, this must have seemed an unnecessary inducement to matrimony); the retirement pension was to be paid in full from the beginning of the scheme, instead of being scaled up over a period of twenty years; and the central authority was the Ministry of Pensions and National Insurance (MPNI), not a Ministry of Social Security. In 1946 and the following years, war pensions to the disabled were of great importance. It was decided that the Assistance scheme should be separately administered, like the Unemployment Assistance Board of the 1930s, to keep the topic out of politics.

Unlike commercial insurance, the insurance scheme was not financially watertight: money was to be paid in from the Exchequer and the Reserve Fund, and part of the individual's contribution was to be paid into the fund for the new National Health Service; but the principle of contributions from the employee, the employer and the state was preserved, and

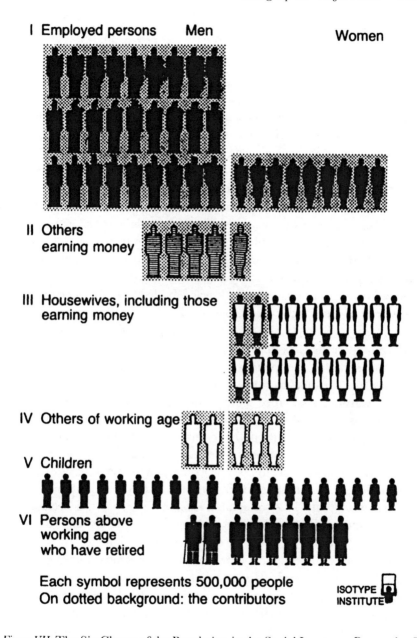

I Employed persons   Men   Women

II Others earning money

III Housewives, including those earning money

IV Others of working age

V Children

VI Persons above working age who have retired

Each symbol represents 500,000 people
On dotted background: the contributors

ISOTYPE INSTITUTE

Figure VII The Six Classes of the Population in the Social Insurance Proposals of 1944

Source: Social Insurance: Brief Guide to the Government's Plan, issued by the Minister of Reconstruction, HMSO, 1944.

Note: This popular version of the Plan cost 3d. Note the Isotype technique for the presentation of statistics.

a new principle was that the amount of benefit was to be enough 'to maintain health and working capacity'.

Schedules set down the amount of contribution and benefit in great detail: for an adult man in full employment, the initial rates of contribution were employee: 4s 9d; employer: 4s 0d; Exchequer: 1s 1d. The balance of payment had therefore shifted from the state, which now provided only 10 per cent of the total, to the employee and employer. Every employee had an insurance card – self-employed people kept and stamped their own cards -and the benefits payable were clearly set out. The standard rate of benefit for all contingencies was 26s 0d a week for both sexes. For an adult dependant, there was a payment of 16s 0d, and for a child dependant, 7s 6d. It was relatively easy for people to calculate what their entitlement was, and what they would receive in return for contributions.

The National Assistance Act 1948 introduced complementary provisions for people who, for one reason or another, were not adequately covered by the insurance scheme. It was subtitled 'An Act to terminate the existing Poor Law' and section 1 began, 'The existing Poor Law shall cease to have effect'. The change of terminology to 'Public Assistance' in 1930 was ignored in the Labour Government's determination to sweep away a system it regarded as repugnant. Some Labour MPs from working-class families, had personal experience of its operation.

The wartime Assistance Board was replaced by a new body, the National Assistance Board. It was to 'promote the welfare' of 'persons in Great Britain who are without the resources to meet their requirements, or whose resources . . . must be supplemented to meet their requirements'. The NAB was not merely to keep recipients at a minimal subsistence level, but positively to promote their welfare; and the provisions applied irrespective of any kind of qualification except that the recipient be human, and on British soil. 'Requirements' were to be defined by the NAB, and there was provision for an appeals procedure.

The grants were to be made in money. In the United States and some other countries, experiments were being made with vouchers for particular purposes, such as clothing or food; but it was decided that families were the best judge of their own needs, and that payments should be made in cash, not in kind. If some misspent the money, that was a small price to pay for the preservation of individual choice and the minimization of bureaucracy.

Under Part III of the Act, every local authority was to provide two classes of accommodation: 'residential accommodation for persons who by reason of age, infirmity or any other circumstances are in need of care and attention which is not otherwise available to them'; and 'temporary accommodation for persons who are in urgent need' (section 29). 'Part III accommodation' as it became known, was to be of a new and better standard. Aneurin Bevan introduced these clauses in the House of Commons with the words, 'The workhouse is to go.'

Part III of the Act also made provision for non-residential services: local authorities were to have 'power to make arrangements for promoting the welfare' of disabled people, including those who are blind, deaf, dumb or otherwise handicapped. Provision could include workshops, work at home, helping in the sale of the products of such work, and the provision of recreational facilities. Local authorities might give financial support to voluntary organizations for some of these purposes.

An interesting contrast between the National Insurance Act and the National Assistance Act is in the degree of delegated legislation. The insurance scheme was set down in terms of actual sums of money, because of the heavy expenditure involved. As adjustments were made in contributions and benefits, for inflation or other reasons, new legislation was necessary. The National Assistance scheme was intended to have much smaller financial implications (since most of the population would be eligible for insurance benefits) and the main purpose was the enabling of local authorities to develop residential and community services as required. It therefore set down principles, and left the details to be worked out.

Disease

The National Health Service Act 1946, laid down a commitment to the health of the nation in the following terms:

> It shall be the duty of the Minister of Health ... to promote the establishment ... of a comprehensive Health Service designed to secure improvement in the physical and mental health of the people ... and the prevention, diagnosis and treatment of illness ... the services so provided shall be free of charge, except where any provision of this Act expressly provides for the making and recovery of charges (section 1).

Plans for a National Health Service had been long discussed, and involved complex issues. The main problems were the status of the large and prestigious voluntary hospitals, which were engaged in teaching and research, and were unwilling to be downgraded, as they saw it, to the status of the former Poor Law infirmaries; the interests of the local authorities, which had done much to improve these same infirmaries, and did not wish to lose jurisdiction over them; and the resistance of medical specialists and general practitioners, who wanted to preserve a degree of professional autonomy, and were unwilling to become employees in a salaried service.

Discussions and negotiations with these and other professional groups, such as opticians, dentists and nurses, began early in 1943. The Brown Plan of 1943 reputedly provided for the continued independence of the large voluntary hospitals, which would take patients from the Health Service on contract, but this plan was never published. The Willink Plan of 1944, produced by a Conservative Minister of Health and published as a White Paper,[5] set down the principle that good medical facilities should be available to all without regard for the patient's ability to pay. It was acknowledged that the existing services were fragmented and limited in scope. A national service would be set up, but both patients and doctors would be free to use it or not – there would be no compulsion. The question of whether the general practitioner service should be salaried or paid on a per capita basis was left open.

Intense public debate was in progress when the war in Europe ended, and the Labour Government took office. Aneurin Bevan became Minister of Health, and the negotiations got tougher. Bevan, formerly a miner from South Wales, had his own very strong views about both the abolition of the Poor Law and the need for a National Health Service. His father, also a miner, had died from pneumoconiosis -- and without compensation from the mine owners, because the condition was not then scheduled as an industrial disease.[6] The medical establishment initially regarded him as an enemy: he was to prove a highly intelligent and skilled negotiator with a thorough grasp of principle. He held long and protracted negotiations with all the interest-groups involved, chaired many committees and conferences himself, and drove a more radical scheme through with the minimum of concessions. The National Health Service Act became law in 1946, but the date when it was to come into operation was delayed until 5 July 1948. This was because new machinery had to be set up, there were major staffing implications, and it was necessary to co-ordinate the legislation with the National Insurance Act and the National Assistance Act, which had the same appointed day.

In the final plan, all types of hospitals were brought under the control of the Ministry of Health, but with two kinds of status. Most hospitals, whether previously voluntary, municipal or private, were placed under the management of Regional Hospital Boards. There were 13 RHBs, the areas being based on the 13 Civil Defence Areas set up in wartime. At a lower administrative level, hospitals were administered by Hospital Management Committees, each being responsible for a small group of hospitals in a particular area.

In an ingenious compromise, the major voluntary hospitals, which carried on most of the medical training and research, were exempted from this structure and designated 'teaching hospitals'. The basic plan was for each RHB to have one such hospital as its centre, working with a university medical school. Teaching hospitals were to work in partnership with the RHBs, but to be administered separately by Boards of Governors responsible directly to the Minister of Health. All hospitals in England and Wales were brought into the NHS apart from a few small private or charitable hospitals which were 'disclaimed' by the Minister, usually at their own request.

Consultants were to be employed by the RHB or the Board of Governors, but were allowed to work on a sessional basis which left them time for private patients. Hospital care was to be without basic charges, though there was provision for amenity beds (section 4) and private beds (section 5); but any bed set aside for private patients was to be made available if necessary for 'any patient who urgently requires accommodation on medical grounds, and for whom suitable accommodation is not otherwise available'.

Local authorities, which lost their hospitals when the Act came into force, became responsible for a consolidated range of public health services – district nursing, health visiting, midwifery, maternity and child welfare, home helps, ambulance services, vaccination and immunization. They were to organize health centres (a development strongly opposed by most general practitioners) and they acquired sweeping, if somewhat obscure powers, under section 28 of the Act, which ran:

> A local health authority may with the approval of the Minister, and to such extent as the Minister may direct, make arrangements for the purpose of the prevention of illness, the care of persons suffering from illness or mental defectiveness, or the after-care of such persons.

The NHS Act provided a broad framework, but allowed for a

considerable degree of delegation. It left scope for the local authorities to innovate, scope for the Minister to require them to provide certain services, and scope for these services to cover any kind of care or treatment not provided by the hospital service. The section was designated to run parallel with section 29 of the National Assistance Act, described above, which gave the local authority similar powers in relation to people suffering from long-term disability or infirmity. Though the services were as yet undeveloped, these two sets of provisions provided a basis for the development of community care.

General practice was to be administered by Executive Councils, one for each local authority area. There were separate committees for medical, dental, pharmaceutical and supplementary ophthalmic services. The national Medical Practices Committee was responsible for the provision of medical practices – designating new ones in under-doctored areas, and closing down practices in areas where in their judgement there was a surplus. General practitioners, who had previously bought and sold their practices, were compensated for the loss of right to do so. Aneurin Bevan commented on the NHS Act afterwards:

> The field in which the claims of individual commercialism come into most immediate conflict with reputable notions of social values is that of health. . . . Preventable pain is a blot on any society. Much sickness, and often permanent disability arise from failure to take early action, and this in its turn is due to high costs and the fear of the effects of heavy bills on the family. You can always 'pass by on the other side'. That may be sound economics. It could not be worse morals.[7]

Idleness

Contrary to many of the fears expressed during the war, the maintenance of full employment was not to prove a problem in post-war Britain. The Coalition Government had committed itself in the White Paper of 1944[8] to a basically Keynesian analysis. However, it was notable that, whereas Beveridge was insistent on a policy of 'full employment', the official document spoke only of 'high and stable employment'.

Government spending was high, particularly in the public sector, as the mines, the electricity and gas industries, the iron and steel industries and the railways were nationalized. There was no lack of work to be done in reconstruction, and a high employment rate was to continue through to the early 1970s. Though there were more than two million unemployed in 1947 – the main year of demobilization – they were quickly absorbed back into the work-force. Overall economic planning brought new industries to the former distressed areas. There was work for almost everyone who wanted it, and the trade cycle, which had dominated economic thinking in the 1930s, appeared to have disappeared for all time. There was considerable optimism that planning and regulation could create economic stability, and prevent the recurrence of widespread economic distress.

Ignorance

Like the NHS Act, the Education Act of 1944 was the result of long and careful consultation with professional and other interests and similarly it steamrollered a variety of patchy provision into a national system. Free education was to be provided all the way from the nursery level, through primary school, to three kinds of secondary school and beyond, to further and higher education.

The Act usually bears the name of R. A. Butler, the Conservative Minister who presided over its passage through Parliament. It was the result of protracted discussion and the work of two influential committees. The McNair Committee had formulated an ambitious plan for teacher training, including extended grants and maintenance awards for students in college, links between the training colleges and universities, and a longer and more liberal training, lasting for three years instead of two.[9] The Norwood Committee had laid down principles for secondary education for all children. Education was to be for three purposes: for work, for citizenship and for the individual – 'to help each individual to realise to the full the powers of his personality'.[10] It was recommended that the existing mix of grammar schools (fee-paying for most pupils), central schools, technical schools, commercial schools and senior elementary schools should be shaped into three kinds of secondary school available without fees: grammar schools for the more intellectually minded; technical schools for those who would benefit from a technological education and 'secondary modern' for the rest. There was to be 'parity of esteem' between the three groups, and children would be tested and directed to an appropriate school at the age of eleven.

Subsequent criticisms of the tripartite system in education and the 11+

examination have been so devastating that it is necessary to stress how advanced these proposals were at the time. Butler was a Conservative with marked Liberal leanings (perhaps that is why he narrowly failed to become Prime Minister). He believed that education was the key to a better society. In the 1930s, a few working-class children had struggled through to university level by means of scholarships. Now the whole education system was to be open to all on the basis of merit. The nation would have the benefit of the best brains and talents. Individual children would be able to make the best of their ability.

The 11 + examination was to be a means of distinguishing what the planners were convinced were three basic types of ability: the academic, the technological and the practical. The Hadow Report of 1926, the Spens Report of 1938 and the Norwood Report of 1943 – all produced by committees with eminent educationalists among their numbers – had agreed that the age of eleven was the right point for a break in the educational process, and that children of different types of ability might be distinguished at that point. What was new in 1944 was the determination to give them all equality of opportunity, with parity of esteem between the different types of school.

The McNair and Norwood proposals formed the basis of a White Paper, *Educational Reconstruction*,[11] issued in 1943. The proposals had the support of all the main political parties, and formed the basis of the new law.

So the Butler Act reached the statute book even before the end of the Second World War. The three types of secondary school were specified, the Board of Education was upgraded to a Ministry, plans were laid to raise the school leaving age from 14 to 15 and eventually to 16,[12] grants were provided for further and higher education, and education became a right instead of a privilege. As Pauline Gregg comments:

> The right to organised education has been one of the most keenly fought and most cherished prizes of the working classes; every section of the British working class movement since the Industrial Revolution has claimed the right to education, and has ascribed to it a remedial quality that would help the worker to better his own material condition, raise his class socially, and introduce justice and humanity over the land. . . . The belief in education as a philosopher's stone was naive, at times pathetic . . . and yet it has proved a mighty warrior for the working classes, and as a social leveller, it is matched only by wealth.[13]

Squalor

The Town and Country Planning Act of 1947 was similarly the result of long deliberation and the process of political consultation with the professions. In this case, there were three key reports: Barlow, Scott and Uthwatt. The Barlow Report of 1940 on the Distribution of the Industrial Population[14] acquired a new significance as factories moved out into the rural areas, bombing destroyed the fabric of the inner cities, and major replanning became imperative. After the Beveridge Report, it was seen as the major key to the defeat of his fifth 'giant'.

Sir Montagu Barlow and his colleagues had argued that the 1930s had been a period of haphazard growth, and that a small country with limited land at its disposal could not afford to continue unrestricted and unplanned building. Urban sprawl, ribbon development along main 'arterial roads', ramshackle developments of which Peacehaven in Essex was named as the prototype, could all be held in check by proper planning. The Barlow Report listed the advantages of population concentration: the proximity of production to markets, low transport costs, the availability of labour. The disadvantages were high site values in city centres, traffic jams and the steady exiling of the working population to the outer suburban areas, with consequent costs and fatigue in the daily journey to work. London and the population drain to the south-east were already special problems.

The Barlow Report argued that it was possible to achieve a balanced distribution of population. The members commended attempts which had been made before the Second World War to disperse industry and provide living accommodation within reach of work – the 'garden cities' of Welwyn and Letchworth, the satellite towns of Wythenshawe, near Manchester, and Speke, near Liverpool, the trading estates; but there was a need for a national plan. Members of the Barlow Commission differed in the degree of control which they thought necessary – the majority settled for a National Board with powers over London, with a remit which could be extended to other areas by Orders in Council. The minority wanted a Ministry with national planning powers.

The Scott Report of 1942[15] was concerned with the preservation of the countryside. While some of its recommendations (like the proposal that rural telephone boxes should be painted green instead of red, so that they might better blend with farms and fields) suggested a somewhat romantic view of country life, the basic findings were practical enough. The rural population was often assumed to have no problems. In fact, much rural housing was of a very poor quality; many people in rural areas still lacked main drainage, gas and electricity. The Scott Committee recommended that the standards which had been achieved in the towns should be extended to the country, which was underprivileged by comparison. This implied the nationalization of the essential industries, since it was improbable that private companies would go to the expense of extending supplies to sparsely populated areas. The Scott Report was also concerned with questions of rights of way and access, Green Belts round the towns, and the development of national parks, for the benefit of town dwellers and country dwellers alike.

The Uthwatt Report of 1942[16] was concerned with Compensation and Betterment: a dry title for an important subject. The Committee found that the powers of local authorities to undertake redevelopment were inadequate in view of the extent of wartime damage and the replanning which was necessary. The Uthwatt Committee recommended that local authorities should have sweeping powers of compulsory purchase – not merely for slum areas, but wherever it was necessary to replan whole areas for shopping centres, housing estates, roads and other purposes. There would be compensation for those whose property depreciated in value due to new developments such as roads or the building of new housing estates, and betterment charges against those whose property increased in value. A subsequent White Paper on land use was much debated. Of all the measures of social reform in the post-war period, this one most directly affected private property and individual ownership.

The main conclusions of Barlow, Scott and Uthwatt went into the Town and Country Planning Act of 1947. A Ministry of Town and Country Planning had already been set up in 1943 to deal with wartime land problems, and this was put on a permanent basis. All local authorities were required to prepare plans for their own areas. The Board of Trade was to approve new industrial projects, and there were to be grants and loans to attract industries to what were scheduled as Development Areas, to secure 'a proper distribution of industry'. New Towns were to be built, with full provision for work, residential areas and community life, to relieve the congestion on the cities. A National Parks Commission was set up, and the Nature Conservancy Council, which developed research on river and air pollution, litter and noise, was also established.

A Welfare State?

The social legislation of 1944–9 was evolutionary rather than revolutionary, in the sense that it built on the legislation of the pre-war period, but made it more comprehensive and more rational. A muddle of provision which had developed empirically was replaced by a coherent network of co-ordinated services. It was the result of an unprecedented process of public discussion of a kind which was both informed (since the outstanding experts were involved in each field) and democratic. In each policy area, the process was built on past experience. Nothing was done in haste, and nothing was done without due consultation with all the interested parties. If the planners got it wrong, as they did in some instances, it was not through lack of consideration or lack of advice.

The 1940s were a period of great social idealism, and this was not confined to any one political party. All parties were united in the intention of bringing about a more secure and egalitarian society. While the return to power of the Labour Party in 1945 gave the plans a more radical impact, they were not exclusively Socialist plans. The legislation did not, of course, produce a Welfare State overnight. Getting the legislation through Parliament was only the first step, and there were major problems ahead.

CHAPTER ELEVEN

Problems of Expansion

In the early post-war period, there was much discussion of 'Social Reconstruction'. This was not simply a matter of moving from a wartime to a peacetime footing: the aim was to create fundamental changes in the organization of society, and to heal the divisions between the social classes. Once the legislation had set out the framework and the powers, there was a massive amount of detailed work to be done at both national and local level to set up the new machinery of state.

The financial cost was high, and in setting up this new structure of services, Britain was borrowing against the future. War had left the economy in massive deficit. Britain had been virtually a front-line battle station for the Allied nations, and exports had all but ceased during the war years, while the labour force had been organized for war purposes, and was disorganized and de-skilled for the new peacetime world. President Roosevelt had promised Prime Minister Churchill a continuation of Lend–Lease (by which the United States provided Britain with consumer goods it could not produce under wartime conditions) after the end of the war to ease the transition back to peacetime conditions; but Roosevelt died, and was succeeded by Truman. Churchill was voted out of power, and was succeeded by Clement Attlee. The relationship between the American and British Governments changed abruptly from wartime collaboration to peacetime commercial trading. Barbara Castle, then a newly elected Labour MP, and later a leading Labour minister, recalls this as a direct action by the Truman administration to create difficulties for a Socialist Government in Britain, insisting that 'even ships which were already crossing the Atlantic changed their nature' as they became conveyors of goods which had to be paid for on docking rather than of a gift from one ally to another.[1] Britain lacked hard currency, and vital supplies were involved.

So Britain faced the transition to peace and a new social order in acute financial difficulties. Food rationing had to continue, and was not finally abolished until 1951. Even bread was rationed. There were shortages of many kinds of basic commodities, the price of consumer goods soared, and taxation increased. There were repeated coal and power cuts – particularly severe in the bitterly cold winter of 1947. The Chancellor of the Exchequer, Sir Stafford Cripps, was known as 'Austerity Cripps'. The first Labour Government with a clear majority in the House of Commons started with popular support for its social programme; but by 1951, its popularity had evaporated in the face of continuing economic difficulties, and Winston Churchill was back in Downing Street. However, both Conservative and Labour governments accepted the framework of welfare legislation – it was part of the 'consensus government' which was to characterize the next forty years. There were some differences of emphasis – characteristically, Conservatives looked at cost, while Labour looked at benefits; but the battle against Beveridge's Five Giants continued.

When the new legislation came into effect in the late 1940s, the administrative implications were staggering. Boards, Committees, Advisory Councils and other bodies were created. Tens of thousands of staff had to be recruited or transferred from old organizations to new ones, to learn new jobs and new ways of working. What was a Regional Hospital Board, and how should it function? How did the work of the Welfare Department of a local authority differ from that of Public Assistance? How did a secondary modern school differ from the senior section of an elementary school? How could the enormous and pressing need for family housing be met, when whole areas were devastated and needed to be replanned? There was no experience of such large-scale organization to draw on, and much to be learned.

Government and local authorities looked to the universities and colleges for training and research. Economists, sociologists and other social scientists found a new focus of interest, and the study of Social Policy and Administration mushroomed.[2] The new specialists devoted themselves to the study of 'social engineering' – how to develop the new services, identify the problems, and improve the quality of care. The result of this concentration of academic effort was a new flood of publishing – some of it critical, much of it impatient with the slow pace of progress; but few of the new social engineers doubted that the machine they had to tune was basically well designed.

Because this was a period of sustained high employment, 'Idleness' and 'Want' were not major problems. There was work to be had, and the National Insurance scheme was not unduly strained. Though there was a growing concern that the National Assistance scheme was not the minor service of last resort which Beveridge had envisaged (too many people, particularly old people, were claiming because benefits were below subsistence level), the scheme was viable. The other three 'giants' were more immediately resistive: in the Health Service, Town and Country Planning, and in the field of Education, there were fresh problems to be faced.

The National Health Service

The NHS initially offered a service which was 'free at the point of delivery'. Aneurin Bevan made it clear that it was not a free service, because the public paid for it through taxation and insurance. The point was that individuals did not have to pay directly when they were sick, or in proportion to the services they needed. This principle was questioned as early as 1949, when Bevan fought his Labour colleagues to prevent a small charge of one shilling on medical prescriptions, and to prevent the imposition of a financial limit on Health Service expenditure. Other Ministers complained that the NHS was 'the sacred cow' of Labour policy, since the claims of other essential services such as housing and education and investment for industry were set aside as the health costs soared. Disputes with Hugh Gaitskell, Stafford Cripps's successor as Chancellor of the Exchequer, played a major part in Bevan's resignation in 1951.[3]

Bevan argued that the high costs of the NHS were only a temporary phenomenon. The hospital and specialist service accounted for more than two-thirds of the total cost in 1950–1. When outdated hospital premises, such as the former mental hospitals and the Public Assistance hospitals, had been brought up to an acceptable standard, and the backlog of untreated sickness had been dealt with, Britain would be a healthier nation, and costs would fall. Both Beveridge and Bevan had concentrated on the problems of making and keeping the working population fit for work, with the assumption that this would reduce absenteeism and increase national productivity.

This view was supported by the Guillebaud Committee of 1956[4] which examined NHS expenditure, and found that it had risen by 70 per cent since the introduction of the service in 1948. The conclusion was that the five years under review had been a period of inflation, and of working through short-term problems, but that there were no grounds for charges of extravagance, and the basic administrative structure of the NHS was sound.

But the opposition was gathering. The medical profession, which had assented to the scheme in 1946 with the greatest reluctance, repeatedly pressed for higher salaries, and in 1951, the British Medical Association threatened to withdraw from the NHS altogether: an eventuality which was seemingly only averted by a very large salary award in that year. Pharmaceutical costs spiralled, as they did in all countries. This was a period of great advance in pharmacology, as the antibiotics and the neuroleptic drugs were developed and refined. In 1952, the Churchill Government introduced charges for dentures and spectacles, thus breaching the principle of a service free at the point of delivery to the patient.

Right-wing critics became active. In February 1952, *The Times* published two articles on 'Crisis in the Welfare State',[5] arguing that Britain could not afford the extensive services planned in the post-war period. Two leading Conservatives, Iain Macleod and Enoch Powell, published a pamphlet[6] soon afterwards arguing that health and social services should only be provided by the state on a test of need – a view which ran completely counter to the Beveridge principles, and raised left-wing hackles about means-testing.

In the Health Service field, the political debate was both protracted and bitter. The opening attack came from John Jewkes, Professor of Economic Organisation at Oxford, who thought the problems were by no means of a temporary nature. They indicated 'a steady and continuous struggle on the part of the British Government to restrain the demand for medical services'. The choices were to restrict capital construction (in effect spending money on current account which should have been put aside for improving the infrastructure); to impose charges for specific services; or to restrict the services to special groups.[7] Jewkes, later the author of *A Return to Free Market Economics*, was followed by other free marketeers from the Institute of Economic Affairs. An influential paper was *Health Through Choice*,[8] which complained of 'a strange neglect of economic principles' in the introduction of a scheme which was free at the point of delivery, and deprecated the intervention of a third party, the state, in the relationship between doctor and patient. 'Consumer sovereignty' could be ensured only by the application of the laws of supply and demand, which meant paying directly for service received.

To this, Richard Titmuss responded by arguing that the simple laws of supply and demand could not operate in the Health Service: the patient could not exercise a free choice, because medicine had become highly technical, and he had to be able to trust his doctor; but could he trust his doctor in a free market, where the doctor–patient relationship was dominated by financial considerations? The result would be 'fee-splitting, commission-taking, canvassing, the dispensation of 'secret remedies' and the employment of unqualified assistants'.[9]

The conflict between Professor Titmuss and his supporters and the Institute of Economic Affairs was to develop with considerable personal bitterness;[10] but one basic fact gradually emerged. Quite independently of the philosophical and political positions taken up by the protagonists, it became clear that the high costs of the NHS were not a temporary phenomenon, for a reason which neither Beveridge nor Bevan seems to have fully understood: *health services are self-expanding.* That is, the better a country's health services, the more will be needed. The reason for this is that good health services keep alive people who would otherwise die: handicapped babies survive, people who would have succumbed to the acute diseases of middle age live on to experience the chronic diseases of old age, old people live longer. Good health services do not produce a fit and healthy population overall: they produce an ageing population with a higher proportion of handicapped and infirm people.

The cynical version of this unhappy truth is the old Health Service slogan 'The only good health service is in the Congo'. Countries with very little in the way of health care for the general population can run very good acute services, because the potential population of chronic sick simply dies off. A more balanced view is that good and freely available health services do increase the national well-being. The fact that patients live on who would otherwise die is not a 'problem' but a proof of success. It is true that this success has to be paid for, and some limits have to be set to health service expenditure. However, throughout this period, Canada, the United States and Sweden spent considerably in excess of 6 per cent on health services, while Britain's expenditure remained below 5 per cent.[11]

Much of the subsequent history of the health services has been influenced by the need to preserve the acute (mainly hospital-based) services in the face of the increasing cost of advanced medical technology, while making less expensive provision outside the hospital sector for the growing volume of chronic need for care: in the main for physical and mental handicap, mental illness, and the infirmities of old age. These services, frequently neglected by local authorities before 1948, were often known as the 'Cinderella Services'. Though they achieved theoretical parity of esteem with the acute services in 1948, this was not to last. By 1962, considerations of the problems of expense and administrative fragmentation brought about a reversal of policy in which, slowly and inexorably, the care of the chronic sick was largely returned to the local authorities.

In 1962, the publication of *A Hospital Plan*,[12] sponsored by Enoch Powell as Minister of Health, proposed new measures for 'the effective use of hospital beds'. Small local hospitals – the former cottage hospitals and small Public Assistance hospitals – were to be closed. Hospital care was to be increasingly concentrated in large District General Hospitals, which would offer fewer beds, but improved medical technology and expanded out-patient services. To parallel this, there would be a sharp downward revision in geriatric, mental handicap and mental illness beds. Provision for these patient groups would be developed by the local authorities.

The Hospital Plan made a major change in the function of the hospital. Previously, hospitals had been centres to which patients went when they were sick, for medical treatment and nursing care. Now the hospital function was to be diagnosis, assessment and clinical intervention, rather than long-term care.

The results of this change have been profound. There were sufficient medical reasons for shortening patients' length of stay in some circumstances – antibiotics reduced the risk of infection after an operation or after childbirth, and new and powerful drugs controlling mood swings, such as tranquillizers and anti-depressants, made it possible for many mentally ill and elderly confused people to sustain life in the community once a routine of medication had been established; but there was continuing concern about the care of the chronic sick in view of the slow expansion of the community services. Attempts to pass the 'Cinderella Services' back to the local authorities in a social rather than a medical context were to create many problems. Professor Titmuss had some stinging comments to make:

If English social history is any guide, confusion has often been the mother of complacency. In the public mind, the aspirations of reformers are transmitted by the touch of a phrase into hardwon reality. What some hope will one day exist is suddenly thought by many to exist already. All kinds of wild and unlovely weeds are changed by statutory magic and comforting appellations, into the most attractive flowers that bloom, not only in the spring, but all the year round.[13]

So 'that exotic hot-house climbing rose, 'The Welfare State" was to be followed by 'the everlasting cottage trailer, "Community Care"', which would in fact have the effect of transferring chronic patients 'from trained staff to untrained or ill-equipped staff, or no staff at all'.

The official plans for community care were set out in 1963 in a companion document to the *Hospital Plan*. This was entitled *Health and Welfare: the development of community care*.[14] It lacked the conviction and force of the *Hospital Plan*, consisting only of general statements on the desirability of community care for physically and mentally disabled people and the elderly, and detailed returns from local authorities on the services they hoped to provide. Though the statistics were revised annually for some years, little attempt was made to explore and account for anomalies in provision, and there was no direct funding: earmarked grants from central Government for particular local authority services, which enabled Government to set and maintain standards, were abolished. Local authorities were given a block grant, and could decide for themselves how they allocated it. The Ministry of Health did little more than suggest guidelines.

By 1965, the National Health Service was well established, and immensely popular with the general public. It had a remarkable success in the fields of general practice and acute hospital treatment; but it was not the service envisaged twenty years earlier. Means were already being found to limit the costs of an ever-expanding service; and the debate had become highly politicized.

Housing

One of the most acute needs at the end of the Second World War was the need for housing. There were still serious slum clearance problems from the pre-war period. There had been virtually no building for six years. Nearly half a million houses had been destroyed or rendered totally uninhabitable, and many more were badly damaged by bombing. There had been two million marriages in the wartime period, so many young couples, separated by war, were setting up house for the first time and ready to start a family. The birth rate went up sharply – to a peak of 20.7

per thousand population in 1947. The phrase 'homes for heroes' remained in currency to haunt politicians – and particularly Aneurin Bevan, who, as Minister of Health, was responsible for Housing as well as for the NHS.

The Town and Country Planning Act of 1947 had set out a framework on the lines proposed by the Barlow and Uthwatt Reports. The immediate need was to meet the housing shortage. Under the Labour Government, the emphasis was on local authority housing, and no longer just for 'the working classes'. The Housing Act of 1949 laid down the principle that housing need rather than social class was to be the main criterion, and local authority Housing Departments worked on complex points systems which included social as well as economic indicators. In the immediate post-war period, the emphasis was on temporary solutions: bomb damage was swiftly repaired to provide reconditioned houses, families were housed in Nissen huts in abandoned Army camps, and the first 'pre-fabs' were provided, with a predicted 12–15 years of life. Some were to last much longer. At the same time Rent Restriction Acts kept down rents in the private sector.

New housing began to be constructed as soon as the labour force was reorganized. Between 1950 and 1955, well over a million new council houses were built, the peak figure being 300,000 in 1953.[15] After that time, there was a change in policy from the immediate satisfaction of housing need to an improvement of housing stock. The Housing Rents and Repairs Act of 1954 assisted house-owners and private landlords by making larger improvement grants available, and so enabling older houses to be brought up to standard. At the same time, local authorities began to develop ambitious plans for high-rise flats, and the New Towns began to take shape.

The reasoning of the Barlow Report led inevitably to plans for high-rise flats. It was necessary for the labour force to be near industrial centres to reduce fatigue and the cost of travel; land was expensive and in short supply in a crowded island. It therefore made sense to build upwards rather than outwards. In addition, local authorities were concerned to provide accommodation quickly and cheaply, and there were techniques of prefabrication available which were particularly suitable for this kind of construction. Half a dozen large construction firms virtually cornered the field, and obtained most of the contracts.[16]

It was some years before the problems became apparent: the isolation of mothers with young children who could not go out to play; the isolation of old people, who could not face the stairs or the lifts; the poor quality of construction, and the lack of imagination in design; the vandalization of walkways and stairways. Public dissatisfaction with high-rise council flats reached its peak in 1968, when a gas explosion at Ronan Point caused one corner of a block to collapse like a pack of cards. Though the blocks created in the 1950s and 1960s are still occupied in many areas, housing authorities now tend to be more careful in allocating suitable tenants.

New Towns such as Stevenage, Corby and Milton Keynes were created under the New Towns Act 1946. They were a development from the 'satellite towns' and the 'garden cities' of the pre-war years. Some twenty were set up in all, eight of them round London, catering for a total population of about three million people. The initial problems of siting were severe: it was necessary to avoid first-class agricultural land, places of historical interest and beauty spots, and there were environmental interests and transport links to be considered. On the whole, the New Town policy has worked well: industry and housing have been successfully combined, and genuine communities have developed. Though many people have doubts about living in a totally planned environment, preferring communities which grow naturally, the standard of provision has been good, and the combination of housing and employment opportunities has in many cases developed successfully.

Up to 1957, the emphasis in national housing policy was strongly on local authority provision. In the privately rented sector, maintenance costs had risen sharply, and there had been a long period of rent restriction. Public opinion was sharply against 'Rachmanism' – exploitation by landlords who harassed their tenants into leaving so that they could sell the property or raise rents. But many tenants had a protected status, so that the owners could neither sell their property nor afford to keep it in good repair. There was a gradual realization that many private landlords were not wealthy and exploitative. They were people of limited incomes whose capital was tied up in an asset they could not realize. The Rent Act of 1957 was based on the simple economic theory that the abolition of rent restrictions would increase private sector provision by bringing market forces into play; but this did not occur. The next few years were to see the virtual disappearance of rented accommodation except at the top and the bottom ends of the market, because of more general economic trends.

In the late 1950s, interest rates rose, inflation set in and house prices rose sharply. In 1945, only some 26 per cent of dwelling-houses in England and Wales were owner-occupied; but this figure rose to 47 per cent by 1966. A house became the best hedge against inflation, and mortgage relief made home ownership profitable in periods of high taxation. After 1955, the number of local authority houses built annually was sharply reduced, while the private rented sector almost ceased to exist.[17]

Education

The Education Act of 1944 had provided a structure for a service which would give every child equality of opportunity all the way from nursery school to university. The main lesson to be learned in this field was that equality of opportunity was not enough.

The 11 + examination soon came under fire. The Act had proposed that grammar schools, technical schools and secondary modern schools were to have parity of esteem, but reality denied the statement. Despite efforts to upgrade secondary modern schools, to provide them with equipment and sports facilities equal to those of the more prestigious grammar schools, the pecking order remained obstinately unchanged. And was it really possible to classify children – to make decisions about their education which would affect their whole lives – at the age of eleven? The pre-war pundits had thought this reasonable. During the 1950s, the evidence grew that some children developed later than others; that the 11 + tests were often unreliable; that the children of 'bookish' parents did better than those from homes where books were unknown; that it was easier to get into grammar schools in some areas than others. Some children were coached, and some parents moved house to get into one of the better endowed areas.

In 1945, the Labour Government had accepted the principles of the Butler Act; this may have been, because many of their leaders were themselves 'public school products';[18] it may have been because they respected the quality of teaching in grammar schools, and did not want to damage the academic standing of these schools; it may have been because the Butler Act had laid down an acceptable basis for the Education Service, and there was too much other legislation in progress to plan major changes so soon. But while the National Union of Teachers and some Labour backbenchers argued for 'multilateralism' – more than one stream under · the same roof – it was not until 1951 that the Labour Party manifesto included a demand for comprehensive schools, and Labour lost that election.

From that time on, policy on secondary schools showed a clear political split. Labour championed comprehensive schools on the grounds that the tripartite system was socially and educationally divisive. The Conservatives championed the grammar schools on the grounds that the divisions were real. But the edge was taken off the controversy by the gradual abandonment of the 11 + examination. Schools experimented with transfers at 13 +, 14 +, 16 +. Some universities and colleges began to accept students with 'unorthodox' academic backgrounds. Educational opportunity diversified, rather than being channelled through the narrow gate of a single examination. But in the 1950s and early 1960s, there was still a sharp awareness of the problems of children in the secondary modern stream This led to the publication of two reports from official committees – the Crowther Report of 1959 and the Newsom Report of 1963.

The Crowther Report was entitled *15 to 18* and subtitled *Education in a Changing Word*.[19] It was concerned with further education opportunities for young school-leavers (at this time, the minimum school leaving age was still 15). Britain was lagging behind other countries – particularly Germany, which had made a remarkable economic recovery in the years since the war – in further education and apprenticeship schemes. The Crowther Committee outlined a twenty-year plan for developments in intermediate technology covering building, plumbing, carpentry, basic engineering skills, the catering and grocery trades, and other trades. These involved day-release and block-release schemes, with the aim that every young person should have the opportunity of acquiring relevant skills after taking up employment. These proposals, which were fully implemented, have achieved relatively little public recognition, but have had a far-reaching effect in changing the occupational structure. Previously, the bulk of the working population was unskilled. Since the implementation of the Crowther report, young people have had the opportunity to acquire a trade or craft after leaving school through a technical college or College of Commerce.

The Newsom Report was concerned with 'children aged 13 to 16 with average or less than average ability'.[20] Its title was *Half Our Future* because these children represented 'half the pupils in secondary schools – half the citizens, workers, mothers and fathers of the future'. The Newsom Committee stated that there was 'much unrealised talent . . . among boys and girls whose potential is masked by inadequate powers of speech and the limitations of home background'. The second volume of the report is drawn from case-studies and survey data: the children were divided into three groups according to ability: the 'Browns' the 'Joneses' and the 'Robinsons'. The 'Robinsons', who represented the lowest quartile, were smaller, lighter in weight, came from larger families, were more likely to have unskilled fathers, lived in poorer neighbourhoods, were given less homework, were more likely to leave school early and without qualifications, and were much less likely to belong to school societies or youth clubs, or to become prefects. It was a compelling picture of educational rejects who became social rejects. The recommendations included raising the school leaving age to 16 (which took a further nine years), measures for making teaching more relevant and linking it to youth employment, the avoidance of excessive grading, and 'a working party on general social problems in slum areas' – the proposal which led to the setting up of the Plowden Committee, whose report will be considered in the next chapter.

A further notable development in this period was the Robbins Committee Report on Universities.[21] This opened up the other end of the educational spectrum, and marked the high point of optimism in the educational field. By 1963, the children born at the time of the post-war 'population bulge' were approaching university age, so pressure on universities and other centres for higher education was increasing. The Robbins Report started from the premise that 'a highly educated population is essential to meet competitive pressures in the modern world', pointing out that university education was available to a much larger section of the population in both the United States and the USSR, and that other countries were planning a considerable expansion. Britain needed new universities, and quickly. There should be broader courses for first degrees, designed to develop student potential rather than to instil information. Postgraduate education and research should be developed. Grants for vacation study and other activities, such as field work, should be made available. Staff-student ratios 'should not be allowed to deteriorate'.

The result was immediately accepted by the Government, and there was a national enthusiasm for new universities. Some of these, such as Aston, Strathclyde and Salford, were former Colleges of Advanced Technology, which kept their technological emphasis. Others were new creations, variously dubbed 'Plateglass' or 'Newbridge' universities – East Anglia, Essex, Kent, Lancaster, Sussex, Warwick, York – which inclined to a more traditional model. There were experiments in plenty – in new types of courses, in new combinations of subjects, in new modes of organization. At the same time, there was a parallel expansion in other forms of higher education: technical colleges became Polytechnics, and Colleges of Further and Higher Education were set up.

The period from 1945 to 1965 was a very exciting one in the field of education – a time when all things seemed possible, and many of them were already happening. Conservatives looked for the implementation of the Butler system. Labour looked for a healing of the divisions in society. The emphasis varied from education as a means of personal fulfilment to education to meet national manpower needs. There was much debate about C. P. Snow's 'Two Cultures' – the liberal and the scientific – and the means of bringing them together; about comprehensive schools and grammar schools, about ROSLA (which meant 'the raising of the school-leaving age') and the proper age of transferring children from one type of school to another. There were experiments with Sixth Form Colleges. But very few voices were raised to query whether the money was well spent, or whether education could fulfil all the hopes which were placed upon it.

The Sixth Arm of the 'Welfare State'

It was becoming apparent that there was some truth in the assertion that the welfare legislation primarily benefited the middle classes rather than the poorer sections of society. As T. H. Marshall was to comment later, this is inevitable when services previously confined to the lower income groups are extended to the whole population.[22] If the stigma of means-testing was to be removed, then some relatively affluent people would benefit: that was the consequence of providing services as of right rather than as of charity. All the same, there was an uneasy recognition that articulate people who could understand how the services worked, knew where to go for assistance, and could talk to professionals such as teachers and doctors as social equals, fared better than inarticulate people who lacked these advantages. So developed the idea that the five major social services were not enough: there was a need for a sixth service which could act on behalf of those who lacked the knowledge, initiative and energy to act for themselves.[23]

This was the rationale behind the rapid development of social work in the late 1950s and 1960s. In the immediate post-war period, Eileen Younghusband of the London School of Economics had produced two reports which demonstrated that social work was useful, but that it was not yet a unified profession.[24] Medical social workers, psychiatric social workers, probation officers and child care officers were being trained on separate courses, and found it difficult to communicate with one another. Many people in social work posts were unqualified or underqualified. They were lowly paid and lacked support services, such as car allowances or secretarial assistance. As a result of this analysis, the first generic course for social workers, in which those intending to enter different specialisms trained together at a postgraduate level, was set up at the LSE in 1954–5.[25]

At the same time, the separate organizations for different kinds of social workers had set up a Standing Conference, and began to produce their own literature on ways and means of working together. One of the problems which had emerged as the social services developed was that a single client or family might be visited by several social workers with different trainings and of varying degrees of competence, all giving different, and possibly conflicting, advice. The solution to this was seen as the case conference, in which workers would meet together and pool their knowledge of a case, choosing one of their members as the key worker. The journal *Case Conference*, founded in 1953, spread the new philosophy.

Government was cautious. In 1955, a working party was set up on 'Social workers in the local authority health and welfare services' – its remit officially restricted to these two underdeveloped fields, where qualified social workers were a rarity. Eileen Younghusband, who had hoped for a much broader-based enquiry, was disappointed, but accepted the chairmanship in the hope that the working party's findings would be relevant to the whole of social work. The Younghusband Report,[26] published in 1959, made proposals for a massive expansion in social work employment in local authorities; the provision of adequate support services; a new qualification, the Certificate in Social Work, which could be taken in two years in Colleges of Further Education; a national training council, to guarantee standards, and a National Institute of Social Work Training (the word 'Training' was later dropped) as a central staff college. While the universities, which could take only limited numbers of social work students, continued to provide courses of a higher academic level, the proposals for a second level qualification met with instant public approval. There were two full columns on the Report in *The Times* on 5 May 1959, and the leader on the same day expressed the view that the report 'fittingly inaugurates the second decade of the Welfare State'. There were debates in the House of Commons and the House of Lords. One Conservative MP thought it the greatest social document since the Beveridge Report, and the Government spokesman in the Lords called it 'a great and absorbing human document'.

The main proposals were implemented in the Health Visitors' and Social Workers' Training Act of 1962. As Eileen Younghusband had forecast, the students taking the new shorter courses soon outnumbered the university-trained students, and went into all kinds of social work, not only to the local authority health and welfare departments. The National Institute was set up in London, and social work entered on a new phase of unification and professional development. The Sixth Arm of the 'Welfare State' was in place.

Success at Last?

In 1965, Professor T. H. Marshall of the London School of Economics summed up sixty or seventy years of 'the story of social policy' with the judgement that social welfare, once confined to 'the helpless and hopeless of the population', had been steadily extended to all citizens. There had been 'a convergence of principles and an integration of practices' to which all political parties had made some contribution: 'there is a growing measure of agreement on fundamentals. It is realised that many of the old antitheses are largely imaginary. . . . There is little difference of opinion as to the services that must be provided, and it is generally agreed that, whoever provides them, the overall responsibility for the welfare of the citizen must remain with the state.'[27]

Marshall thought that there was a new understanding of community living, and a new willingness to share. Britain had moved a long way from the 'naked "cash nexus" described by the Poor Law Commission in 1909' to a recognition of citizens' rights and duties. The public/private welfare debate was no longer important, and the arguments put forward by MacLeod and Powell against the extension of public welfare services were simply irrelevant.

Events were swiftly to prove him wrong. 'Consensus politics' in domestic policy certainly held in theory until the Thatcher Government substituted 'conviction politics' in 1979,[28] but the practical limitation and contraction of the public health and social services began almost before Marshall's book had reached the bookstalls.

CHAPTER TWELVE

Problems of Contraction

Labour won the General Election of November 1964. As in 1945, the economic situation was highly unfavourable. According to R. H. S. Crossman, 'The incoming Prime Minister was presented with a Treasury memorandum showing an £800 million deficit on overseas payments . . . and even after the "Paris Club" of central bankers agreed, early in November, to make another £142 million loan to Britain, with a prospect of a further £215 million from the International Monetary Fund, the pound continued to weaken'.[1]

Harold Wilson's administration of 1964–70 was followed by the Conservative administration of Edward Heath from 1970 to 1974. Labour returned to power from 1974 to 1979. Labour was thus in office for ten years out of fourteen between 1964 and 1979. During this period, the pressures for social reform continued, but were increasingly countervailed by international pressures on the British economy and the growing strength of the views of the New Right. The promises of 1948 began visibly to fail.

Race, Gender and Equality

The influx of immigrants from the 'New Commonwealth' had begun soon after the Second World War. The workers came from India and Pakistan, from Ceylon (Sri Lanka), from the West Indies, from Africa and other countries in the hope of better living conditions, often taking the more poorly paid jobs and moving into the worst housing. Britain needed their labour, but by the mid-1960s, the numbers were growing, swelled by wives and children who came to join the workers, and the problems were multiplying. As early as 1958, there were riots in Notting Hill which were thought to have had a racial element,[2] and conflict grew as the immigrants competed for better jobs and for housing.

The Race Relations Acts of 1965 and 1968 set up the Race Relations Board (now the Commission for Racial Equality) and made it unlawful to discriminate on grounds of colour, race or ethnic origin in the provision of goods, facilities, housing accommodation or land. Machinery for conciliation was set up to resolve conflicts, but a breach of the provisions constituted a civil offence which could lead to a court action and the award of damages. Discriminatory advertisements were prohibited.

Though both Labour and Conservative leaders were in favour of measures to promote racial harmony, there was a considerable undercurrent of popular resentment against 'the blacks'; and Enoch Powell, then Conservative MP for Wolverhampton, touched a raw nerve in 1968 when he advocated mass repatriation. Powell's speech at Birmingham opposed the provisions of the Race Relations Bill then going through Parliament. He warned that its implementation would 'risk throwing a match into gunpowder'. Britons would become 'strangers in their own country'; and he added 'Like the Roman, I seem to see the Tiber foaming with much blood.'[3] This classical allusion (Powell had at one time been a Classics professor in the University of Sydney) was lost on the Press, and possibly on the public. What became known as the 'Rivers of Blood' speech greatly inflamed racial conflict.

Richard Crossman, then Secretary of State for the Social Services, wrote in his diary a few days later: 'There's no doubt how last week has got to be described. It was Powell week, and we are still absolutely dominated by the effect of his Birmingham speech. There he is with his 40–50,000 letters streaming in, the marches from the docks and from Smithfield, all part of a mass response to a very simple appeal: 'No more bloody immigrants in this country!' I haven't spoken to anyone who has talked to Enoch since his sacking.'[4] Powell had been summarily dismissed from a post in the Shadow Cabinet. Though the shock value of the 'Rivers of Blood' speech was high at the time, the immigration issue never again excited so much popular opposition.[5] After the 1971 Immigration Act, which limited the numbers of immigrants, the problems of ethnic minorities merged into the more general problems of poverty, decaying urban areas, and the maintenance of public order.

The movement to secure equal opportunities for women took a different and less explosive course.[6] The Labour Party had long had a commitment to 'equal pay for equal work' and this was achieved (at least in theory) with the passing, after a long parliamentary campaign, of the Equal Pay Act 1970. The Equal Opportunities Commission, which is concerned with discrimination against women in employment, was set up in 1975. There was some discussion at the time on the possibility of setting up a single board to deal with both racial and gender discrimination, on the American model; but the organizations representing the ethnic minorities were opposed to this. They argued that the situation was different from that in the United States. Ethnic minority groups were relatively small in Britain, and most of their members were immigrants. Most women in Britain were British born, and they totalled more than half the population. It was thought possible that complaints from women would swamp any joint machinery which was set up. (It was also the case that some of the ethnic minority groups, coming from male-dominant cultures, were not necessarily enthusiastic about equal opportunities for women.)

With many frustrations, and in a relatively unspectacular way, the work of the two Commissions has achieved a framework for a greater measure of equality of opportunity in Britain, and neither has been seriously challenged to date, though discrimination still takes many forms, not all of them capable of legal prohibition.

The 'Rediscovery of Poverty'

In 1966, two Fabian academics from the London School of Economics, Peter Townsend and Brian Abel-Smith, published a study on poverty, *The Poor and the Poorest*,[7] which demonstrated that the growth of affluence had left whole classes of society in poverty – particularly large families on low incomes, and those on National Assistance. A powerful argument for increased family allowances and a minimum income level, or alternatively a state supplement to low incomes, was carried forward by the Child Poverty Action Group (CPAG).

Pressure-group tactics were not new. What was new was that British pressure groups, learning from their American counterparts in the Civil Rights movement and the War on Poverty of the Kennedy–Johnson era, now enlisted the help of the media, and acquired a new skill in presentation. CPAG and the Low Pay Unit produced a stream of pamphlets based on research in the Fabian tradition to hammer home the message that poverty had not been defeated, and that much more should be done for people in need. Television, radio and the daily newspapers brought the issues to the attention of the public. Conservative and Labour ministers were bombarded with research material, focusing on one type of benefit after another, in an attempt to raise allowances and humanize a benefit system which was already showing signs of rigidity. CPAG had marked successes in improving access to and take-up of benefits, in securing new forms of allowances and easier conditions for awards. Training courses were introduced for Social Security staff, in which they were required to undertake role-play exercises, and to find out what it was like to be on the other side of the counter. The Welfare Rights movement developed branches in most areas of the country, giving advice to those in need of benefits. The Law Centre movement provided advice on legal issues to people who could not afford the ordinary processes of law. The Low Pay Unit carried out research on families with small incomes.

But the CPAG campaigns, despite their immediate successes, produced two adverse long-term effects: first, the policy of 'disjointed incremental-ism' – fighting the case for one specific benefit after another on a narrow front – meant that the benefit system grew more complicated, and benefits for one type of need got out of step with those for others. The simplicity and comprehensibility of the Beveridge system was lost. Second, in dealing a blow to complacency about the 'Welfare State', the campaigns provided ammunition for the opposition. It was very easy to turn 'There is still much to be done' into 'The Welfare State has failed'.

The failure of the Welfare State was a favourite theme of the Institute of Economic Affairs, founded in 1964, which became the academic branch of the New Right. A flood of papers and pamphlets on monetarist lines countered the literary flood from CPAG and its allied groups, arguing a very different case: freedom involved choice, not state monopoly; com-petition meant greater efficiency; Britain must shake off the shackles of the Socialist-inspired bureaucracy. State welfarism was restricting choice and stifling enterprise. The IEA Hobart Papers, with titles such as *Housing and the Whitehall Bulldozer*, *After the NHS* and *Growth Through Competition* were widely circulated. While the Fabians and the CPAG concentrated on the needs of the underprivileged sectors of society, the IEA argued that Britain was becoming affluent, so that extensive compulsory welfare systems were no longer necessary.

The Move to Selectivity

Though the academic debate took place on overtly political lines, the necessity of abandoning Beveridge-type universalism was reluctantly recognized by the Left as well as the Right. In November 1967, the financial situation worsened sharply. Sterling was devalued, and public expenditure cuts became necessary. Labour was in power at the time, and it was a Labour Secretary of State for the Social Services, Michael Stewart, who convened a conference of senior academics and civil servants only a fortnight after devaluation to discuss a new policy situation. Britain's international trade position was increasingly unfavourable and, for demographic reasons, the social services would be under increasing strain. The birth-rate had dropped, and the proportion of old people in the population was rising rapidly. That meant that a smaller economically active population would have to support a larger dependent population. In these circumstances, no government could continue to expand the social services in response to all the demands which were being made upon it. Expansionism – the cry of 'More money, more staff, more training' – would have to be replaced by a bleak attention to priorities.

The hard reality of democratic government was that no political party could hope to remain in power if it continued to raise taxes: the general public wanted a welfare system, but was not, in the last resort, prepared to pay for it. The only way to improve, or even maintain, the services in a situation of increasing demand and restricted resources was through the voluntary social services and charitable giving.

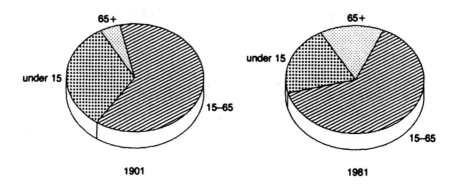

Figure VIII Age-structure of the population, 1901 and 1981
Source: Annual Abstract of Statistics 1989, table 2.3.

The message was unpopular, but the facts seemed incontrovertible. The result was a fierce debate in the Labour ranks on the subject of 'universality or selectivity'?[8] In *Social Services for All?*[9] a Fabian symposium on the issues published in 1968, Peter Townsend argued that the debate was really about 'the kind and quality of society we wish to achieve in Britain', not about cash limits; but most writers were prepared to accept some degree of selectivity. Brian Abel-Smith described the 'slogans of the Beveridge era' as outmoded. There had never been 'social security from the cradle to the grave', and we had never abolished means-testing. Mike Reddin attempted to add up all the different forms of means-testing then in operation – for rate and rent rebates, home helps, day nurseries, children in care, educational maintenance, uniform grants, school meals, welfare foods for expectant mothers, contraceptives, residential care and other services. He estimated that there were at least 3,000 different tests, with different criteria and conditions. No one in authority appeared to be concerned about the cumulative effect on claimants, or the anomalies and illogicalities created.

Most of these Fabian writers were prepared by 1968 to accept some degree of selectivity. The broad outlines of 1948 had been replaced by an increasingly complicated welfare machine which seemed to be ill-adapted to meeting the needs of disadvantaged people. The way forward seemed to consist of two moves: a thorough reorganization of the services to make them more responsive and more efficient, and the development of new forms of special benefits for special needs.

Administrative Reorganization in the 1970s

Social policy in the early 1970s was preoccupied with questions of reorganization. It was evident that the existing provisions in the health and welfare services were becoming cumbersome, and hampering development, but it was hoped that new administrative structures could cure the problems. The major reorganizations of the period 1970–5 came in three areas: the local authority Personal Social Services, the National Health Service, and the structure of local authorities.

The Personal Social Services
The Younghusband Report of 1959 had created a second tier of social workers, and done much to improve the supply of qualified staff; but it was

clear that the services needed to be better organized. They were scattered between local Health Departments (dealing with sickness and maternity work), Welfare Departments (dealing with disability and the chronic infirmities of old age), Children's Departments (rapidly developing work with families where children were at risk), Education Departments (dealing with children in the school system) and Housing Departments (dealing with homeless families, rent arrears and evictions). An inter-departmental committee, composed of distinguished public figures, not civil servants, was set up in 1965 under the chairmanship of Sir Frederic (later Lord) Seebohm, and reported in 1968.[10] Its terms of reference were 'to review the organization and responsibilities of the local authority personal social services in England and Wales, and to consider what changes are desirable to secure an effective family service'.

The Committee's work was thorough, though the members were denied the opportunity to commission fresh research: they were told that this would be too expensive, and that it would take too long. The chief problem facing them was how to combine the scattered social work services of local authorities, and whether to place them under the aegis of any one of the 'parent' departments – Children, Health, Welfare, Education or Housing. Their conclusions were as follows:

1 There should be a new local authority department to provide 'a community based and family-oriented service available to all'.

2 This department should be free-standing, and not under the supervision of any other department.

3 It should combine the social work of Children's Departments and Welfare Departments, both of which would disappear; Educational Welfare and Housing Welfare; and certain elements of the work of Health Departments: mental health care, home helps, day nurseries, residential Homes.

4 This new Department should be headed by a Director of Social Services, with chief officer status – i.e., equivalent to that of the Director of Housing or the Director of Education or the Medical Officer of Health.

5 The Social Services Department would have total responsibility for the social needs of the area: not only for those covered by statutory requirements, but for any needs which might arise.

6 The new framework was to be underscored by the concept of reciprocity: the Social Services Department would act as a powerhouse

to ensure 'the greatest number of people ... giving and receiving service for the benefit of the community'. Individual volunteers would work with social workers, carrying out tasks and maintaining contact with clients under social work direction. Voluntary organizations would be funded and supported by the local authority, and would be free to criticize and stimulate the local authority into new forms of action.

These recommendations[11] became the basis of the Local Authority Social Services Act of 1970. The Bill had a stormy passage in two respects: first, there was immediate and powerful opposition from the medical organizations, which regarded social work as 'the handmaid of medicine', and wanted this new area of work to reinforce the dwindling empires of the Medical Officers of Health, soon to lose most of their public health work to restructured Hospital and Community Services. Second, though a Labour Government was in power at the time, it was clear that a general election was imminent, and that the Bill might fall. If the Conservatives were returned to power, it was thought that the Bill might not be reintroduced in the face of pressure from the medical profession.

The rapid and successful passage of the Bill owed much to the political energy of Lady Serota, a Labour peer and former Leader of the London County Council, who was instrumental in securing parliamentary support and parliamentary time for it. The Act received the royal assent on the day Parliament was dissolved.

When the new Directors of Social Services were subsequently appointed they found that much was expected of them. They had taken on very broad responsibilities involving an unknown volume of work. They had been told that there was no additional money available – the reorganized service was expected to be less costly, not more so; and they took over staff of very varying capacities and relatively narrow experience. There were new and heavy responsibilities. The Social Services Departments had to take over the management of the former approved schools for delinquent and neglected children under the terms of the Children and Young Persons Act 1969, and the development of services for disabled people under the terms of the Disabled Persons Act 1968. Both involved major changes with which the former Children's Departments and Welfare Departments had barely begun to cope.

In 1971, the year in which the Local Authority Social Services Act came into force, the unification of social work was finally achieved. The Act provided for the setting up of the Central Council for Education and

Training in Social Work (CCETSW), with responsibility for the validation of courses, the maintenance of professional standards, and the accreditation of qualified entrants to the profession. At the same time, the British Association of Social Workers (BASW) was formed from the amalgamation of the existing professional associations for psychiatric social workers, child care officers and almoners (now hospital social workers). Social workers in hospitals ceased to be employed by the National Health Service in 1974, and were transferred to the staff of the local authority, so that the local authority is responsible for hospital teams as well as area teams. In England (though not in Scotland, where developments had started earlier and taken a different course) probation officers kept their own professional organization, and continued to be 'officers of the Courts'.

The demand for qualified social workers continued to rise. In 1971 CCETSW opted for a single qualification – the Certificate of Qualification in Social Work, which was awarded to all students on approved courses, from the two-year 'Younghusband' courses to Master's degrees in universities. In 1975, a new Certificate of Social Service, based on day-release for staff already in employment was introduced. The problem for CCETSW has been to secure as wide a base of training as possible, and the Council, constantly aware of the problems of expanding its work in a period of financial retrenchment, has opted for breadth rather than depth. The post-qualification courses recommended by the Seebohm Committee, which would have gone far to iron out the inequalities in basic social work education, have not materialized. The vast majority of social workers do not yet have the opportunities of advanced training available to nurses, prison officers or the police.

The National Health Service

One of the first ominous signs of a changing economic climate was the introduction of charges for medical prescriptions by the Labour Government in January 1968. The argument proceeded on the now familiar lines of economic necessity versus social justice; but despite the strong opposition of the then Minister of Health, Kenneth Robinson (who had been Aneurin Bevan's parliamentary secretary in 1948) and of other Labour MPs, the selectivists won. There were exemptions from charges for patients over retirement age, and for those with chronic conditions; but prescriptions, like dentures and spectacles, were no longer 'free at the point of delivery'.

Reorganization would, it was hoped, bring about a more effective service. The NHS Act 1946 had set up a tripartite structure – hospital, local authority and general practitioner services – but there were few links between the sections. The three arms of the NHS grew steadily apart and, by the early 1960s, there was widespread unease about the basic structure. The Porritt Report of 1962[12] was the first to suggest thorough revision. The issues were debated for some years, while successive governments, both Conservative and Labour, issued two Green Papers and a White Paper.[13] The final White Paper of 1972 put an end to protracted discussion, and led to the National Health Service Reorganization Act of 1974. A new structure was set up, consisting of Regional Health Authorities, Area Health Authorities and District Management Teams, the special status of teaching hospitals disappeared, and the former hospital services became 'Hospital and Community Services'. This meant that local authorities now lost all their health services apart from what had become minor environmental services – pollution, food and water inspection and so on. The position of Medical Officer of Health was replaced by that of the Community Physician, on the staff of the District Management Team. Health visitors and district nurses were removed from local authority staff to form 'primary care teams' attached to general practice. By this time, though general practitioners had defeated the intentions of the framers of the NHS Act 1946 by refusing to join health centres run by the local authorities, they had responded well to Government initiatives which enabled them to set up health centres for group practice under their own control. The pattern of GP care was therefore moving from that of a single doctor working alone to that of a team with support staff.

These changes were accompanied by an extensive retraining programme for senior hospital staff. This embodied a new management philosophy set out in what was known as the 'Grey Book',[14] largely the product of the American firm of management consultants, McKinsey and Co. It relied on currently popular concepts of consensus management and travelling leadership.

The lack of a clear management structure, and the cumbersome nature of a four-tier system soon defeated the innovators in the extended Hospital and Community services. In 1979, a Royal Commission reported that 'we need not be ashamed of our health service, and there are many aspects of which we can be justly proud'[15] but criticized the top-heavy administration, and the failure to make swift decisions. In 1980, in a further revision, Area Health Authorities were abolished, and District Health Authorities set up to make major policy decisions at the local level.[16]

Local authorities

The county and county borough structure had worked well since its inception in 1888, but the distribution of the population was changing. City populations had for the most part ceased to grow. There was talk of 'inner city decay' and 'exurbanisation'. Communications were vastly improved, and the distinction between town and country was no longer clear-cut. As Dr Hedley Marshall of INLOGOV, the Institute of Local Government Studies, noted, 'the defects in the eighty-year-old structure were becoming more apparent. Local government areas no longer corresponded to the settlement pattern. Nor was there consistency in size, population or financial resources. . . . Overspill, changes in life styles, and particularly the advent of the motor car, made it impossible for local authorities to solve their problems within their own boundaries'.[17]

The Redcliffe-Maud Commission[18] recommended the abolition of county boroughs, and the introduction of a new administrative framework. Their proposals were largely implemented in the Local Government Act of 1972. For most of the country, county councils took over the major responsibility of local government for rural and urban areas alike. In the major conurbations of Merseyside, Greater Manchester, West Yorkshire, South Yorkshire and the West Midlands, a two-tier system was established; metropolitan county councils took overall responsibility for strategic planning, police, passenger transport, and certain other matters best administered over a wide area, while metropolitan boroughs within their boundaries were responsible for such services as education, social and personal health services, and housing. This structure was similar to that in London, where the Greater London Council had been established in 1965 as a joint structure covering the work of the London Boroughs.

The distinction between metropolitan councils and metropolitan boroughs was not clear-cut, since there were joint powers in many areas of work, and a balance had to be worked out in practice. In addition, in both metropolitan and non-metropolitan counties, some powers, chiefly concerned with issues of housing, public health or environmental protection, were delegated to district or parish councils operating at lower levels.

The most controversial effects of the changes at the time were the redrawing of boundaries and the changing of some traditional shire titles, some of which have since been changed back again as a result of protest; but the major effect was in the strength of the new metropolitan counties. As J. D. Stewart predicted, party political interests became much more pronounced in these large authorities – and in the 1973 elections, all the metropolitan counties, in addition to the Greater London Council, were Labour controlled.[19] Thus the Local Government Act of 1972 set the stage for the conflicts which were to take place between central and local government in the 1980s.

EPAs and CDPs

The Seebohm Committee had recommended that Social Services Departments should be 'community based'. Hospital Services became 'Hospital and Community Services' under the NHS Reorganization Act of 1974. The theme of 'community' was also evident in two notable social experiments of the late 1960s and early 1970s, Educational Priority Areas and Community Development Projects. The EPA scheme owed much to the Plowden Report, *Children and Their Primary Schools*, published in 1966.[20] Lady Plowden and her colleagues were concerned with primary education as the most basic step in educational and social opportunity. They argued that 'equality of opportunity' was not enough. The main problems lay in the decaying areas of the inner cities. There were areas in which the children never had a chance to grasp the opportunities which were theoretically available to them. There were old 'board school' buildings dating from the days of the 1902 Education Act, with poor equipment and outdated books. In such schools, the turnover of teachers tended to be high, and few of them lived in the local community. Many pupils came from home backgrounds where education was neither understood nor valued. The Plowden Committee was much influenced by developments in the United States, where community work was developing rapidly in the inner cities, and 'Head Start' programmes offered special tuition to underprivileged children, particularly blacks and Puerto Ricans. The Plowden Report stressed the importance of nursery education – the origins of inequality start young. They asked for a policy of 'positive discrimination' for designated 'areas of disadvantage', and for local diagnosis of the needs and the possible achievements, rather than 'standard national formulae'. They recommended community schools, where parents could become involved in the educational process, and the school would be part of the locality.

As a result of these recommendations, a national experiment was set up, in which five Educational Priority Areas were designated, and special services set up in partnership with university departments of Education.[21]

Much enthusiasm developed for 'community schools', in which parents and other adults could take part, and children would learn in the context of their own cultural group. The supporters of EPAs were keen that the experiments should be broadened into a national policy, but the money was never available for the findings to be applied nation-wide. Even if this could have been done, there were two sources of doubt: was it desirable to socialize children into the local area, when the population was increasingly geographically and socially mobile? And could the educational system alone really change society? There were no more EPAs, and subsequent research has cast doubt on the validity of some of the data.[22]

Under the Heath Conservative administration of 1970–4, a very different approach to education emerged. The authors of *The Black Papers on Education*[23] alleged that state education was failing; that educational standards, measured in terms of the three Rs, had actually declined since the First World War; that 'permissive educational practices' resulted in 'a vacuum into which the worst features of the pop and drug world can enter'. They took the view that postgraduate training of teachers was unnecessary, that the school-leaving age should go back to 14, and that discipline and sound drilling in the fundamentals had been abandoned in the search for social egalitarianism.

The *Black Papers* were strongly opposed by many educationists, who found the arguments élitist and retrogressive, and the material highly inaccurate in detail.[24] Nevertheless, they were to have a long-term effect on the education system in influencing policy decisions in the 1980s.

In the early 1970s, the enthusiasm for social change moved from the Department of Education and Science to the Home Office, which sponsored an ambitious scheme for Community Development Projects. Twelve CDPs were set up in run-down areas in different parts of Britain. In each, an action team of community workers was appointed to attempt the revitalization of the area, and a research team was appointed to analyse the work of the action team and to report on the findings.

Alex Lyon, who was Minister of State at the Home Office at the time, described the CDP scheme as 'the brain-child of a remarkable civil servant, Derek Morrell'.[25]

Those projects ... were designed to put teams of articulate young people into areas where the population, though deprived, was inarticulate, to help those people to express their own sense of grievance, and to put pressure on the authority to do something about the situation. The teams have been successful in carrying out that task to the extent that many local councillors wish they did not exist.[26]

Between 1969 and 1975, large sums of government money were spent on CDP work. The articulate young people went to work with a will, setting up advice and opinion centres, tenants' groups, welfare rights centres, adventure playgrounds, leafleting, organizing protests, marching. CDP workers saw themselves as 'change agents'. They saw it as their task to 'fight the system', to oppose social control, to 'lead the march on the Town Hall'. The late 1960s were a time of social revolt, and CDP was in the forefront, with the cry of 'Power to the people'.

Martin Loney charts the story of the rise and fall of CDP.[27] The reasons for its fall were many. Derek Morrell, the gifted civil servant who might have steered it on manageable lines, died suddenly. The Home Office support thereafter was less than whole-hearted. Central Government increasingly withdrew, leaving the twelve action and research teams largely to their own devices. Most of the teams made no attempt to co-operate with the existing workers in their areas – local government councillors, social workers, voluntary organizations – in their enthusiasm for growth through conflict. As one of the more moderate research directors commented, 'A constrained, harassed and politically sensitive system does not welcome outside pressure which appears to raise conflict, increase sectionalism, add to the insatiable demand which outstrips resources, and generally threaten the representative system.'[28]

Councillors complained of 'long hair and earrings among project members'.[29] There was certainly a culture clash; but beyond that, and the disintegrating relationships with the local authorities, were more serious problems. CDP was set up to test whether an enthusiasm for public participation and a small input of resources could revitalize deprived areas. The answer which emerged in a flood of pamphlets and reports from all twelve areas was that the task was impossible. The problems were not local in origin. They derived from national problems: low incomes, unemployment, housing shortages, lack of economic opportunity. Some (though not all) of the teams became dominated by militant neo-Marxists, who saw political revolution as the only solution.[30]

If this development was unwelcome to a Conservative Government, it was equally unwelcome to their successors. It was a Labour Home Secretary, Merlyn Rees, who decided to end CDP funding in 1975, and there was no final evaluation of the work which had been done. In the

United States, the great 'War on Poverty' had already ground to a halt. The world was changing.

The five EPAs and the twelve CDPs covered only small designated areas. Though there were lessons which could be drawn from both sets of experiments, no major changes resulted. The schemes were in fact little more than tokenism – a gesture to an expansionist philosophy which could no longer be sustained. The initiative passed to the Urban Aid funds, which concentrated on reviving industry in inner city areas rather than on stimulating public participation.

Conservative Policy in the 1970s

The 'welfare consensus' held in the Conservative administration of 1970–4 under the premiership of Edward Heath. Sir Keith Joseph, as Secretary of State for the Social Services,[31] was concerned to improve the services within the resources available. He was impressed by the arguments of the Child Poverty Action Group concerning the need to improve access and take-up of social security benefits, and initiated a campaign to ensure that all those who were entitled to benefits knew of their entitlement, and were encouraged to claim. Posters and new, readable leaflets written without jargon were sent to every post office, and leaders of local communities – councillors, doctors, teachers, clergy – were circularized and asked for their help in making the benefits known.

The Family Income Supplement scheme (FIS), introduced in 1970, provided extra money for families on low incomes – a means of improving benefits which had been advocated by some Fabians as well as by some members of the Conservative Party. Though other Fabians argued that this would depress wages, and advocated a minimum income scheme, the objection was raised that this would price workers of limited capacity, such as some mentally and physically handicapped people, out of the employment market altogether.

Another Conservative innovation at this time was the Family Fund, specially dedicated to the needs of families with handicapped children. It was decided that this fund should be administered through a charitable trust rather than through statutory channels, and the Joseph Rowntree Memorial Trust took on the considerable task of organizing it nationally. Though the Family Fund is not widely known by the general public, it has been extensively used to provide for special needs – a car, a house extension, extra clothing or holidays – for hard pressed families.[32]

In June 1972, Sir Keith Joseph promoted a major research initiative on 'Transmitted Deprivation'. According to the then Chairman of the Social Science Research Council, the aim was to call attention to 'the persistence of deprivation, despite general economic advance, and to the evidence that the same families tended to be deprived generation after generation'.[33]

At this time, theories about the 'culture of poverty' were much in vogue in the United States. It was postulated that poverty and deprivation were learned in childhood, and passed from one generation to the next. In Britain, a joint working party was set up between the Department of Education and Science and the SSRC, and an ambitious research programme was set up. In fact, the initial review of existing research by Rutter and Madge spelled out the inadequacy of the theory to meet the facts. In an exhaustive survey of research on economic status, housing, crime, psychological disorder, parenting behaviour, multiple problem families, the status of ethnic minorities and other issues, the authors pointed out that though there was much evidence of inequality in Britain, it was not only a matter of economic inequality; and that while there were 'continuities over time', these were by no means all due to familial influences. There were regional continuities, like the persistently high unemployment rate in Scotland, or the persistently high delinquency rate in London; and there were ethnic continuities, like the poor housing and employment status of many West Indian families.[34]

A major programme of social research was carried out over nearly ten years, and a final report summarized the findings.[35] These, though interesting and valuable to social scientists, did not answer the original question in the form in which it had been put. Sir Keith wanted a clear-cut answer which could be translated into positive terms for a targeted group of 'deprived' families. He did not want to be told that the question was a good deal more complicated than he had thought, and that the answer lay in an improvement in the social services as a whole. It may have been with this experience in mind that he insisted on changing the title of the Social Science Research Council to the Economic and Social Studies Research Council (on the grounds that social research was not 'scientific') and reduced its budget. As in the case of Community Development Projects, social research workers had not come up with the answers which the Government of the day wanted. Some took the view that the Government had been asking the wrong questions.

A New Round of Cuts

If the economic crisis of the mid-1960s provided the first major rethinking of 'Welfare State' principles, the oil crisis of 1973 was to precipitate the second. The sudden increase in prices by the Middle Eastern oil producers had profound effects on the economies of most industrialized countries. According to Denis Healey, who was Labour Chancellor of the Exchequer at the time, the increase in oil prices added £2.5 billion to Britain's current account deficit, increased the cost of living by 10 per cent, and reduced the Gross Domestic Product by 5 per cent, all in a single year.[36]

Healey provides a thoughtful analysis of how Keynesian economic principles were breaking down: Keynesian theory ignored institutional factors, such as the power of the trade unions; and it started from an assumption of national economic self-sufficiency. The theory had worked well enough in the United States in the late 1930s (when it was the basis of Roosevelt's New Deal); but Britain in the 1970s had powerful trade unions, and over 30 per cent of the Gross Domestic Product was dependent on exports. Industrial stagnation had been assumed not to co-exist with rampant inflation, but now Britain was suffering from both simultaneously. The international currency markets were in turmoil, production in Britain lagged behind that of powerful competitors. When the country's currency reserves were endangered, Healey was forced to ask the International Monetary Fund for a loan; but the IMF was American-dominated, and the United States was still opposed to socialism in Britain. The loan was granted – on condition that Britain made severe cuts in public sector expenditure. According to Healey, it was repaid before the Labour Government left office in 1979; but public confidence in Labour's ability to handle the economy had been badly shaken.[37]

'Zero growth . . . times of economic stringency . . . given the financial situation . . . cutback . . . restraint. These were the key terms of 1975', began the editorial preface to the *Year Book of Social Policy in Britain 1975*. In the following year, the editors commented that 'The economic descent from affluence to poverty has been more devastating than . . . seemed possible'.

Labour was still in power in the winter of 1978–9, typified by the Press as 'the Winter of Discontent'. Attempts to control inflation were failing, and the Government's limitation of wage increases to five per cent produced a wave of strikes. Britain's industrial output fell, and many services were disrupted. The trade unions were flexing their 'industrial muscles' and strikers included not only the road transport workers, who demanded a pay rise of 25 per cent, but also ambulance staff, water and sewerage staff, grave-diggers, dustmen and school caretakers – people whose refusal to work had immediate public impact. Ironically enough, it was the action of these relatively poor groups which created a revulsion against the power of the unions. As sick people were refused hospital admission, water supplies became polluted, bodies remained unburied, sacks of rubbish piled up in the streets and children were sent home from school, public alarm grew and became a major factor in Labour's electoral defeat in May 1979.

The Conservative Party manifesto promised the control of inflation, curbs to the power of the trade unions, the maintenance of the rule of law, support for family life and better health and education services. It was expected that a Conservative Government would reduce welfare spending, and stress the values of self-help and private enterprise rather than those of community and social concern; but in the next eighteen years, the changes in social policy were to be much more fundamental than a mere shift in political orientation. The attacks of the New Right, which argued for the diminution or even the abolition of the welfare services, were gaining force in the second half of the 1970s, and a new and powerful ideology was to give them political legitimacy.

CHAPTER THIRTEEN

Breaking the Consensus

'I set out to destroy socialism because I felt that it was at odds with the British character', Mrs Thatcher said in retrospect, 'Consensus is the absence of principle and the presence of expediency.'[1] Under the Conservative administrations of 1979–83 and 1983–7, productivity increased, income tax was slashed, and members of the public queued to acquire shares in public utilities – telecommunications, British Airways, gas, electricity, water. The average wage increased by more than the rate of inflation, and fortunes were made out of property. 'Popular capitalism' became the aim, and to some extent the reality; but this was also a time in which unemployment grew to frightening proportions, and beggars reappeared on the city streets. It became fashionable again to talk of 'the poor' as a single class, and of 'scroungers' and 'layabouts' who would not work. Greed and acquisitiveness were extolled as virtues, and the gap between rich and poor got wider.

The Reasons for Change

Despite Mrs Thatcher's very personal style of government, the reasons for change were very much broader than her own convictions. Technological change, in particular the increasing ease and falling costs of international communications, meant that the decisions of individual national governments were no longer the main determinants of social policy. By 1979, the big industrial conglomerates were already exerting their influence across national borders, and there was no longer any major opposition to international capitalism, for communism was clearly failing, though the Iron

Curtain and the Berlin Wall would not fall for another ten years. As investment moved freely from country to country, national governments concentrated on competitiveness for the survival of their economies. This was seen in terms of 'shaking out' industry, producing a lean economic machine and cutting production costs.[2] As John Peterson comments, 'most states appeared to lose both the will and the capacity to steer their domestic economies'.[3]

Britain was not alone in moving to a market model for social policy; and in Western Europe, the matter was complicated by the developing structure of the European Economic Community, which Britain had joined in 1973. The Conservative Party's marked nervousness about closer links with Europe was chiefly due to two factors – the fear of losing national sovereignty, and the knowledge that directives from Brussels would increasingly infringe that sovereignty by insisting on common standards of consumer and worker protection. For the general public, the issue was kept at the level of appeals to the Union Jack, the magical quality of the pound sterling, and complaints about directives on the contents of sausages and the curve of bananas; but for many 'Eurosceptics', the real issue was the ability of British industry to keep wages down and hours of work long.

In 1979, it was in any case clear that Britain's welfarist philosophy had to be challenged and tested. The Labour Government had virtually collapsed under wave after wave of industrial action. As we have seen economic factors were working against a welfare philosophy as early as 1965, when it became apparent that public expectations were running ahead of public willingness to bear taxation. Promises had to be made to win an election, but as international competition for markets became sharper, governments found it increasingly difficult to redeem the promises; and politicians who did not redeem their promises were unlikely to be re-elected. Labour costs had to be kept low – and that meant breaking the power of the trade unions and allowing unemployment to rise. A promise to reduce taxation was popular – but that meant reducing the burden of welfare. The welfare system must therefore be supply-led, not demand-led. It was with these imperatives in mind that the Thatcher Government took office.

The theoretical underpinning for this stance was provided by the Institute of Economic Affairs and the Adam Smith Institute, two right-wing think-tanks which had produced a flood of pamphlets elaborating on the views of two prominent American monetarists, Milton Friedman[4] and F. A. Hayek.[5] It was argued that the 'Wenceslas myth'[6] of the state as universal provider must be checked; that state services are inherently paternalistic, frustrating personal independence and enterprise; that they place too much power in the hands of professionals such as doctors, teachers and social workers; and that privatization is therefore in the public interest. A cash nexus between professional and customer (patient/student/client) puts power and dignity back into the hands of the individual by allowing freedom of choice. Rewarding those who show enterprise will in time create a more prosperous state, to the benefit of all: by means of the 'trickle-down' or 'echelon' effect,[7] prosperity will in time permeate right through the economic system to the poorest. A genuinely free market will produce a state of spontaneous order or *catallaxy*[8] in which regulation and planning are largely unnecessary, and the response to consumer demand is swift and efficient. Government can thus withdraw from the arena of social policy, leaving consumers to make their own decisions with a minimum of public service intervention.

These were the principles on which the Conservatives set about breaking the social policy consensus.

Rolling Back the Boundaries

In his first budget speech, Sir Geoffrey Howe, the new Chancellor of the Exchequer, spoke of 'rolling back the boundaries of the public sector'.[9] For a time, almost any move towards dismantling the 'welfare state' seemed possible. On 9 September 1982, the Cabinet considered a paper by the Central Policy Review Staff which suggested a number of ways of cutting welfare expenditure: allowing the attrition of social security benefits by not increasing them in line with inflation; charging full market fees (then £12,000) for higher education, with a system of scholarships and student loans; a voucher system for primary and secondary education; the wholesale replacement of the National Health Service with a private insurance scheme. Some members of the Cabinet were appalled, and they argued successfully that the time was not yet ripe for such wholesale measures; but the Prime Minister was not pleased. It was later reported in the *Economist*, which leaked information about the document to its readers, that she and the Treasury ministers were 'furious' that the discussion was blocked. The byline in the *Economist* was 'Thatcher's Holocaust'.[10] If the Conservatives were to roll back the tide of welfare, they would have to do it in a way which did not cause a public outcry, riots and election defeat.

For this reason, the first two Thatcher administrations did not fully grasp the nettle of administrative change. Up to 1987, social policy was largely determined by budgetary allocation and drastic expenditure cuts, not by the traditional routes of academic analysis, public discussion and parliamentary process. People who took any interest in social policy except with a view to financial cut-back were known as 'Wets'. The main areas in which changes with social policy implications took place before 1987 were unemployment, housing, Social Security and local government, and in each case, the main means of change was economic leverage.

Shaking Out the Labour Force

The Conservative Party fought the 1979 General Election on a Saatchi and Saatchi campaign with the slogan 'Labour isn't working', and a poster showing a long dole queue. The figure for the registered unemployed then stood at 1.2 million. By the third quarter of 1984, the official figure was over 3 million, and the basis of calculation had been redrawn to exclude a further 300,000.[11] The constant 'massaging' of unemployment statistics in the 1980s was the subject of much criticism from social scientists and the media.

The unemployment rate did not begin to fall until 1987, and problems were very much worse in the industrial north than in the more prosperous south-east. The rationale for allowing unemployment to increase was that it was necessary to shake out industry and produce a leaner, more efficient workforce, and that unemployment was the best weapon against inflation; but there was a heavy price to be paid in social distress. For some years, the burdens fell mainly on the poorer sections of the population. It was not until the 'shake-out' began to affect 'Essex Man' – the newly affluent members of the middle classes in the Home Counties, with their large mortgages and hire-purchase commitments – that there was a public outcry.

Unemployment was a powerful weapon against the trade unions. The Employment Act of 1980 restricted picketing, which had led to some angry scenes in 1978–9. The Employment Act of 1982 went further in outlawing political strikes, and – still more drastically – rendering Union funds liable to confiscation if the Union supported unlawful action.

The miners' strike of 1984 was a crucial test of political strength.[12] The strikers were warned grimly that this time there would be no 'beer and

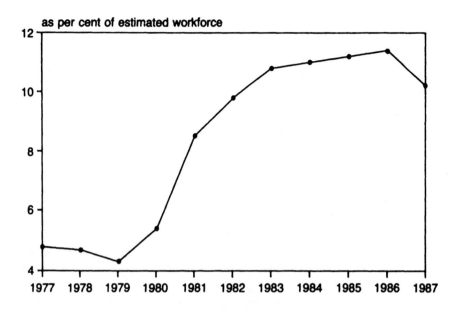

Figure IX Unemployment, United Kingdom, 1977–87
Source: Annual Abstract of Statistics 1989, table 6.6.

sandwiches at Number 10' as under recent Labour Governments. The coal industry was overmanned, unprofitable pits had to be closed. There were alternative sources of energy – notably cheap oil – and coal could be imported more cheaply from abroad. In the resultant industrial battle, Arthur Scargill and the leaders of the National Union of Mineworkers refused to condemn the use of violence, and lost the support of the Labour Party, while the Government enforced management's 'right to manage' by the deployment of huge police pickets. Law and order were restored at the cost of badly damaged industrial relations, and the power of organized labour was decisively broken.

Some rise in unemployment was inevitable. A similar trend affected most industrialized countries in this period, irrespective of political ideology, as a result of three new economic factors: 'stagflation', or world-wide inflation co-existing with economic depression; rapid developments in information technology, which led to redundancies in many white-collar occupations as clerks and junior managers were replaced by computers; and the movement towards economic integration in the European

Community, which focused attention on the need to 'keep Britain competitive'. The problems and the pressures were not wholly of the Conservative Government's making, and anxiety about the country's economic stability kept the Conservatives in power, even though there was mounting opposition to their social measures.

Cutting the Social Security Budget

Since the early 1950s, the majority in the Conservative Party had been opposed to universalist social security on the grounds that it sapped the moral fibre of the nation, and created dependence on the state. In the event, the Thatcher Governments judged it wise to maintain the system, despite its soaring cost. High unemployment rates, early retirement and the existence of very low-paid jobs, all officially tolerated if not encouraged in the interests of keeping down inflation, meant increased claims for unemployment benefit, retirement pensions and Family Credit. Single parenthood was increasing, and the Single Teenage Mother became the symbol of Conservative frustration with a social security system which they resented paying for, but could not axe.

In financial terms, the social security system was easily the largest of the social services.[13] In the mid-1980s, it absorbed nearly 30 per cent of all public expenditure, and cost nearly as much as health, education and welfare combined. In 1982, there were 22 different benefits, administered by an army of 90,000 staff, and covering a wide range of individual and family needs. Nearly three-quarters of all household units received some of their income from social security benefits, and 11 per cent received 90 per cent or more of their income from benefits. No government could make major cuts in this system without risking the loss of power.

Unemployment benefit was maintained without recourse to the kind of wholesale cuts in basic benefits which had been implemented in the 1930s; but a series of regulatory measures made cuts without the need for parliamentary approval. The link between the rate of long-term benefits and earnings was abandoned in 1980, and that between short-term benefits and earnings in 1982. From 1984, benefit was paid fortnightly in arrears, making a saving of £8.5 million. The installation of wire grilles in some DSS offices testified to the deterioration of relations between officers and clients.

Other minor savings were made by transferring the cost of the first eight weeks of sickness benefit to employers; paying child benefit four-weekly in arrears instead of weekly; cutting eligibility to housing benefit under a revised scheme introduced in 1984; and 'fiscal drag': delaying upratings in benefit required to keep pace with inflation.

Despite these measures, the Social Security budget continued to grow. The cost was consistently higher than Government estimates, and repeated attempts to target limited amounts of money to the most needy groups failed. Reductions in the health and social services, particularly in residential care, shifted costs to the Social Security budget. Cuts in public sector expenditure proved much easier to plan than to implement.

It was not until 1986 that the Government, which had by then been in power for seven years, was ready to make a direct legislative challenge to the 'welfare state' through new legislation. The Social Security Act 1986 was the only major measure of this kind passed before the General Election of 1987. This Act had been a long time in drafting. Reducing the public's dependence on welfare benefits was regarded as a priority from the day the Conservatives took power in 1979, and it was clearly expected to be a vote-winner. A Review Body was set up, chaired by a minister, to look at the options. Its findings were hotly contested by the poverty lobby, which adduced evidence and calculations to show that the recommendations were anti-social and unworkable; but they reached the House of Commons substantially unaltered.

The Bill was condemned by the poverty lobby; the Select Committee on Social Services pleaded for caution in view of the complexity of the issues and the unknown nature of the consequences; and there were some stormy scenes in the House of Commons. Nevertheless, the Bill, unaltered in its major provisions, became law as the Social Security Act 1986. There were four main sets of provisions: the introduction of personal pensions, the creation of the Social Fund and the abolition of certain grants and benefits. Personal pensions schemes, referred to as 'the earner's chosen scheme', enabled individuals to contract out of the state pension scheme and to make their own arrangements with private insurance companies, to whom the state would also pay an appropriate contribution. Pensions would be attached to the individual and not to the place of work, with advantages in an increasingly mobile society where people could be expected to change jobs several times during their working lives.

The Benefits Agency was set up as an autonomous agency at one remove from government – much like the Unemployment Assistance

Board of the 1930s. The Social Fund, 'the most vilified proposal to emerge from the Social Security Review'[14] was instituted for single social security payments, such as grants for beds, gas or electric cookers, and heaters to people in need. It was to be strictly cash-limited, and there was no provision for an appeal procedure. Recipients were be expected to pay the money back, and this or any other kind of social security payment might be recovered from a dead person's estate if he or she had concealed assets.

The categories of grants abolished included two universalist grants introduced under the Beveridge Plan, the death grant and the maternity grant. Those in genuine need could apply to the Social Fund, but the benefit would be means-tested – and repayable. No benefits were to be payable to persons engaged in trade disputes – another means of damaging the trade unions, whose members had been accustomed to claim benefit while picketing. Students' entitlement to benefit in vacations, which had helped many students to survive on inadequate grants without getting into debt, was also abolished.

Restricting the Local Authorities

The local government reorganization of 1974 had created the Greater London Authority, and powerful metropolitan councils in conurbations in the Midlands, Lancashire and Yorkshire. After Labour's defeat in the General Election of 1979, these bodies found themselves on an early collision course with the Thatcher Government, which was determined to reduce their power. The Public Sector Borrowing Requirement was severely restricted, and the Rates Act of 1984 introduced 'rate-capping'. As a result, they could neither borrow the money they required for development, nor pass the cost on to the rate-payer.

Some councils lurched to the political left – notably in Liverpool, where the 'Militant Tendency' gained control, continued high spending, and left the city virtually bankrupt by 1986. With their finances drastically reduced, local authorities resorted to frantic expedients to maintain essential services – selling and leasing back their own town halls, playing the stock market. Conservative politicians repeatedly attacked the local authorities, claiming that many of the Labour-dominated councils were wasting the rate-payers' money, and that the true bastion of democracy was Parliament, not the local councils. The ventures of what they termed the 'Loony Left' in supporting minority groups – Asians, blacks, single parents, feminist and 'gay' groups – were derided, and claimed to be remote from the interests of solid working-class opinion.

The Greater London Council and the metropolitan councils were abolished in 1986. Except for certain joint functions such as transport, control was handed back to the individual borough councils. The GLC, damaged by a judicial decision which defeated its 'Fare's fair' campaign for flat-rate fares on public transport in the London area, went out in a blaze of fireworks; and London's County Hall, where Ken Livingstone and his supporters had defied the Parliament on the other side of Westminster Bridge, was put up for sale. [15]

A Property-Owning Democracy?

One of the strongest planks in the Conservative platform was the powerful image of a property-owning democracy through the 'right to buy'. Mass home ownership, like mass share ownership, was encouraged to give individuals a stake in the country, and to create popular capitalism. Within a few days of the first Thatcher Government taking office, an announcement was made on plans for the sale of Council houses. Predictably, the better properties in the more favoured areas sold quickly (at low prices to sitting tenants) and the policy was very popular among former tenants, some of whom improved their properties in ways which the local council would not have been able to finance. Double glazing, new heating systems and car ports added to the amenities of some very basic housing. From the Government's point of view, the policy achieved the aim of weakening local authorities, most of whom could not build more council houses because the proceeds of sales went into their growing deficits.

Home ownership became a national passion. It was widely said that 'property prices never go down' and that 'a house is a hedge against inflation'. Financial measures kept the interest rate low, and made mortgages more attractive. Property prices soared, demand was further strengthened, and a spiral began. In many areas, house prices doubled within a single year as the 'ripple effect' spread from the London area and the highly industrialized south-east to other parts of the country. Fortunes were made, particularly by large commercial companies which could afford to acquire large blocks of property. On a smaller scale, the rise in house prices benefited individuals who could afford to move from a high-cost area to a low-cost one, or those who inherited property which could be turned into disposable income.[16]

Between 1979 and 1987, home ownership increased from 55 to 64 per cent of housing tenure, while public housing starts dropped from 107,000 to 30,000 in the same period.[17] The restriction in housing starts and the sale of about one million council houses substantially reduced the availability of low-cost housing. A Department of the Environment survey in 1985 estimated that the condition of public housing was deteriorating, 85 per cent being in need of repair and maintenance.[18] The run-down inner city estates, where nobody wanted to buy the properties, were an increasing problem.

Mounting Protest

Despite the fact that many people had become more affluent under the first two Thatcher Governments, public opinion polls in the 1980s, such as those reported in *British Social Attitudes*,[19] consistently showed that the Government's policy for the health and social services did not carry public support. Respondents questioned about priorities in public spending repeatedly placed the Health Services and the Education Services at the top of their list of preferences, and said that they were prepared to pay for them in increased taxes; but this attitude was not reflected in election results. Until the economic bubble burst, many voters seem to have been mesmerized by economic prosperity, fear of the EEC and the Tories' firm conviction that they were saving England. Mrs Thatcher's speeches on 'The Revival of Britain' (subsequently published) matched her triumphalism over the successful outcome of the Falklands war.[20] All the same, there was a growing disquiet about the Government's methods of operation.

A New 'Quangocracy'
Soon after the 1979 General Election, over 200 'quangoes' or advisory bodies were summarily abolished. Many of them had specialized knowledge and experience. One was the Personal Social Services Council, which was working on the development of local authority and voluntary social services. Another was the standing Royal Commission on Income and Wealth, the Diamond Commission, which had produced a series of

major reports on the distribution of wealth and the persistence of the gap between rich and poor.

An avowed aim of the Conservative administrations of the 1980s was to 'bring Government nearer to the people' by cutting public sector services which were regarded as self-perpetuating monopolies, remote and inaccessible; but they brought into being a style of management by a variety of unelected bodies, all subject only to central Government control. A report in *The Independent* commented:

> According to *Public Bodies*, the Cabinet Office's guide to departmental non-governmental organizations, there were 1,412 quangoes in 1992. They had 114,000 board members and staff, and spent £14 billion ... £10.5 billion of which was taxpayers' money. 40,000 of the posts were directly in the gift of ministers and the Prime Minister. To these ... must be added the NHS, whose £12 billion budget is distributed through bodies ... all now devoid of public accountability.[21]

Official Statistics

Two phrases much used in Government circles of the time were parodied in the television series *Yes, Minister*: the 'need to know' and 'being economical with the truth'. The first implied that information might be restricted; the second, that it was not always necessary to tell the whole truth, even if the partial truth might be misleading. The handling of official statistics illustrates both points. In the 1980s, when the Government should have welcomed 'feed-back' on its social policies from expert bodies, voluntary organizations, academics and other sources, their contribution to social analysis was drastically reduced. Hugo Young comments that 'In a climate in which everything was political, detachment was held to be a chimera, and objectivity a fraud, and the classes who claimed these virtues lost their foothold in public life.'[22]

Regular sources of official information became less helpful to social analysts. The Civil Service strike of 1981 was a preliminary to the disbanding of the Civil Service Department, and to substantial cuts in Civil Service staffing. A White Paper of 1981 endorsed the recommendations of Sir Derek (later Lord) Rayner, Chairman of Marks and Spencer, that official statistical services should be cut by 25 per cent. Sir Derek laid down the principle that 'information should not be collected primarily for publication. It should be collected because Government needs it for its own business.'[23] One could scarcely have a clearer indication of the restriction of the 'need to know'.

Concern among statisticians at the deterioration in public statistics was expressed in October 1989 by Sir Claus Moser, formerly head of the Government Statistical Service, and Sir David Cox, former president of the Royal Statistical Society, who made a public appeal for an independent body to monitor the Government's use of statistics.[24] There was no official response.

In the absence of official enquiries and accurate statistics, it is difficult to judge the severity of the hardship caused to the poorer members of society by the social policies of the 1980s. The Government was certainly not very interested in finding out. Charges that 'the rich got richer while the poor got poorer', and that destructive social policies were leading to the creation of a new and deprived underclass, contradicted the assumptions of Hayek's 'trickle-down' philosophy. Those who tried to provide the evidence that this was happening got short shrift.

The Black Report

A Working Group on Inequalities in Health was set up by Sir Douglas Black, Chief Scientist to the DHSS. It included several eminent academics, and provided detailed evidence of inequalities between the Registrar-General's five occupational classes: for instance, that the risk of death before retirement was two and a half times as great for Social Class V (unskilled manual workers) than for Social Class I (professional and managerial workers); and that sickness and medical consultation rates were consistently higher for Social Classes IV and V than for Social Classes I–III. Despite the status of the Working Group, and of the Chief Scientist himself, the DHSS refused to publish the report. It was distributed to enquirers only in a photocopied form, with a foreword from the responsible minister stating that it was 'quite unrealistic'. A Penguin paperback edition edited by Professor Peter Townsend, who was a member of the Working Group, had wide sales.[25]

The Scarman Report

The Brixton Riots of April 1981, which sparked off other urban riots, notably in Toxteth, Liverpool, were analysed in a report by Lord Scarman, an eminent appeal judge and chairman of the Law Commission.[26] Lord Scarman was at pains to make it clear that, though there was an ethnic element in the riots, they were not specifically racial riots. There was a real crisis in the inner cities. While the Rule of Law had to be maintained, a more conciliatory attitude on the part of the police and better social conditions in poverty-stricken urban areas with a large ethnic population could help to prevent further outbreaks of violence. His conclusion was:

> The inner city is crucial for the future of the British nation. The inner cities are the testing ground where the character of Britain will be determined. This is because of their population mix, their high rate of unemployment and their substandard physical environment. Most importantly, our fellow citizens who live here see themselves at a disadvantage compared with the rest of us, and many of them attribute their disadvantage to racial prejudice ... We must tackle the crisis of the inner cities, not because we are frightened of conflict, but because we are all fired by conscience and a passion for justice.[27]

Faith in the City

In the absence of a Government inquiry, the Archbishop of Canterbury, Robert Runcie, set up his own Commission on the problems of what were termed 'Urban Priority Areas'. The members of the Commission included some leading social scientists. The first section of their Report (1985) consisted of a closely argued analysis of the problems of poverty and deprivation in Britain:

> To describe UPAs is to write of squalor and dilapidation. Grey walls, littered streets, boarded-up windows, graffiti, demolition and debris are the drearily standard features.[28]

Using six social indicators of deprivation derived from previous work by the Department of the Environment, the analysis built up a factual and convincing picture of inequality – of areas of an increasingly affluent Britain where people lived on very low wages in substandard housing, where crime, vandalism and family breakdown were the rule rather than the exception, where there was 'a general frailty of civil order':

> The more recent history has been one of growing inequality – in life chances, income, housing, education, public services, and the general level of civic amenity.[29]

The response from Government was dismissive. The protest from the Church, like those from the universities and other concerned institutions, fell on deaf ears. One Cabinet minister described the Report as 'Marxist'.

The 1987 Election

Despite considerable public protests about the direction of Government social policy, the Conservatives were returned to power for the third time in 1987. Until that time, the structure of the Education Services, the National Health Service and the community care services had remained largely intact, though all three were affected by derestriction and the pressure towards private enterprise. A parliamentary majority of 102 gave the Conservatives the opportunity to carry through more drastic measures. Between 1987 and 1989, legislation passed very rapidly and without much public discussion was to apply the *coup de grâce* to these key services. Though Mrs Thatcher resigned in 1989, and government under her successor, John Major, was much less abrasive, the policy of replacing national structures by a pluralistic public/private mix was to continue unchanged.

CHAPTER FOURTEEN

Dismantling the Framework

In retrospect, it is clear that the breaking down of what were seen as the bureaucratic monopolies of the 'Welfare State' in education, health, community care and housing was a long and consistent process. The years 1987–9 were the time of legislative change, but developments from 1979 to 1987 provided a piecemeal introduction to the changes, and developments from 1989 to 1997 under the Major Governments translated the changes into practice. The resignation of Mrs Thatcher in 1989 made no great difference. At least as far as the health and social services were concerned, Mrs Thatcher was correct when she told a *Newsweek* reporter that 'There is no such thing as Majorism"[1]. All the major changes had been piloted through Parliament by the time John Major took office.

The model employed was that which had already been used for the former public utilities, such as telephones, gas and electricity, where Government had already withdrawn from day-to-day participation in service provision, exerting only a regulatory power. OFTEL (1984), OFGAS (1986), OFFER (electricity, 1988) and other semi-autonomous agencies were the prototypes. While market forces would not operate unrestricted, a national framework of provision was replaced by a decentralized network of agencies which came to be known as *quasi-markets*,[2] in which purchasers would be able to make their choice from the services of providers. Essential to this concept was the *purchaser–provider principle*, first enunciated by Lord Rothschild as adviser to the Cabinet: that the roles of purchasers and providers should be clearly separated.

The intention was to introduce competition, and theoretically to improve choice for the consumer. The consequences of this policy, based on classical economic theory, have been profound.

In the sections which follow, the implementation of this policy in the key services of the 'Welfare State' is traced through the five Conservative administrations from 1979 to 1987, and followed by comments on the Major years.

Re-shaping the Education Services

Conservative policy in the 1980s was beset by a basic paradox: on one hand, there was considerable pressure from the Department of Education for the restoration of traditional approaches: topic teaching and group projects were discouraged. Subject teaching, formal class instruction and a highly competitive system based on examination results were back in favour. Grammar schools were preserved, and private schools flourished. There was considerable pressure on Colleges of Education, which had their budgets severely cut, to reduce theoretical work – particularly that based upon the suspect areas of Psychology and Sociology – and to concentrate on school-based practice. 'Hands-on' experience was stressed, and educational theory was largely dismissed as time-wasting.

At the same time, there was much emphasis on 'relevance', and in particular on the relevance of technology. Education became valued primarily as a preparation for employment. In 1982, an extended Manpower Services Commission with a £2,000 million annual budget took many young people off the unemployment register (thereby improving the unemployment statistics) but largely bypassed the Education Services. The new City Technology Colleges bypassed the secondary school system entirely, offering training of a strictly practical nature, closely tied to local industrial needs under the direct control of the MSC. Most of the 14 colleges set up under this initiative were adaptations of local schools rather than new establishments.

The Education Act 1988 provided for the virtual dismantling of the local authority education services, from primary schools to polytechnics.[3] Finance was delegated directly to secondary schools and to primary schools with over 200 pupils, including voluntary schools, so that all became 'grant-maintained'. Local school management or 'LMS' became the norm; but while the local education authorities lost power and responsibility to the individual schools, being responsible only for allocating the 'general schools budget' and approving plans, there was a second paradox in education policy: while some power and responsibility went down to the schools, and there was at least a gesture in favour of 'parent choice' and parents in management, much more power went into the hands of central government. A National Curriculum was established for all children aged 5–16, and the Secretary of State was given power to prescribe programmes of study, attainment targets and assessment. The National Curriculum Council and the Schools Examination and Assessment Council were to dominate the work of schools and the lives of schoolchildren on a hitherto unprecedented scale (much closer to the highly prescriptive systems in France and Germany than to British tradition). The work of these agencies encountered massive resistance from the teaching profession, including boycotts of assessment procedures and threats of strikes. The Act also abolished the Inner London Education Authority, which had an outstanding record in the educational field.

Thereafter, there was increasingly firm central control over what the schools taught, and how it was to be tested. The Education Act of 1992 instituted regular inspections of schools, and put pressure on local authorities to maintain standards by threatening special government Education Associations to take over failing schools. OFSTED, the Office for Standards in Education, became the centre for a rigorous régime of testing, and results were published in the form of league tables. There were constant disputes with the teaching profession. Teachers complained that the tables were statistically crude, and the criteria used cruder. The National Union of Teachers repeatedly threatened to boycott the procedures. Debates were to fill the pages of the *Times Education Supplement,* and to occupy national teachers' conferences for years; but with minor adjustments (such as allowing seven-year-olds to complete their test papers in pencil) the plans were followed through.

Polytechnics were at this time funded by local authorities, and shared in the financial restrictions of the local authority sector, but they were at least valued as teaching practical subjects. Universities, funded fairly generously by previous governments, faced a drastic reversal of conditions. In 1980, they were given a month in which to plan 18 per cent cuts in expenditure over a three-year period.[4] Since the largest budget item was that of staff salaries, and most academics then had security of tenure, the cuts were only made possible by extensive early retirement schemes, without regard to the effects on teaching and research.

Throughout the university system, funding was used to create pressure to contract the humanities and the social sciences (with the exception of Economics) and to expand technological subjects. Subject areas like Classics, Ancient and Mediaeval History, Philosophy and Theology virtually disappeared from many universities. Even the pure Sciences – Biology, Chemistry and Physics – were badly affected. In all, some 10,000 university staff left, and the older universities suffered with the new ones. In 1985, the University of Oxford refused to award an honorary degree to Mrs Thatcher for her work as prime minister – a decision which led to heated correspondence between her supporters and her detractors in the Press.[5]

Structural changes in further and higher education followed. The Education Act of 1993 set up a new Higher Education Funding Council in place of the University Grants Committee, with more members drawn from the business world than from the universities. This body became responsible for both the existing universities and the polytechnics, which had been removed from local authority control in 1988 and were now renamed universities. The Act also gave the HEFC power to institute 'efficiency studies' and systems of inspection not too different from those set up in schools. Though the end of the binary system and the widening of access to university education was generally welcomed, there was widespread concern that the effect of these measures would be further to destroy the quality of university teaching. The columns of the *Times Higher Education Supplement* soon began to resemble those of the *Times Education Supplement* as protests against the new assessment procedures spilled over into its columns. There was much concern that distinction between institutions devoted to academic excellence and research and institutions devoted to vocational training was being lost; but the pass had long since been sold, since universities had become entrepreneurial institutions devoted to the service of industry, and it was difficult to preserve academic excellence as staff–student ratios worsened, and more students were crowded into less space with fewer books. The practical and immediate results of the 1993 Act were to level down rather than level up; and to introduce into the university sector, which had previously been largely self-governing, a level of control which negated a cherished academic freedom.

Breaking Up the National Health Service?

When the Thatcher Government came to power in 1979, there was a rapid expansion in private health insurance, and in the construction of private hospitals, in the expectation that the NHS might be suddenly dismantled; but this did not occur. Mrs Thatcher was forced by public pressure to assure the nation that 'I have no more intention of dismantling the health service than of dismantling Britain's defences'.[6] Nevertheless, the Government's plans for the health services, as for other public services, involved bringing in the efficiency and competition of the business world, and ultimately breaking up what was seen as a state monopoly in the hands of professional vested interests. Finance was sharply cut. Health authorities were told to use privatized services wherever possible, putting such services as laundry, rubbish collection and catering out to tender, and were urged to seek new money for themselves. Some of the London hospitals made their books balance by charging very high fees to foreign patients. Private wings and private beds flourished, providing accommodation and services well above the NHS level. Other hospitals, more modestly, rented space to flower shops, gift shops and hairdressers on their premises, and this did have the effect of improving facilities for patients. In the practitioner services, prescription charges were increased, dental and opticians' charges were increased and, in 1989, free optical tests were discontinued except for special groups.

The cumbersome four-tier structure of the Hospital Services was reduced to three tiers in 1982,[7] and Sir Roy Griffiths, deputy chairman of Sainsbury's supermarket, was brought in to examine the management problems of the NHS with a small group of businessmen: the consensus management set up under the principles of the 'Grey Book' had proved unworkable. Government assumed that Sir Roy and his advisers would be able to recommend ways of ensuring 'quality control'. If supermarkets could provide fresh, quality food and household goods for shoppers on a day-to-day basis, why should the health and community services not be assessed in the same way? Sir Roy had to explain to Mrs Thatcher and her Cabinet that the 'purchaser–provider principle' might work for buying sugar or soapflakes, but was much more difficult to apply to the provision of health care.[8]

The Griffiths Report of 1983[9] proposed a new structure: a district general manager would become responsible for resource management for all the services of a district, co-ordinating the work of sector managers and handling a fixed budget. 'Travelling chairmanship', the consensus system introduced by the 'Grey Book' of 1972, was replaced by more robust philosophy of 'the buck stops here'. The duty of a manager was to manage, not to agree with colleagues. The majority of the new 'Griffiths managers' were recruited from industry and commerce, or from the medical profession. NHS administrators and nursing administrators were generally less successful in obtaining posts. All new appointees were given four-year renewable contracts. This provided an incentive to produce rapid results, but did not encourage long-term planning.

An immediate result was the very rapid sell-off of psychiatric hospitals. New district managers, committed to the rapid improvement of a stream-lined acute hospital service, saw the closure of entire hospitals as an opportunity to fill the yawning gaps in their budgets. Between 1984 and 1990, 20,000 psychiatric hospital beds were closed, and the demolition squads moved in, reducing many hospitals to rubble.[10] Most of the sites were sold off for housing or leisure centres. The hospital service no longer took responsibility for the care of patients whose needs were primarily for nursing and social care.

Under the National Health Service and Community Care Act of 1990, District Health Authorities were enabled to become NHS Trusts, 'to own or manage hospitals, or other facilities previously managed by health authorities, or to develop new facilities'. This effectively took whole districts out of the management of the regional authority, and gave them their own budgets. NHS Trusts were required 'to keep their revenue, income and expenditure account in balance'. They were given consider-able freedom in handling their own finances, subject to the ultimate con-trol of the Secretary of State (in practice, the Department of Health). All the members of the NHS Trusts were nominees, not elected representatives.

Family doctor practices, like Hospital Trusts, could opt out of the Health Service framework (in this case their Family Practitioner Commit-tee). They were given power to administer their own budgets, and buy in services from hospitals and the private sector as required for their patients: subject, of course, to cash limits.

These sweeping changes met with strong opposition from the medical and nursing professions. The Royal Colleges and other professional bodies pleaded for pilot programmes to test the changes before they were applied across the country, but with no effect.[11] Public debate tended to focus on finance rather than on issues of principle or patient care. Many commentators queried whether the funding would be adequate, and there was an uneasy and mounting conviction that it would not. The applicants for NHS Trusts and fund-holding practices flew the entrepreneurial flag, often in the hope that their enterprise would be rewarded with more generous financial allocations to prove the new system a success.

It was assumed that Trusts and fund-holding GP groups would know how to use resources to the best advantage. Fund-holding general practitioners could decide whether to send patients to hospital (and to which hospital to send them), buy in different kinds of specialist care, and control their pharmaceutical bills. Many doubts were expressed in the Press on the wisdom of the new system, chiefly expressing fears that the new diversified structure introduced a system of rationing in which the NHS Trusts and GPs had to make unpopular decisions about the services they could offer patients, while Government exercised a strong financial and regulatory control. Nevertheless, the changes went ahead. The National Health Service had been the largest employer in Europe. By April 1992, the purchaser/provider split was operative in all health authorities, and there were about 160 Trusts and 600 fundholding practices.[12]

'Care in the Community'

The Local Authority Social Services Act of 1970 had set up strong and independent Social Services Departments of local authorities to take responsibility for a wide array of social services. Most of the directors were social workers, and the staff provided what in the United States is called 'direct service', advising and helping clients in both domiciliary and residential services.

Social workers were one of the early targets of the 'New Right', which saw their activities as typical of the 'Nanny State'. In 1979 and 1980, the columns of the *Daily Telegraph* were regularly occupied with articles deriding the Seebohm structure and arguing for its abolition.[13]

Funds for social work education and training were cut to a minimum. The Central Council for Education and Training in Social Work had been encouraged to develop an elaborate plan for the development of its work, and estimated the costs at £50 million. The Government offer in 1988 was £1 million.[14]

A strongly legal element was introduced into the work of social workers in respect of mentally ill clients and neglected or abused children. The

1983 Mental Health Act gave 'approved social workers' power of compulsion in the admission of mentally ill people to hospital, while a series of highly publicized cases of child abuse – Jasmine Beckford, Tyra Henry, Beverley Lewis and others[15] – gave the impression to the public that social workers were negligent or inefficient in guarding children's interests. The Children Act of 1989 set up a new and complicated set of provisions for the protection of children by the courts. Social workers could no longer determine what was best for a child's welfare. They became responsible for bringing evidence to the courts (and could be blamed if the evidence was not sufficient for the courts to make the right decision). As social services budgets shrank, more emphasis was placed on these statutory duties than on the human relations tasks of helping clients and their families to live in the community.

The final and most drastic change came from another direction: the problems relating to community care. As the policy of running down long-stay hospitals developed, the Government faced sharp criticism from several sources. In 1985, the all-party House of Commons Social Services Committee reported that there was 'a crisis in the community'. Mentally ill people, and people with severe social problems, were being discharged from hospital without proper after-care. There was a marked increase in homelessness – even on Parliament's doorstep, for as the Committee pointed out, London's Cardboard City was only a stone's throw from the House of Commons. Mentally ill people were being sent to prison, which was 'inappropriate', and there was a great increase in family stress, as relatives desperately tried to cope with problems beyond their capacity. The report called unequivocally for Government action and increased local authority expenditure.[16]

In 1986, the Audit Commission for Local Authorities tackled the same theme in a report[17] which stressed that even in financial terms, the situation needed remedial action, particularly in relation to elderly infirm people. Neither local authorities nor hospital authorities were dealing adequately with the need for social care. Two inadequate services were 'struggling along in parallel'. There were 'perverse incentives': many people were being forced into expensive residential or nursing homes in the rapidly growing private sector. When their savings were exhausted, the cost fell on the Social Security budget, so it had merely been transferred from one account to another; and since the care offered by private homes was almost exclusively residential, it could hardly be described as 'care in the community'.

Again the problem was handed to Sir Roy Griffiths. He substantially supported the views of the Select Committee and the Audit Commission, and added some stinging comments of his own – for instance, that community care was 'everyone's poor relation and nobody's baby'. His conclusion was that community care for all client groups should be transferred to the local authorities: though this was unpopular with a Government bent on reducing local authority power, there was no viable alternative. Bowing to the Cabinet demand that he explain his plans in supermarket terms, he recommended 'Packages of care' for clients to be designed by Social Services Departments. Some elements might be provided by other agencies, including those in the private sector.[18]

These recommendations were incorporated into the NHS and Community Care Act of 1990, but implementation was twice deferred in response to a variety of protests from local authorities, medical and social work organizations, and did not finally come into operation until 1993. The result was that many Social Services Departments virtually ceased to practise direct service to clients: they became purchasers of services provided by a variety of other agencies, some of the traditional voluntary and charitable kind, others set up on a commercial basis.

The End of State Housing

Monk and Kleinman comment that the Conservatives regarded public housing 'as symptomatic of a wider malaise of dependence on the welfare state . . . a weakening of the moral fibre of the working classes'.[19] Little remained of Council housing by 1988; but the Housing Act of that year set up a system whereby whole estates or blocks of housing which could not be sold off could be transferred to Housing Action Trusts. 'Tenants' Choice' (popularly known as 'Pick a Landlord') would safeguard the rights of tenants. This scheme was not a success. Large Scale Voluntary Transfers (LSTVs) in which local authorities sold off whole estates, sometimes for only a nominal fee, became a common way of dealing with the 'difficult' estates, and a 'rent to mortgage' scheme was later introduced to accelerate the sale of Council houses.

Thatcher to Major

In other aspects of the economic and social life of Britain, the time of the third Thatcher administration was a time of crisis. In 1988, the economic bubble burst. The years of boom were followed by a catastrophic recession. Company liquidations soared, small businesses crashed. The housing market collapsed. Many home owners were faced with 'negative equity', a situation in which their mortgage was greater than the current value of their property. Building society repossessions for non-payment of mortgage interest, which had stood at only 2,500 in 1979, nearly doubled by 1989; and by that time, more than a quarter of a million houseowners were more than six months in arrears with their mortgage payments.[20] The Government's economic policies had been profitable and attractive as long as share prices and house values were rising; but many people found that that they also involved the risk of financial hardship, the loss of a family home, and possibly bankruptcy.

The final blow came with the introduction of the Community Charge, popularly called the 'poll tax', under an Act of 1989. Domestic rates, based on greatly increasing house values, were abolished and, instead, all adults were required to pay a flat rate charge. The charge, set by the local authority, could vary from area to area and from year to year. The millionaire owner of a mansion paid exactly the same charge as the former mental hospital patient crowded into a corner of a lodging house. The scheme proved unworkable, not only because of its inequity, but because of difficulties in administration. People move, houses do not. Local authorities were to waste much time and money in trying to trace non-payers, and cases were still coming to the courts ten years later. Second thoughts produced some exemptions, such as those for people in nursing homes for the elderly, and reductions were introduced for students, unemployed people and those on very small incomes – though even they were required to pay 20 per cent of the charge.

The stated aim was to make local government more responsive to the wishes of the people; but the effect was to shift the burden of local taxation from the wealthy owners of large properties to the poorer sections of the population. Though the legislation went on to the Statute Book, the country simply refused to accept it. There were riots in Trafalgar Square in 1990, and many thousands of people met the flat-rate tax with an equally flat refusal to pay.[21] Some were still refusing to pay years after the 'poll tax' was abolished.

Support for Mrs Thatcher began to dwindle. There was a period of frantic Cabinet re-shuffles, in which John Major, who had been Foreign Secretary for only three months, became Chancellor of the Exchequer, and impressed the House of Commons with a sound and steady budget; but it was the end of an era. On 25 October 1989, Margaret Thatcher went, and John Major took her place.

The classic advice of senior civil servants to ministers is 'Don't rock the boat'. Between 1979 and the end of 1989, the boat had been well and truly rocked. Consensus was replaced by competition, compassion by commercialism and community values by cut and thrust. In the jargon of the media, hardly a week passed without a new 'crackdown' being 'unveiled'. Words like 'radical' and 'reform', which historically belonged to policies designed to produce social betterment, were used to describe procedures in which the social advances of a century and a half were torn up by the roots.

The eight years of the Major administrations were to be more emollient than the Thatcher years, but through them the policy of privatization continued without interruption. The new prime minister was an unusual Conservative leader. He was the only member of his Cabinet who had ever been unemployed, and he came from a modest suburban family.[22] In interviews, he promised 'a genuinely classless society'; but there was to be no U-turn in social policy. The consensus of social policy analysts appears to be that the Major Governments of 1989–92 and 1992–7 were largely concerned with consolidating the Thatcher legacy.[23]

The overall effect of the new policies was to fragment large organizations and institutions, and to replace them with a moving network of purchaser/provider relationships. These are necessarily difficult, if not impossible, to document on a national scale, particularly in view of the deterioration in national statistics; but there was no doubt at all about the Conservatives' resistance to the European Union's programme for improving working conditions.

The Social Chapter and the ERM

At the Maastricht Summit of December 1991, there was pressure from the other member states of the European Union for British agreement to the 'Social Chapter' or Protocol on Social Policy. The terms of this document were very general: it provided for the improvement of the working environment, better health and safety provision for workers, equality for men and women in terms and conditions of work, and a shorter working week. The signatories were committed to accepting 'by means of directives, minimum requirements for gradual implementation'. The British delegation refused to sign. The final solution was to detach the protocol from the other agreements. It was signed by the other eleven states of the European Union, and Britain was the only exception. John Major came home saying that he had won 'game, set and match'; but the refusal damaged Britain's standing in Europe.

Worse was to come. Britain was in deep economic recession, and interest rate policy was constrained by the country's participation in the Exchange Rate Mechanism (ERM), by which the currency had to be maintained at a particular parity, narrowly defined. Falling tax revenues and higher Social Security bills made public sector borrowing a matter of deep concern. The Public Sector Borrowing Requirement (PSBR) for 1992 showed a deficit of £37 billion, and the projected deficit for the following year was £50 billion. Speculation that Britain would be forced to devalue grew through the summer of 1992, forcing repeated denials from ministers; but on 'Black Wednesday', 16 September 1992, Britain finally withdrew from the ERM. At the time, this was seen as a defeat for the Government, but paradoxically, in the long term it proved to be decisive in reversing the economic malaise, and thus keeping the Conservatives in power.

Unemployment and Social Security
Economic decline meant higher Social Security bills. John Major said in 1993 that 'every prime minister wishes to achieve full employment', but his Cabinet still took the Thatcherite view that high unemployment was a price worth paying for the defeat of inflation. The price was proving to be a heavy one. The number of claimants for unemployment benefit rose by almost a million during Major's first term of office, to reach 2.6 million. Social Security expenditure amounted to one-third of all Government expenditure, rising rapidly in the early 1990s as the recession deepened.

To the left of the Conservative party, there were people who wanted to build a more positive welfare policy. In his Budget statement of December 1993, Kenneth Clarke as Chancellor of the Exchequer stated categorically, 'This Government will never take part in any attempt to dismantle the welfare state. We want to see a better welfare state, well-run, well-judged, and one that meets the priorities of modern society.'[24] He introduced Work Start, a new policy for the long-term unemployed, speaking of 'the need to build bridges out of dependency'; but though there was a good deal of talk about how to deal with unemployment and the Social Security budget, there was comparatively little action in this period. All in all, there was a great deal more talk than action. Conservative politicians had used unemployment as a weapon to beat the trade unions – and it was a weapon which many were not prepared to give up, even in the face of disproportionately high public expenditure.

During this period, public criticism mounted on the subject of 'pensions mis-selling'. The personal pension scheme introduced in the Social Security Act of 1986 had encouraged people to contract out of the state pension scheme, Many people subscribed to pensions schemes offered by private insurance companies, some of them considered highly reputable concerns, and found that they were substantially mis-led as to the benefits they would actually receive. This became a national scandal, much exposed by the Press.[25] Companies were eventually ordered to make restitution, and at the end of the millennium, the Private Investment Agency was still levying fines on those who delayed in doing so.

NEW INITIATIVES

Behind the adherence to Thatcherite principles in the time of the Major Governments, there was a kinder and more homely philosophy struggling to get out – provided that its execution did not cost too much, or upset the extreme Right. The Community Charge was first modified by a cut of £140 in March 1991 (financed by an increase in Value Added Tax) and then replaced by a Council Tax, a graduated property tax based on property values, from November 1993. A White Paper on Open Government made it clear that 'official statistics were also required for the citizen' and an *Official Statistics Code of Practice* reminded Government statisticians of the importance of producing reliable and objective data.[26] The Conservative Party was more interested at the time in two measures which expressed John Major's own philosophy: the Citizen's Charter, and the 'Back to Basics' campaign.

The Citizen's Charter
This initiative neatly combined business principles with a gesture to human rights and citizen participation. John Major himself was

enthusiastic about the idea of improving the quality of public services and included the idea of the Charter in his speech to the Conservative Central Council on 23 March 1991. For Major it was an important plank of his own approach. He believed that ordinary citizens were much less concerned about the ownership and control of services than about the quality of the services provided. While much energy had been expended on privatisation, little attention had been given to how quality was to be ensured and measured, and how citizens were to be recompensed when it failed to maintain standards.

The Citizen's Charter initiative aimed at raising standards and giving guarantees of service quality, but critically without raising public expenditure. It paralleled consumer-orientated approaches being adopted in business and seemed to offer a new dimension to the agenda inherited from the Thatcher years. The Downing Street Policy Unit and individual ministers worked frantically through 1991 and 1992 to produce a scheme.[27] The Citizen's Charter Unit was set up in 1992 under the Cabinet Office with promises of new performance standards, particularly in education, health and transport.[28] The Charter aimed to give service users guarantees on everything from the length of time they would have to wait for hospital treatment to the recompense they could expect in the event of their train journey being delayed. Fifteen charters for different public services were issued in March 1992, shortly before the General Election.[29]

While some dismissed this initiative as merely cosmetic, it did mark a distinct shift away from the profit-orientated policies of the Thatcher period. A £5 voucher as an apology for a late train might not be much consolation to a traveller who had missed an appointment or a connection, but it indicated that quality of service mattered. If it was a minor application of the ideas of quality control which were being developed on the political Left, it was at least a start.

Back to Basics

This campaign arose from a speech at the Conservative Party Conference in 1993, when John Major made a plea for the 'old values' of decency and courtesy. The phrase 'back to basics' was taken up enthusiastically by the conference and began to be seen as a new way forward for the Government. It was originally intended to relate to issues of law and order, to restore a society where vandalism and petty pilfering were frowned upon, elderly people could cross the road in safety and women could walk safely at night. One might question whether it was ever a policy in any substantive sense; but it was a theme which Major and his advisers thought would appeal to the general public. *The Times* noted 'a nostalgic Party conference speech which won him affection and time',[30] but two days later, a comment suggested a political vacuum: 'the oratory at the conference which evoked a roseate past has no vision of a better future'.[31] Unfortunately, 'Back to Basics' carried two risks: first, that the government might be seen as moralizing, or telling people how to behave: press and public were quick to interpret it in terms of sexual behaviour rather than public safety, and minority groups bristled at the possibility of government intervention in their private lives; second, that the unrelenting scrutiny of the increasingly hostile media would reveal individual examples of ministers whose behaviour was not according to what were (wrongly) assumed to be sexual standards. Charges of ministerial hypocrisy followed; but the really damaging scandal was not concerned with issues such as homosexuality, adultery or prostitution. It was the 'Cash for Questions' issue, which surfaced in 1995, and which involved the rights and integrity of Parliament itself. If members of Parliament were alleged to be accepting bribes from unscrupulous industrial magnates, the flag of the free market had been unfurled once too often. 'Back to Basics' quietly subsided, and so did the Major Government.

John Major was a genuinely popular public figure – the decent 'grey man' who had taken on the difficult task of following the Iron Lady, and had stayed the course; but his Cabinet and the Conservative party were not popular: rent by dissension, harried by scandal, deserted by both the media and the industrialists, they knew by 1997 that their period of power was over. It was time for extensive re-thinking, and New Labour was waiting in the wings.

CHAPTER FIFTEEN

New Labour – New Social Policy?

Labour had been waiting in the wings for a long time; but the Labour Party had changed radically during the long years in opposition. There was no question of going 'back to Beveridge', or to the social policy confusions of the 1970s. New Labour had done some intensive re-thinking, and evolved new lines of policy.

Neil Kinnock had reorganized and re-shaped the Labour Party; but after its defeat in the 1992 election, he resigned, and went to Brussels. His place as leader of the party was taken by John Smith, who commanded much public confidence and affection, but who died suddenly in May 1994. John Smith's major political achievements were to take the first steps towards the introduction of OMOV (one member, one vote) as party policy, and to set up the Social Justice Commission. OMOV removed the trade unions' block votes at party elections, freeing Labour from the threat of domination by the 'hard Left'.[1] The Social Justice Commission, headed by Sir Gordon Borrie, set about the task of assessing the principles on which a rapidly changing society might be made more efficient and more equitable.

The Social Justice Commission

The Commission was set up on the fiftieth anniversary of the Beveridge Report. John Smith's message to its members directed them to counter 'the bankrupt dogmas of the free economy' and to plan the development of 'an intelligent welfare state'. They were to study 'the scourges of poverty, unemployment and low skills' and to maximize 'our most precious resource – the extraordinary skills and talents of ordinary people'. They were charged to produce a long-term strategy for Britain, not for one parliament or for one party.

The Commission reported five months after John Smith's death. The chief conclusion of their report was that 'There is no going back to the stability and security of the 1950s and 1960s' because the world had changed. There had been three kinds of revolution: an *economic revolution* on a global scale in finance, competition, skill and technology which emphasized the need for innovation and adaptability. In future, most people's work-patterns would be fragmented. 'The notion of 'a job for life' has disappeared, and employment insecurity affects us all.'[2] A *social revolution* had resulted from demographic changes, changes in family structure and women's employment, and the development of a 'multicultural, multiracial, multilingual and multi-faith society';[3] while a *political revolution* involved 'a challenge to old assumptions about Parliamentary sovereignty and . . . the growing centralization of government power'. Britain must play 'an active and positive role shaping the European Union' and power must also be devolved to the local level, so that people can 'have more say about the things that are important to them, from schools to pensions'.[4]

The report follows a prescription for 'a middle-sized country on the edge of Europe with a relatively weak economy'.[5] People must recognize that they have responsibilities in addition to rights and 'the values of social justice' must be promoted. These are defined rather cautiously as the equal worth of all citizens; the equal right to meet basic needs; the spreading of opportunities and life-chances 'as far as possible' and the reduction 'and where possible elimination' of unjustified inequalities. There can be no going back to Beveridge: this is a different world – though the Commission preserve the idea of fighting Beveridge's 'Five Giants' and add a sixth giant, Discrimination.

Apart from these general statements, the analysis is primarily in terms of concern for economic productivity and 'keeping up with Europe' – a theme developed in a study from the London School of Economics Welfare State Programme.[6] It is taken as fundamental that Britain must be competitive and prosperous in order to be able to afford a welfare state of any kind. The Commission sets out a new framework for 'Full Employment in Modern Economy'. This involves a high and sustainable growth rate; the maintenance of low inflation; the expansion of the service sector to compensate for the decline in manufacturing; 'life-long learning' to improve the skills of Britain's work-force; the re-integration of the long-term unemployed into the labour market; economic aid for disadvantaged areas; and a new flexible working pattern.

Government must take an active part in labour market regulation, because this is 'a mark of a civilized society'. Discrimination must be fought, whether it is practised against women, against men, against minority groups, against disabled or older people.

The Commission repeatedly stresses that there is no future for 'romantic notions about the re-creation of the male breadwinner earning a family wage. The old jobs which offered a reasonable wage to men without a good education will not return, and nor will women's entry to education and training be reversed.'[7] 'Work-rich' families will be those in which both parents work. The problem lies with 'work-poor' families. Women married to unemployed men are only one-third as likely to be employed as women whose husbands work. Employment will be 'flexible', but periods out of employment can be used for further training and for 'family needs' such as child care and the care of elderly relatives.

'An intelligent welfare state' must provide for the new learning-and-working patterns. The Commission argues that the post-war 'welfare state' was passive: it existed to meet conditions where the main (usually male) breadwinner was not able to provide for his family. Today, the welfare system must be active – not filling gaps but helping people back to self-improvement and self-support, offering 'a hand-up rather than a hand-out',[8] and a 'Welfare to Work' strategy. One of the major problems is that, while work-patterns have become increasingly fragmented, the Benefits System has remained rigid, treating people as either 'in work' or 'out of work' – while at least three-quarters of a million part-time workers do not fall clearly into either category. The need is for 'a stable and predictable base against which people can deal with change'.[9]

The Commission had a very difficult task. Their brief was to work out the framework of a fair society with only a very limited remit, and with little idea when or if their ideas would be taken up. The sections are uneven, but the general picture of a rapidly changing society, where people live insecure and rapidly changing lives, emerges clearly enough. The *New Statesman and Society* called the report 'Labour's currant bun',[10] but it jolted the Left out of some outworn assumptions. The task of the next Labour Government, dealing with fragmented families with fragmented work patterns and fragmented learning opportunities, was not going to be easy.

Tony Blair and the 'Modernizers'

By the time the Social Justice Commission reported, the Labour Party had moved on. Heated debates with the 'Traditionalists' had brought the 'Modernizers' to the fore, headed by a new kind of Labour leader. Tony Blair stood outside many Labour traditions, and had experienced 'no historic battles on the picket lines'.[11] He was born in 1953, the year of Elizabeth II's Coronation, and was an Oxford undergraduate when the Oil Crisis ended the expansion of the 'welfare state': he represented a new generation, untrammelled by old debates and old prejudices, who wanted a more fundamental break with Labour's past than the Social Justice Commission had envisaged.

Blair's first biographers have spent much effort in trying to define the sources of the political and social values which he brought to the Labour Party. He has acknowledged the influence on his thinking of John Macmurray, a Christian Socialist in the tradition of William Temple and R. H. Tawney. In *The Self as Agent* and *Persons in Relation*, Macmurray, a distinguished Scottish philosopher of the 1940s and 1950s, attacked Adam Smith's defence of selfishness, 'social and self-love are the same', holding that people's personalities were created by their relationships in families and communities. Tony Blair read Macmurray's work as a student at Oxford, and has acknowledged that it was a formative influence – 'not the details but the general concept'.[12] In 1996, he provided a foreword to a selection of Macmurray's writings, in which he identified 'the crucial political question of the twenty-first century: the relationship between the individual and society . . . the task is to construct a new settlement for each individual and society today'. Macmurray insisted that fellowship and freedom in society involved a balance between rights and responsibilities.

This was the philosophy which Tony Blair and Gordon Brown took to the United States in January 1993, soon after Bill Clinton's election as President. They met the new president and his adviser, Amitai Etzioni, and discovered a philosophy so close to that of John Macmurray that Blair and Clinton were often saying the same thing in very similar words.[13] Etzioni, successively professor of Sociology at Harvard, Columbia and George Washington Universities, had made a heavyweight attack on the economists' view of human nature as essentially individual and acquisitive. In *The Moral Dilemma* (1988), he insisted that 'there is a key role for moral values ... and social bonds'. Communities are 'social webs of people who know one another as persons, and have a moral voice'. He insists that there must be a balance between individual rights and social responsibilities. In *The Spirit of Community*, he has a memorable analogy, picturing human society (or its leaders) as riding a bicycle 'forever teetering in one direction or another' between the two.[14]

Another important influence on Labour's re-thinking came from theoretical sociology. Anthony Giddens, now Director of the London School of Economics, has been described (in a book of which he is part author) as 'Tony Blair's favourite sociologist'.[15] In a series of books written since 1984, he has developed a coherent and persuasive theme:[16] the globalized modern world differs radically from all previous stages of history. Modern technology, including electronic communication, has 'disembedded' time and space from local contexts of action. In the 'post-modern society'(the words 'modern' and 'post-modern' appear to be used interchangably), we are freed from the traditions, habits, customs and routines which have characterized history for centuries: traditions and beliefs mingle, and people have a new freedom of action. The division between Left and Right is 'still meaningful in politics, but it no longer offers a purchase on some of the most basic political issues we face': human and animal rights, concern for the environment, ethnicity, gender, the relations between rich and poor nations.[17] Though there is 'a Left nostalgia for the welfare state', there should be no need for it in an increasingly wealthy world. Socialism is no longer an alternative to capitalism, and the goal is 'developing a cosmopolitan global society in which wealth generation and control of inequality are reconciled'.[18]

This analysis has proved attractive because it includes a wide variety of current concerns and it may account for the frequent use of 'modern' or 'new' in Labour's policy statements. Giddens' critics stress that it is sociological grand theory, unsupported by empirical verification. Particular arguments are woven into a 'seamless web' of unsupported assertions. The analysis is basically a-historical: it offers no possibility of learning from the mistakes of previous generations, or of planning for the future; and it is determinist: the only future is global capitalism, the only basic aim is wealth creation.[19]

Clause Four

The first major battle confronting the Modernizers was to persuade the Labour Party to change Clause Four, part four, of its Constitution in 1995. This clause committed the party to 'the common ownership of the means of production, distribution and exchange' – in other words, to the public ownership of all major industries and essential services. The campaign for a new Clause Four involved many people – Blair's chief supporters, campaign managers, press aides and constituency parties; but there can be no doubt that the version accepted represents his personal credo: there is a final draft in his own handwriting.[20]

The new Clause Four began, '*By the strength of our common endeavour, we achieve more than we can achieve alone*' – a direct attack on the individualism of the Thatcher era; but it continued '*the rights we enjoy reflect the duties we owe*'. There was to be no concession to welfare dependency. The next section contained a number of notable points:

> A dynamic economy serving the public interest, in which the enterprise of the market and the rigour of competition are joined with the forces of partnership and co-operation to provide the wealth the nation needs, and the opportunity for all to work and prosper, with a thriving private sector . . . where those undertakings essential to the common good are either owned by the public or accountable to them.

By this time, Labour was already receiving overtures from the business world, notably from the managing directors of Sainsbury's and Marks and Spencer. New Labour was to be the friend of the 'thriving private sector', and there is no commitment to re-nationalization of essential under-takings, such as water, electricity and the railways, provided that they are in some way 'accountable' to the public. There is a promise of wealth creation and work opportunities, but no specific commitment to full employment.

> A just society, which judges its strength by the condition of the weak as much as the strong, provides security against fear, and justice at work; which nurtures families, promotes equality of opportunity and delivers people from the tyranny of poverty, prejudice and the abuse of power.

This section echoed the words of the Social Justice Commission, and gave some assurance of a continuing commitment to the under-privileged – and of security in fragmented lives. 'Justice at work' was a cautious reference to the Commission's views on the promotion of Works Councils, a popular alternative to trade unions in the more prosperous countries of western Europe. 'Nurtures families' was a last-minute alteration from 'supports family life' which might have been considered too moralistic for the conference.

> An open democracy, in which the government is held to account by the people, decisions are taken as far as is practicable by the communities they affect, and where fundamental human rights are guaranteed.

This implied open government, and a pragmatic approach to policy-making. It also implied the continuation of government at one remove, presiding over a public–private mix of services through quality control. Though the rationale was different, the idea of 'hands-off' government was accepted as enthusiastically by New Labour as by the Conservatives.

The new Clause Four ended with a gesture towards European integration (but not to the single currency) and international peace. It was adopted by the National Executive of the Labour Party on 13 March 1995, and by a special conference of the party six weeks later, on 29 April. Some members of the conference thought that the new version was anodyne, but a careful reading suggests that it was a very able draft which contains both the essential points of Labour's policy shift and the principles on which policy has been based since it took office in 1997.

The Third Way

Tony Blair has published his own summary of the changes which New Labour intends to bring about in his Fabian pamphlet of 1988. The Third Way is to 'move decisively beyond an Old Left preoccupied by state control, high taxation and producer interests, and a New Right treating public investment, and often the very notions of 'society' and collective endeavour, as evils to be undone'. It is not 'an attempt to split the difference between Left and Right', but about traditional values in a changed world. It is 'a serious reappraisal of social democracy, reaching deep into the values of the Left to develop radically new approaches'.[21] There is no mention of the Liberal Party, or of the Social Democrats, who, under the leadership of Roy Jenkins and David Owen, had tried to find a 'third way' in the 1980s. Tony Blair and Gordon Brown had learned more than community politics from the Clinton administration: the practice of what is known in the business world as 'brokerage politics' or 'dealer politics' – adopting the opposition's best policies. The Conservatives were to complain of this many times, and John Prescott was reputedly concerned about the 'Clintonization' of Labour.[22] The tactics of the boardroom have invaded politics on both sides of the Atlantic. Charles Kennedy, leader of the Liberal Party, has accused New Labour of 'mix and match politics';[23] but if the old polarities of Left and Right are disappearing under global pressures, both 'Third Way' pragmatism and the objections from the other political parties seem inevitable.

The values of the Third Way are the equal worth of each individual, opportunity for all, responsibility and community.[24] The main features of change are 'the growth of increasingly global markets and global culture, technological change, a transformation in the role of women, and changes in the nature of politics resulting from 'the growth of the European Union and a popular loss of faith with distant, unresponsive and often ineffective political institutions'.[25] The Third Way offers 'not a shopping list of fail-safe policy prescriptions, still less an attempt to reinvent the wheel', but a Government prepared to learn the new skills of working in partnership with the private and voluntary sectors, devolving power, co-operating internationally, acting flexibly and 'answering to a much more demanding public'.[26]

Labour in Power, 1997–2000

As Robin Cook said at the time, the new governmental team 'hit the ground running'. Their plans were made in advance, and they were ready to implement them. Any assessment of New Labour's social policy on the basis of its first two and a half years in power must of course be tentative, but there have been no major changes of direction in that time, and no U-turns. Though the Blair Government has made it plain that it needs at least two electoral terms to fulfil its aims, it is at least possible at the time of writing to note the issues which have been regarded as priority, and the directions of change.

The first priority was to ensure a stable and thriving economy without increasing income tax. Favourable global economic conditions and good management have made this possible, though it has meant tight curbs on public expenditure. Despite the curbs, some major measures have had a considerable effect on the quality of life for the working population.

The Conservatives forecast economic disaster if Britain agreed to the European Union's Social Chapter, and John Major battled long and hard to secure exemption at Maastricht; but the new Government signed the protocol in June 1997 – the month in which it took office. The effect was to apply higher European Union standards of acceptable working conditions to Britain over a two-year transitional period.

In another major development, the Human Rights Act became law in November 1998, to take effect from January 2000. This had fundamental implications for the British legal system, which is based on case-law and precedent, not, like that of European countries which had inherited the *Code Napoléon*, on principles of natural justice.[27] Though Britain had signed the European Convention on Human Rights in 1950,[28] that convention was not part of British domestic law, and discrepancies between the two had led to many disputed cases being taken to the European Courts at Strasbourg. The main effect of the Human Rights Act is to introduce principles of natural justice into the British courts, and to outlaw many kinds of social discrimination on the grounds of race, gender and religion without further debate.

The National Minimum Wage Act became law on 31 July 1998. Though the level of £3.60 an hour (painfully negotiated between the Confederation of British Industry and the Trade Unions) was low, it was estimated to give an immediate boost to the earnings of some 1.9 million people, mainly women in the service industries. It meant an end to sweated labour conditions at last.

Unemployment has been steadily reduced, and by the end of 1999 had reached the lowest figure for twenty years on reliable International Labour Office calculations. A New Deal for the unemployed under the age of twenty-five, involving positive help in improving skills and finding employment, is being steadily extended to other groups – lone parents, disabled people, the over-fifties.[29] The sense that New Labour actually wanted people to work, and expected them to do so, has acted as a spur to the economy.

A 'family-friendly' approach has been largely implemented through budgetary measures rather than through legislation. The Minimum Wage and a substantial increase in Child Benefit came into operation immediately following the 1999 Budget,[30] and a further rise in Child Benefit is promised. The Chancellor of the Exchequer, Gordon Brown, has referred to child poverty as 'a scar on the soul of Britain', and plans to eradicate it within twenty years.[31] The Working Families Tax Credit, the Children's

Tax Credit and an Income Support Personal Allowance for the poorest families should lift a million children out of poverty. (These provisions are being largely paid for by the abolition of mortgage tax relief and the abolition of the married couple's tax allowance.)

In addition, there is a National Childcare Strategy, providing up to a million new childcare places for working parents. There is a National Parenting and Family Institute, and a telephone Helpline for parents (0800–800–2222). The Employment Relations Act 1999 set out 'family-friendly work policies' which build on the achievements of the Social Chapter, including the right to training for young workers, paid holidays, maternity and parental leave.

These measures have the potential for a considerable improvement in the quality of life for ordinary people. They have been generally welcomed, and the Government's annual report[32] published in July 1999 might have made more of them. Instead it was framed as a somewhat mechanical summary of the Government's progress in keeping its election pledges. Of 177 commitments in the New Labour Manifesto of two years earlier, 90 were described as 'Done', 'Met' or 'Kept'. 85 as 'On course' or 'Underway', and only two, neither concerned with social policy, as 'Not yet time-tabled'. Items large and small, from 'Reform the Bank of England' to 'Back the 2006 World Cup Bid' jostled for attention, and the document, sold in Tesco's for £2.99, did not attract large sales.

Other Government initiatives have led to controversy. and some to considerable opposition from their own supporters.

A Contract for Welfare

Frank Field, Minister for Welfare Reform, was told to 'think the unthinkable' about pensions. He thought the unthinkable, and the Government found it unacceptable. Mr Field, a poverty campaigner of thirty years' standing, was a universalist in the Beveridge tradition. His plan for universal second 'stakeholder' pensions, funded by contributors, employers and Government was intended to be redistributive, making the wealthy pay for the poor; but it ran into trouble with the Treasury, which rejected it on the grounds of expense, and he did not have the full support of Harriet Harman, his senior as Minister of Social Security. *The Times* commented 'Mr Field seemed at times to be on a moral crusade of almost biblical connotations, while Ms Harman appeared to be more grounded in feminist ideology'.[33] Both left office, and there was criticism of a lack of direction and clarity in the Government's plans.

When Alistair Darling took charge of DSS in the summer of 1988, it was to implement a much clearer and better co-ordinated plan. Pensions became one part of a general 'Contract for Welfare', and the 'stake-holder' scheme postponed for legislation in 2000, when there is expected to be a limited scheme for people earning from £9,000 to £18,000 a year.

The main focus of the 'Contract for Welfare' initiative is an attack on welfare dependency. People who have grown used to living on state benefits are to be encouraged, induced and in the last resort coerced by withdrawal of benefit to become self-supporting. The public has been repeatedly assured that 'help will be targeted where it was most needed'. A series of consultation papers setting out plans for a new range of services, from re-training opportunities to personal counselling, for those of pensionable age, young people, lone parents, the long-term unemployed and people who were disabled or who had long-term illnesses was published. These stressed the importance of work and the ways in which the Government proposed to set about removing barriers to employ-ment.[34] All benefit claimants of working age were to be required to look for work before receiving state help. Alistair Darling introduced the Bill as 'the end of the something for nothing culture', maintaining, 'It is the responsibility of Government to provide positive help: it is the responsibility of claimants to take it up.'[35]

Part V of the Welfare Reform and Pensions Bill included the setting up of a 'Single Work-Focused Gateway' to the benefit system. All claimants except those in narrowly defined categories of physical impairment are required to attend at least one job interview, and further restrictions, including stringent conditions and the withdrawal of benefit, may be applied in the case of those thought to be recalcitrant. The Bill led to a storm of criticism from voluntary organisations, chiefly on the grounds of its inflexibility with regard to disabled people and lone mothers. It had a rough passage in the House of Commons despite the Government's large parliamentary majority. On one occasion, as many as 80 Labour MPs abstained. The House of Lords twice rejected it, chiefly on the initiative of Lord Ashley, the disability campaigner. It was forced through the Com-mons for a third time, and the Lords finally gave way on 10 November 1999, the day before they agreed to the reduction of their own number to 92 life peers.

Education policy

In his leadership campaign of 1994, Tony Blair declared in a television interview that 'Under the next Labour government, education is *there*, right at the heart, and the whole business of government would be to make sure that we raise the skills and talent of the people because that raises their ambitions'. Government education policy has been concentrated on primary schools, providing extra investment for school buildings and reducing class sizes. The delegation of funds to school level has been endorsed, but accompanied by an even tighter degree of central government control.

In the early 1990s, the parliamentary Labour Party had opposed the system of centralized control, competitive league tables, and assessment introduced by the Tories, but Tony Blair was an early convert: he came to the conclusion that parents liked it, and 'It is absolutely vital that parents get as much information as possible.' This was the only major issue on which he disagreed with party policy.[36] £60 million has been committed to a National Literacy Strategy in 1999, and £55 million to a National Numeracy Strategy.[37] 'Literacy hours' and 'numeracy hours' have been prescribed for primary schools to bring British figures for numeracy and literacy up to Continental standards.

New Labour's education policy has so far been distinctly abrasive. The Director of OFSTED, Chris Woodhead, has frequently referred to '15,000 incompetent teachers who should be sacked'. There has been an all-out attack on 'failing schools'. OFSTED 'hit squads' have been called in to reorganize over 200 schools, and 32 schools have been completely closed down.[38]

Secondary school league tables were published on 1 December 1998, accompanied by comments from the Secretary of State for Education and Employment, David Blunkett, that a named school was 'the worst in the country', and named districts had the lowest rates in literacy and numeracy, coupled with the highest rates of truancy. Simon Jenkins in *The Times* commented in 1998 that League Table Day had become 'the annual festival of middle-class prejudices'. Understanding the tables required 'a mastery of differential calculus, the Planck constant, the Heisenberg uncertainty principle and a Downing Street focus group', and did not allow for the fact that children in areas with Britain's worst social problems were hardly likely to score as well as children from 'glorious Buckinghamshire, Cheshire, Barnet, Bromley, where people work hard, live clean and pass their exams'.[39] New Labour has shown a remarkable insensitivity to the very different life-chances of children in different areas of Britain. Though there is a planned New Deal for communities suffering from 'poverty, unemployment, poor skills and education, and decay' (which sounds remarkably like the Community Development Projects of the 1970s), the problems have so far been highly resistant to solution.

David Blunkett has dismissed protests that the teaching profession has been undermined by Government intervention, describing his critics as 'blatant élitists dressed up as well-intentioned liberals'.[40] The Education Framework and Standards Act 1998, heralded as 'the greatest reform in teaching for fifty years'[41] provides for a new General Teaching Council which will have the power to de-register teachers found incompetent. It also provides for 'performance-related pay' in which a breed of 'super-teachers' will be identified on head teachers' assessments and league table results. This proposal raised an immediate outcry from members of the teaching profession who pointed out that the proposals were divisive, and likely to strain relations in the staff room: good teachers are used to working as a team, not as individuals in competition with one another.[42]

The Act also contains provision for 'action zones', in which parents, teachers and community groups will be given grants enabling them to run schools 'in areas where local authorities have failed to raise standards' coupled with renewed publicity about 'failing schools' and 'hit squads'.

The House of Commons Select Committee on Education has recommended the setting up of a team of Commissioners to oversee the work of OFSTED, coupled with some strong comments on its activities.[43] There are reports that the pressure on children, even very young ones, to do well at school, is acute. A paper for the National Early Years Network instances a four-year-old girl who said that she must work 'to pass my Key Stage One tests' – the tests administered to 5–7 year olds. 'Work' meant sitting down with repetitive work sheets which gave them 'clutched pencil syndrome', and were likely to 'switch them off learning' by the age of five.[44]

In the university sector, the Higher Education Funding Council has pursued its own programme of assessment on very similar lines. League tables published in 1999 proclaimed that Imperial College, London was top of the league, 'beating' Oxford and Cambridge – though, as a scientific institution, it does not teach or carry out research in the same range of subjects. One former technical college was 'named and shamed' as the worst in the country.

Health policy

Health, like Employment and Education, has been rated a priority by New Labour. Very large sums of money were promised to the health services, and there was talk of £37 billion over three years; but, in a searching television interview, the Minister of Health at the time, Frank Dobson, admitted that this was 'quite a tight settlement', and that it amounted only to an increase of 3.8 per cent per year in place of the previous Government's 3.0 per cent.[45]

The Government claims to have 'abolished the internal market in the NHS', thus saving £1 billion a year;[46] but, while only some 50 per cent of general practitioners had become fundholders, the Primary Care Act 1998 appears to involve spreading the fund-holding principle to all of them: the difference is that primary care groups, rather than individual practices, will negotiate with the Hospital Trusts; but the pilot projects will take some years to organize. Hospital Trusts are to continue, but according to Mr Dobson, 'GP practices will hold the purse-strings'.[47] The question of whether the purse will be big enough remains unanswered. The setting up of the Institute for Clinical Excellence, on the other hand, has been welcomed by most medical practitioners as providing much-needed guidance on prescribing pharmacological products. Plans for 'High Street health clinics' are in the early stages,[48] but are being strongly contested by general practitioners.

Seventeen new hospitals are under construction. There are to be 'super-nurses' to match 'super-teachers', and 6,000 more training places made available for nurses over the next three years – if the nurses can be recruited.

One of New Labour's election pledges was a blanket pledge to 'reduce hospital waiting lists'. This issue has been pursued with much energy. Frequent media references to waiting list figures have made the pledge almost a test of the Government's efficiency, and the Department of Health has brought considerable pressure to bear on hospitals to achieve it. The chairman of the British Medical Association has asked the Government to 'end this obsession with numbers on lists, and focus on patients who are in greatest need',[49] protesting that clinical practice must not be distorted in order to make a political point. New hospitals take years to build, and skilled physicians and surgeons take years to train. Overall waiting lists, covering procedures from the most urgent and life-saving to the relatively trivial, are virtually meaningless.

The first hospital league tables were published in June 1998, accompanied by 'naming and shaming' of the 'worst' authorities, and threats of 'hit squads' to force improvements. They led to widespread protests from Trusts about the insensitivity and inappropriateness of the criteria used. Frank Dobson's replacement as Health Secretary, Alan Milburn, said soon after his appointment that his concern would be 'Lives, not lists',[50] which gives some hope that the 'league table' approach and the distorting emphasis on waiting lists may give way to more meaningful criteria.

Crime

Before the 1997 Election, Tony Blair promised to be 'tough on crime, tough on the causes of crime' – probably his earliest successful sound-bite. The Blair Government has proceeded to be very much tougher on offenders than either the Thatcher and Major Governments. The Home Secretary has announced in parliament that electronic tagging is a great success in reducing the prison population, and will be extended.[51] He announced on the same day that Britain's first boot camp had earned high praise from the Inspector of Prisons, and that the inmates were reported to enjoy it. A Home Office minister, interviewed at length on ITV on the same day, spoke approvingly of 'punishment', 'retribution' and 'deterrence'.[52] It was quietly decided not to publish a report from the University of Cambridge's Institute of Criminology, funded by the Home Office Research Unit, which stressed the effects of social breakdown, and concluded that harsh and retributive policies did not reduce crime.[53] The proposal to abolish a defendant's right to opt for jury trial has led to sharp protests from the human rights lobby.

Groups in Social Need

One of the most striking facts about New Labour's social policies is that there is little sign of commitment to the vulnerable groups who have traditionally been a matter for Left-wing concern. Many physically disabled people have been distressed by the methods used by the DSS to 'shake out' the disability register. The Benefit Integrity Project (BIP), intended to cut disability benefits by 25 per cent, was finally abandoned in March 1999: 85 per cent of existing benefits had been confirmed, and a further two per cent increased. Of the 13 per cent whose benefits were reduced or stopped, 71 per cent had them restored on appeal, and a few had them increased.[54] Though there have been generously funded new incentives for disabled people to work – subsidies to employers, grants for special equipment, and the opportunity to return to full benefit within a year if the job proves unmanageable – benefits have not been increased beyond inflation, and there has been no extra help for those who cannot work. Proposals to restrict Incapacity Benefit and to abolish the Severe Disablement Allowance for claimants over the age of 20 have caused further alarm.[55] Much of the legal aid system is being abolished. A proposal preserving legal aid for disabled people and those of very limited means in cases of personal injury was not accepted by Government.

The Disability Discrimination Act, which sets up the Disability Rights Commission and provides for improved access to public places and public services for people with mobility, sight and hearing problems has come into effect – but New Labour can hardly take the credit for that: the Act was passed in 1995 by the Major Government. It will be extremely difficult to implement, and the services and agencies which have to comply have ten years in which to do so.

Lone parents (the overwhelming proportion of them lone mothers) will benefit from 'child-friendly' measures such as increases in child benefit and nursery provision, but they too are expected to work and support their children, rather than making a home for them. This is not a policy to be applied with rigour to young women with small children. Proposals for hostel accommodation and training for mothers under the age of eighteen without family support sound like an echo from a moralistic Victorian past. Young mothers have voiced strong objections on television, saying that they do not wish to be forced to bring their children up in hostels.[56]

All people over pensionable age are to receive £100 a year towards their winter heating costs (a bonus which not all need, and some disabled people may need much more) and those over the age of 75 have been promised free television licences – whether or not they find television worth watching, and whether or not their sight is good enough to watch it. The guaranteed minimum income for pensioners (initally £10,000 a year) has received much publicity, but is only an upgrading of Income Support. The question of nursing home costs is far more serious. One of the most draconian measures of the Thatcher era was the abolition of hospital and local authority care for sick and frail elderly people, leaving them to meet the cost of private nursing home care for an indefinite period. The fear of a long final illness and the loss of their homes and most of their life savings is a source of considerable anxiety to all but the wealthy. The Blair Government proceeded soon after taking office to set up a Royal Commission on the Long-Term Care of the Elderly. The Commission reported in March 1998, but its report was not published until March 1999.[57] The recommendations were that the state should share the risk, paying for medical and nursing care, while patient and relatives remained responsible only for 'hotel' care charges. The proposals are known to have met with hostility from the Treasury, and so far there has been no action.

Nor has there been any improvement in conditions for mentally ill people. A review of the 1983 Mental Health Act was carried out, raising hopes that, instead of dealing only with the issue of compulsory treatment for the very small proportion of 'dangerous' patients as that Act did, it would address the needs of the very much larger group who have received only sporadic and fragmented care since the run-down of the psychiatric hospitals. It did not. Proposals reached the Green Paper stage in November 1999, and are concerned only with extending compulsory treatment (on pain of a compulsory return to hospital) for the 'dangerous' in the community. Though there have been headlines in the tabloids stating that 'Community care has failed', the broader issues of community care have not yet received any sustained attention either through research or policy review.

Government ministers are known to be resistant to lobbying on behalf of the needs of particular groups, and to refer enquirers to the Social Exclusion Unit; but that unit already deals with homeless people and asylum seekers, and it is unlikely that it can develop the necessary expertise to help all the other groups who are being marginalized by an excessive emphasis on work as the route to full citizenship.

There has been some debate over whether the Government's hands are tied by its commitment not to increase general taxation in the present Parliament; whether it is trying to capture the core vote (which is not notably concerned about the wellbeing of vulnerable groups) or whether there is a deeper ideological commitment to raising general thresholds rather than eliminating pockets of deprivation. This last may well be the motivating factor.

The End of the Welfare State?

If Anthony Giddens is still the guru of New Labour, we may find a rationale for the abandonment of Labour's traditional social compassion in his argument in *The Third Way: the renewal of social democracy* (1998). He claims that welfare policies are 'essentially undemocratic, depending . . . on a top-down distribution of benefits . . . bureaucratic, alienating and inefficient'.[58] 'In place of the welfare state we should put the *social investment state*, operating in the context of a positive welfare society'.[59] The Beveridge Report he argues, was essentially negative, a matter of combating the Five Giants; but in future, in a positive welfare policy, Want will be replaced by autonomy, Disease by active health, Ignorance by education as a continuing part of life, Squalor by well-being, and Idleness by initiative.

This may make good rhetoric, but it does not square with the facts either of the current state of Britain or of the predictable risks of human life, which were well-known to Seebohm Rowntree and Beveridge. The argument sounds perilously like a new version of the 'trickle-down theory'. It is based on the assumption that unrestricted global capitalism can solve all problems, and that markets will continue to expand indefinitely. A recorded conversation between Anthony Giddens and the international financier George Soros reveals that it is the financier, not the sociologist, who thinks that unrestricted capitalism is not enough, and that world markets must eventually be regulated.[60] If there is another world recession, confident assumptions about the inevitability of growth and the phasing out of welfare services could look very hollow. Giddens acknowledges the risk, but concludes that human life is full of risk. The problem is surely that some people live very much riskier lives than others, and we still need the safety net.

Opposition to the Government's harsher measures is currently growing on the back benches and in the solid Labour constituencies. In the summer of 1999, complaints that the Government was keener on wealth creation and capturing votes from the Conservatives than on relieving social need began to mount.[61] Commentators have suggested that 'the spin-doctors around No. 10' have ignored the traditional Labour commitment to 'less well-off' sections of society, as they are now called, because traditional Labour voters have 'nowhere else to go' – no other major party to vote for on the Left.

There is considerable concern about the introduction of systems of service measurement and quality assessment which are electronically sophisticated, but theoretically elementary and imperfect. They are no substitute for professional knowledge and experience. Many members of the professions, on whose knowledge and judgement so much of the quality of services depends, feel that they are being bullied and harassed in the attempt to make them meet unreal expectations. Inadequate mechanical accounting systems are being used as a substitute for rational planning and development, and power is flowing to the centre, in the hands of a new bureaucracy. The spectre of Jeremy Bentham's Panopticon, the all-seeing government eye, setting standards by remote control, has returned to haunt us in the electronic age.

In his speech to the Labour Party Conference in 1991, Tony Blair made a clear commitment to a set of policies which would create a new sense of community, and end the adherence to purely commercial values:

> This is modern socialism. Its means ever-changing, its purpose ever-constant, founded on the belief that we are more than buyers and sellers in some impersonal market place, not merely individuals stranded in helpless isolation, but human beings, part of a community with obligations to one another as well as to ourselves.

Will New Labour keep this promise?

Quasi-Markets, Quality and Measurement

The breaking up of large government agencies responsible for health, education and social care has been achieved by privatization and Government's determination not to take responsibility for overall financial decision-making. In the hands of the Conservative Governments of 1979–97, the rationale was the application of classical economic theory. In the hands of the New Labour Government since 1997, the rationale has been decentralization, and an expressed intention to locate power closer to the grass roots; but so far, the policy of creating quasi-markets, and the reliance on 'numbers and lists' has been intensified. Recent Social Policy literature on the subject emphasizes both the theoretical weaknesses of this approach, and the anti-social consequences which stem from it.[1]

Julian LeGrand and Will Bartlett, two of the leading scholars working in this field, point out that before 1979, the 'Welfare State' was the biggest area of non-market activity in Britain:

> How much was produced and who got the fruits of production were not the unintended consequences of self-interested decisions made by individual producers and consumers operating in a competitive market. Rather they were the outcome of conscious decisions of politicians, bureaucrats and professionals . . . ostensibly at least intending to work in such a way as to further the public interest.[2]

A market system is not ' the outcome of conscious decisions'. It is only a mechanism. It cannot plan, reason or judge. It has no moral dimension. It works well enough for the provision of consumer goods, but is highly unsuitable for the provision of personal services to vulnerable individuals.

In a classic market situation, the consumer buys a standardized product, such as a bar of soap. The product is definable: it is clear what sort of soap it is, and which firm produced it. It is unlikely that the packet will be found later to contain dog biscuits or macaroni. The quantity of the contents is stated, whether in grammes or ounces. The make of soap is stable over time; the purchaser is familiar with different brands, and has a choice between them. The quality can be checked very quickly and easily, both by the purchaser and by a government regulatory agency; and if the purchaser does not like Brand A, there is no difficulty in moving to Brand B next time. There is immediate 'feedback' to the company marketing the product if the product is unsatisfactory: their sales slump, and if it continues to be unsatisfactory, they go out of business.

In the quasi-markets of the welfare services, these conditions hardly ever apply. There are problems of *definition*: 'health', 'education' and 'social care' are not commodities. They are umbrella terms for a variety of services rendered by a variety of individuals of varying skill, ability and competence through a variety of agencies, many of them now profit-making.

There is a *lack of specification*: because people's circumstances vary, there is no clear statement of what should be included in a 'package of services' for a particular individual, and this will depend on the resources currently and locally available.

Needs change: many of the services are delivered over long periods of time, during which the needs of the user (pupil, patient or client) will vary, and so will the resources available to meet them – often for the worse.

Services are not standardized: users and service-deliverers form relationships of mutual understanding which are broken when provision is contracted or staff on short contracts leave.

Recipients' knowledge of services is often poor: most of them will not have a clear understanding of what is or should be available, and are not in a position to compare quality. They are heavily dependent on professional advice (a point which Professor Richard Titmuss made in *The Gift Relationship* in 1970).[3]

Their choice of services is limited: often the only alternative to taking what is offered is to 'go private'. A true market situation would require the existence of empty beds, vacant school places, extra care workers, to make the choice a real one.

It is difficult to change 'products': there is no problem involved in buying another brand of soap; but changing general practitioners, asking for a second medical opinion, changing schools, replacing a domiciliary service, can all be very stressful. People who need services are often reluctant to criticize and risk losing the good will of the professionals.

These factors alone indicate that the application of a market model to the social services is almost grotesquely inappropriate; but there are also specific disadvantages which do not occur in classic market situations:

The purchaser is often not the consumer: Hospital Trusts, schools, social services agencies will all be purchasers on behalf of patients, pupils (or their parents), clients. Many of these organizations will be both purchasers and providers to other purchasers. The terminology of the 'purchaser/ provider split' is much too simplistic to cover the variety of relationships involved.

There is a pressure for low unit costs: purchasers seeking 'value for money' (now commonly abbreviated to 'VFM') will have an in-built incentive to take the cheapest option. Providers will seek ways of reducing unit costs, and this will frequently involve the creation of larger units – bigger hospitals, bigger schools, bigger nursing homes. Most of the small, homely residential homes for elderly people and mentally ill people set up in the 1980s have already been bought up by large combines for this reason. Another way of reducing unit costs is to employ less well-trained or less-experienced staff to keep down salary costs: the loss of expertise is apparent to the consumer, but the consumer is not the purchaser.

'Cream-skimming' is common: profit-making agencies may take the easier subjects, leaving the 'difficult' cases – the hard-to-teach children, the very sick old people, the people with severe mental illness, the very poor and disorganized – to the voluntary sector. There is nothing very new about the difficulties of placing such people, but the introduction of the profit motive may mean, as it has done often before, that the people in the greatest need are rejected. Even the voluntary agencies may need to reach arbitrary standards to qualify for grants – with the result that the 'difficult' cases drop quietly out of the system.

Planning becomes impossible: if provision is to be left to market forces with only a minimum of government supervision, what is to be done about gaps in provision? Who will identify them, and how will they be filled – particularly if they do not offer rapid and certain profits? How will the whole mesh of producers and providers be analysed, and new providers be encouraged where there is a need for them?

There is no effective feed-back: several writers have pointed out the need for research on what is happening at the point of service delivery, starting with large-scale descriptive studies of 'consumer' experience; but the practical problems of mounting such research are enormous. Projects would be very expensive, findings from particular areas could not be shown to be generalizable, since there is no body of corporate knowledge with which to compare them, and any findings would quite possibly be out of date before they were published. The need for effective feed-back to large industrial organizations was a constant theme of management theorists in the 1960s and 1970s; but if there is no organization, how is the new, moving, constantly-changing pluralistic system to know what it is doing?

Stultification: the lack of stimulation from feed-back means that an organization simply begins to run down.[4] It is likely that in the case of quasi-markets, particular relationships between purchasers and providers will become institutionalized, buttressed by contracts and legal formulae, and a new bureaucracy will develop, as unresponsive as ever to urgent and personal needs.

Measurement and Quality

The introduction of Citizen's Charters was a first attempt to remedy the problems by setting standards for key services. In the 1990s, the quality assurance industry burgeoned: the library of one university (York) lists 716 books and four journals devoted to the subject, and every organization has its quality assurance officers; but the means of trying to assure quality in the social services are often mechanical, and in statistical terms very unsophisticated.

Hospital waiting lists are a prime example: the Government's Annual Report 1998/09 states that the policy is 'now on course', and that waiting lists have been cut by 60,000 since May 1997; [5] but they a very poor index of a hospital's efficiency (would we not expect the best hospitals in terms of clinical practice to have the longest waiting lists?); and they are subject to other pressures, besides those exerted from the Department of Health. Health insurance plans usually specify that there must be a three-months wait for treatment before private treatment can be claimed, and this is an incentive to hospitals anxious to cut costs to keep a list of at least that length, to deter people with private insurance. Hospitals may have an incentive to maintain a waiting list to demonstrate their need for extra staff and extra resources; they may also remove the less urgent cases from a waiting list to make it shorter and please the Department of Health.

League tables which rank the effectiveness of particular facilities in order are very popular with the Blair Government. They are thought to be very popular with the general public. If they are, the reason is probably the current preoccupation with football. When a substantial section of the population sits down every Saturday night to check 'the pools', it is easy to see why the approach might prove appealing; but serious issues of quality in education and health care are not properly determined on the level of a game. League tables are an attempt to quantify quality. The search for simple, measurable criteria which will express the whole range of factors which make up quality has been pursued in government and in social policy research at least since the early 1960s. The effect of over-reliance on such measures can be seriously distorting, because some processes are much more easily measured than others: for instance, measures of treatment in hospital tend to concentrate on surgery, and on operations such as appendectomies and hernia operations, which are fairly standardized. There are no adequate and standardized measurements for mental health care or the rehabilitation of people with physical impairments. In schools, emphasis is placed on GCE passes and truancy rates, not on the broader aims of educating children to understand the world they live in. Often like is not being compared with like, because inputs are manifestly uneven: to compare the record of a hospital or a school in a poor district of a northern town with a large ethnic population with that of a comfortable suburban district in the south is seriously misleading. The subsequent 'naming and shaming' as 'the worst in Britain' and the threat of 'hit squads' can hardly improve morale or performance by harassed staff in the beleaguered institutions. If the aim is to measure the effectiveness of the educational or curative *process*, inputs must be roughly similar to make the measurement of outcomes of any significance. Calls for 'more sophisticated measures' are emerging from the government departments, and the league tables grow ever more complicated, with arbitrary 'weightings' to take account of imponderable factors; but the answer may be to abandon a simplistic policy which is no substitute for experience and encouragement.

Despite the Government's commitment to democracy and decentralization, the use of these quantitative methods is also leading to an unprecedented degree of regulation by centralized authorities, with corresponding alienation of professional and other staff. The Government might ponder on the proposition that 'Quantification is the refuge of bureaucrats.'[6]

Political Parties in Power since 1830

Note: where changes of government or leadership were frequent, this table has been slightly simplified.

Prime Minister	Ruling Party	Dates
Grey	Whig	1830–2
Melbourne I	Whig	1832–4
Peel I	Conservative	1834–5
Melbourne II	Whig	1835–41
Peel II	Conservative	1841–6
Russell I	Whig	1846–52
Derby–Disraeli I	Conservative	1852
Aberdeen	Whig	1852–5
Palmerston I	Whig	1855–9
Derby–Disraeli II	Conservative	1858–9
Palmerston II	Whig	1859–65
Russell II	Whig	1865–6
Derby–Disraeli III	Conservative	1866–7
Disraeli I	Conservative	1867–8
Gladstone I	Liberal	1868–74
Disraeli II	Conservative	1874–80
Gladstone II	Liberal	1880–5
Salisbury I	Conservative	1885–6
Gladstone III	Liberal	1886
Salisbury II	Conservative	1886–92
Gladstone IV	Liberal	1892–4

Rosebery	Conservative	1894–5
Salisbury III	Conservative	1895–1902
Balfour	Conservative	1902–6
Campbell-Bannerman	Liberal	1906–8
Asquith	Liberal	1908–16
Lloyd George	Liberal	1916–22
Bonar Law	Conservative	1922–3
Baldwin I	Conservative	1923–4
Macdonald I	Labour	1924
Baldwin II	Conservative	1924–9
Macdonald II	Labour	1929–31
Baldwin–Macdonald	National	1931–5
Baldwin IV	Conservative	1935–7
Chamberlain	Conservative	1937–40
Churchill I	Coalition	1940–5
Attlee	Labour	1945–51
Churchill II	Conservative	1951–5
Eden	Conservative	1955–7
Macmillan	Conservative	1957–63
Douglas-Home	Conservative	1963–4
Wilson I	Labour	1964–70
Heath	Conservative	1970–4
Wilson II	Labour	1974–6
Callaghan	Labour	1976–9
Thatcher I	Conservative	1979–83
Thatcher II	Conservative	1983–7
Thatcher III	Conservative	1987–9
Major I	Conservative	1990–2
Major II	Conservative	1992–7
Blair	New Labour	1997–

Biographical Notes

These brief notes are intended as an aid to reading the foregoing chapters. They are drawn in the main from the *Dictionary of National Biography (DNB)*, *Who's Who* and *Who Was Who*. These publications should be consulted for a fuller account. Individuals are listed by the name they were generally known by in their career, with later titles in parentheses.

Arnott, (Dr) Neil, 1788–1874, physician and public health reformer, worked with Chadwick and Southwood Smith (q.v.) on the Poor Law Commission and the General Board of Health. Physician extraordinary to Queen Victoria, 1837. FRS, 1838. Member of (General) Medical Council, 1854.

Attlee, Clement Richard (Earl Attlee), 1888–1967, Labour politician. Secretary, Toynbee Hall, Lecturer, Ruskin College Oxford and London School of Economics, MP, member of Coalition War Cabinet, 1940–5, Prime Minister 1945–51.

Barnardo, (Dr) Thomas John, 1845–1905, founder of Dr Barnardo's Homes. Missionary medical student, worked at the Ernest Street Ragged School, founded East End Juvenile Mission, developed Homes for destitute children. Licentiate of the Royal College of Surgeons, 1876, Fellow 1879.

Bentham, Jeremy, 1747–1832, founder of Utilitarianism and writer on jurisprudence, known for the principle of 'the greatest happiness of the greatest number' and the 'hedonistic calculus'. Promoter of the Panopticon (invented by his brother). Author of the *Introduction to the Principles of Morals and Legislation, Principles of Penal Law* and *The Constitutional Code*, among many other works.

Bevan, Aneurin, 1897–1960, Labour politician, former coal miner. Minister of Health, 1945–51, Minister of Labour and National Service, 1951, member of Tribune Group, resigned 1951.

Beveridge, (Sir) William (Lord Beveridge), 1879–1963. Sub-warden of Toynbee Hall, first Chairman of the Employment Exchange Committee. Director, London School of Economics, 1919–37, Master of University College, Oxford, 1937–45. Sole signatory of the *Beveridge Report*, 1942, author of *Full Employment in a Free Society* and *Voluntary Action*.

Blair, Tony (Anthony Charles Lynton), b. Edinburgh, 1953. Called to the Bar, 1976, MP for Sedgefield, 1983. Opposition spokesman on Treasury and Economic Affairs, 1984–94. Leader of the Parliamentary Labour Party, 1994. Founder of 'New Labour'. Prime Minister 1997– .

Blunkett, David, b. 1947. Lecturer, Barnsley College of Technology 1974–87. MP, Sheffield Brightside, 1987. Front-bench spokesman on Health, Education, Employment. Secretary of State for Education and Employment, 1997.

Booth, Charles, 1840–1916, business and pioneer of social research. Author of *Life and Lanour of the People of London*, 17 vols. 1889–1903; member of the Royal Commission on the Poor Laws, 1905–9, cousin of Beatrice Webb (q.v.).

Booth, William ('General Booth'), 1829–1912, founder of the Salvation Army. Methodist itinerant preacher, ran a Christian mission in Whitechapel. Salvation Army launched on military lines 1878. *DNB* calls it 'a world-wide engine of revivalism'. Author of *In Darkest England, or The Way Out*.

Bosanquet, Bernard, 1848–1928, Oxford philosopher and writer on Ethics. Editor of *Aspects of the Social Problem*, giving philosophical backing to the views of the Charity Organisation Society. Friend of C. S. Loch (q.v.).

Bosanquet, Helen (née Dendy), wife of Bernard Bosanquet, supporter of the Charity Organisation Society, member of the Royal Commission on the Poor Laws, 1905–9, author of *Social Work in London*.

Boyson, (Sir) Rhodes, b. 1925, Conservative politician, MP for Brent North. Joint author of the *Black Papers on Education*, author of *Down with the Poor*. Hobby (according to *Who's Who*), 'exciting the millennialist Left in education and politics'. Under-Secretary of State for Education, Minister of State, Social Security, Northern Ireland Office, and Local Government (Department of the Environment).

Brown, Gordon, b. 1951. PhD Edinburgh, 1982. Journalist, Current Affairs editor, Scottish TV. MP Dunfermline East, 1983. Shadow Trade and Industry Secretary, 1989–92; Shadow Treasury Secretary, 1992–7; Chancellor of the Exchequer, 1997.

Butler, R. A. (Lord Butler of Saffron Walden), 1902–80, Conservative politician. Minister of Education, 1940–5, subsequently Chancellor of the Exchequer, Lord Privy Seal, Home Secretary, Foreign Secretary, Master of Trinity College Cambridge.

Castle, Barbara (née Betts) (Lady Castle), b. 1910, Labour politician. MP for Blackburn, 1945–79, Chairman of the Labour Party 1958–9, Minister of Overseas Development, Minister of Transport, Secretary of State for Employment, Secretary of State for the Social Services, MEP.

Chadwick, (Sir) Edwin, 1800–89, senior civil servant. Poor law, factory and public health reformer. Secretary to Jeremy Bentham (q.v.), Assistant Poor Law Commissioner, 1832–4, Secretary to the Poor Law Commission 1834–48, Commissioner of the General Board of Health, 1848–54, dismissed 1854.

Churchill, (Sir) Winston, 1874–1965, MP (Liberal), President of the Board of Trade, 1908–10, Home Secretary, 1910–11 (Conservative), Chancellor of the Exchequer, 1924–9, First Lord of the Admiralty 1939–40, Prime Minister 1940–5 and 1951–5, Leader of the Opposition 1945–51.

Clarke, Kenneth, QC, b. 1940. President of Cambridge Union, 1963. Called to the Bar, 1963. MP Rushcliffe, 1970. Minister of State of Transport (1979–82), Health (1982–5), Paymaster General 1985–7, Secretary, Department of Trade and Industry, 1987–8; Health 1988–90; Home Office 1992–3; Chancellor of the Exchequer, 1993–7.

Cripps, (Sir) (Richard) Stafford ('Austerity Cripps'), 1889–1952, Labour politician and lawyer. MP, Leader of the House of Commons and Minister of Aircraft Production in the Coalition Government in the Second World War, President of the Board of Trade, Chancellor of the Exchequer, 1947–50.

Crossman, R. H. S., 1917–74, Labour politician. Fellow and Tutor of New College, Oxford, assistant editor *New Statesman and Nation,* MP, Minister of Housing and Local Government, Secretary of State for the Social Services, 1968–70.

Darling, Alistair, b. 1953. Lawyer. Shadowed Chief Secretary to Treasury 1996–7; Chief Secretary to Treasury, 1997–8; Minister of Social Security, 1998.

Dobson, Frank, b. 1940. London School of Economics, administrative posts with Central Electricity Generating Board, Electricity Council, Assistant Secretary, Commission for Local Administration. MP 1983, Labour Party co-ordinator 1987–9, spokesman on Energy, Employment, Transport, Environment. Health Secretary, 1997–9.

Farr, William, 1807–83, medical statistician. Compiler of Abstracts in the Registrar-General's Office, 1838–79. President of the Statistical Society, 1871 and 1872. Author of *Vital Statistics*.

Field, Frank, b. 1942. Director Child Poverty Action Group 1969–74; Low Pay Unit, 1974–80. MP Birkenhead, 1979. Chairman, Select Committee on Social Services, House of Commons,, 1987–90; Minister for Welfare Reform (DSS) 1997–8, resigned over pension plans. Author of many publications on poverty, low pay, etc., including *Losing Out: the emergence of Britain's underclass* (1989); *How to Pay for the Future: building a stakeholders' welfare* (1996) and *Reforming Welfare* (1997).

Fry, Elizabeth, 1780–1845, Quaker prison reformer. Wife of banker Joseph Fry. Formed association for improvement of female prisoners in Newgate Prison, 1817. Instituted an order of nursing sisters, some of whom went to the Crimea with Florence Nightingale (q.v.).

Galton, (Sir) Francis (1822–1911), biologist and founder of the Eugenics School, cousin of Charles Darwin. Worked on genetics, credited with the discovery of fingerprinting. Author of *Hereditary Genius*. General secretary of the British Association, 1865–7, consulting editor of *Biometrika*.

Giddens, Anthony, sociologist, b. 1938. Lecturer, University of Leicester, Simon Fraser University, Vancouver. Lecturer and Reader, University of Cambridge, 1968–85, Co-founder of the Polity Press, 1984. Director, London School of Economics, 1997. See Bibliography for publications.

Griffiths, (Sir) Roy, 1926–94. Deputy Chairman, Sainsbury's. Deputy Chairman, National Health Service Management Board 1986–94.

Hall, (Sir) Benjamin (Baron Llanover), 1802–67. MP, opponent of the General Board of Health 1848–54, when he represented the existing water and sewerage authorities. Described in S. E. Finer's *Chadwick* as 'the prince of London rabble-rousers'. President of the reconstituted General Board of Health, 1854, Privy Councillor, 1854, Chief Commissioner of Works, 1855–8.

Halsey, A. H., b. 1923, Professor of Social and Administrative Studies, University of Oxford, 1978–90, Professorial Fellow of Nuffield College.

Research publications on education and social class. Directed research on Educational Priority Areas, and edited EPA publications.

Hannington, Wal, 1896–1966, leader and organizer of the National Unemployed Workers' Committee Movement, member of the Central Committee of the Communist Party. Led Hunger Marches in the 1920s and 1930s. Author of *The Problem of the Distressed Areas, Ten Lean Years,* and *Unemployed Struggles 1919–1936.*

Harman, Harriet, b. 1950. Lawyer, Legal Officer National Council for Civil Liberties. MP Camberwell and Peckham, 1997. Secretary of State for Social Security, 1997–8. Dismissed over pensions issue.

Healey, Denis (Lord Healey), b. 1917, Labour politician, MP. Institute of Strategic Studies, Secretary of State for Defence, Chancellor of the Exchequer, 1974–9, Chairman of the Interim Committee of the International Monetary Fund, 1977–9.

Heath, (Sir) Edward, b. 1916, Conservative politician, MP, Parliamentary Secretary to the Treasury and Government Chief Whip, 1955–9, Lord Privy Seal, Secretary of State for Industry, Leader of the Opposition 1965–70, Prime Minister 1970–4.

Hill, Octavia, 1838–1912, housing reformer and supporter of the Charity Organisation Society. Managed property for John Ruskin and subsequently the Ecclesiastical Commissioners on the principle 'not alms, but a friend'. Member of the Royal Commission on the Poor Laws, 1905–9. Co-founder of the National Trust.

Hyndman, Henry Mayes, 1842–1921, Socialist writer and propagandist, leader of the Social Democratic Federation (Marxist) until 1914. Responsible for the SDF social survey which attracted the attention of Charles Booth (q.v.).

Joseph, (Sir) Keith (Lord Joseph), b. 1918, Conservative politician. Fellow of All Souls College, Oxford, Minister of Housing and Local Government, Secretary of State for Social Services, for Industry, for Education and Science.

Kay, James (afterwards Sir James Kay-Shuttleworth), 1804–77. Medical practitioner, worked with Chadwick and Southwood Smith (q.v.) on the Poor Law Commission and the General Board of Health, subsequently moved into the field of popular education.

Keynes, John Maynard (Lord Keynes), 1888–1946, Cambridge economist. Editor of the *Economic Journal*, Secretary of the Royal Economics Society, author of *A Treatise on Money*, 1930, *General Theory of Employment, Interest and Money*, 1936. Adviser to Government, involved in German reparations after the First World War, American Lend–Lease, Bretton Woods agreement and setting up of the International Monetary Fund after the Second World War.

Lansbury, George, 1859–1940, Labour leader and politician. Member of Poplar Board of Poor Law Guardians, member, Royal Commission on the Poor Laws 1905–9 (signatory to the Minority Report), MP for Poplar and later Bow, Christian pacifist, joint founder of the *Daily Herald.*

Lawson, Nigel (Lord Lawson), b. 1932, scholar of Christ Church, Oxford. Editorial staff, *Financial Times,* 1956–60; City Editor, *Sunday Telegraph,* 1961–3; Editor, *The Spectator,* 1966–70. MP 1974–92; Financial Secretary to the Treasury, 1979–81; Chancellor of the Exchequer, 1983–9.

Lewis, (Sir) George Cornewall, 1806–63, son of Thomas Frankland Lewis (q.v.), succeeded his father on the Poor Law Board, (1839–47). Chancellor of the Exchequer, 1855–58, Home Secretary, 1859–61, Secretary of State for War, 1861–3.

Lewis, (Sir) Thomas Frankland, 1780–1855, MP, Joint Secretary to the Treasury, 1827, Privy Councillor 1828, Treasurer of the Navy, 1830, Chairman of the Poor Law Commission, 1834–8.

Lilley, Peter, b. 1943. 'Economic consultant on under-developed countries', 1966–74; investment adviser on energy industries, 1966–72; chairman, Bow Group, 1972–5; Chairman, partner and director of London Oil Analysts' Group; MP St Albans, 1983–97; MP Harpenden 1997. Secretary to the Treasury, 1987–9; Secretary of State for Trade and Industry, 1990–2, Social Security 1992–7, Deputy Leader of the Conservative Party, 1997. Publications include *Delusions of Income Policy* (with Samuel Brittan, 1977); *Thatcherism: the next generation* (1990).

Livingstone, Ken, b. 1945, teacher, local government leader and Labour politician. Councillor, Lambeth and Camden Borough Councils, Leader of the Greater London Council 1981–6, MP for Brent East since 1987. Author of *If Voting Changed Anything, They'd Abolish It,* 1987. Elected Mayor of London, 2000.

Lloyd George, David (Earl Lloyd George), 1889–1943, Liberal politician. MP, President of the Board of Trade 1906–8, Chancellor of the Exchequer, Minister of Munitions, Prime Minister 19116–23.

Loch, (Sir) Charles Stewart, 1849–1923. Secretary to the Council of the Charity Organisation Society, 1875–1914, strongly opposed to state intervention in welfare. Initiated the *Charities Register* and the *Charities*

Digest. Member of the Royal Commission on the Poor Laws, 1905–9: the Majority Report was largely his work.

Major, John, b. 1943, career at Standard Chartered Bank. Member, Lambeth Borough Council 1968–71. MP Huntingdon, 1983; Chief Secretary to the Treasury, 1987–9; Foreign Secretary, 1989; Chancellor of the Exchequer 1989–90; Prime Minister 1990–7.

Malthus, (Rev.) T. R., 1766–1834, mathematician and demographer. Fellow of Jesus College, Cambridge. Author of the *Essay on Population,* 1798, and subsequent revisions.

Mayhew, Henry, 1812–87, journalist and sometime editor of *Punch.* Author of *London Labour and the London Poor.*

Melbourne, Lord (William Lamb) 1779–1848, Whig politician. Home Secretary 1830–4, Prime Minister 1834–8, Leader of the Opposition, 1838–42.

More, Hannah, 1745–1833, writer and social reformer. Member of the 'Blue Stocking Society' of literary ladies, and of the Evangelical Clapham Sect. Organized schools and women's groups in the Cheddar Valley.

Moser, (Sir) Claus, b. 1922, Director, *The Economist,* Director, Central Statistical Office and Head of Government Statistical Services, 1967–78, President Royal Statistical Society, 1978–80, Warden, Wadham College, Oxford.

Nicholls, (Sir) George, 1781–1865, Director, Birmingham Canal Navigations, Superintendent, Birmingham Branch of the Bank of England, Poor Law Commissioner, 1834, Permanent Secretary of the Poor Law Board, 1848.

Nightingale, Florence, 1820–1910, reformer of hospital nursing. Visited the hospital at Kaiserwerth, near Dusseldorf, 1850 and 1851. Superintendent of the Hospital for Invalid Gentlewomen, Chandos Street, London. Expedition to the Scutari Hospital in the Crimea, 1854. Nightingale School and Home for Nurses, St Thomas's Hospital, London, founded, 1854.

Orwell, George (real name Eric Blair), 1903–1950, journalist and writer. Author of *Down and Out in Paris and London, The Road to Wigan Pier, Animal Farm.*

Powell, Enoch, 1912–98, Conservative politician. Professor of Greek in the University of Sydney, Australia, 1937–9. Rose from Army rank of private to brigadier in the Second World War. MP 1950. Financial Secretary to the Treasury, 1957–8, Minister of Health, 1960–3.

'Rivers of Blood' speech on immigration, 1968. Became Ulster Unionist.

Ricardo, David, 1772–1823, economist, MP, author of *Principles of Political Economy and Taxation*, in which he developed 'The Iron Law of Wages'. Colleague of T. R. Malthus (q.v.).

Rothschild, Nathaniel Mayes Victor (Lord Rothschild), 1910–90. Research chemist and industrialist, Chairman, Shell Research Ltd., Director General, Central Policy Review Staff 1971–4, adviser to the Thatcher administrations.

Scarman, Leslie (Lord Scarman), b. 1911. Barrister, High Court judge, Lord Justice of Appeal. Chairman, Law Commission, President, Constitutional Reform Centre.

Seebohm, (Sir) Frederick (Lord Seebohm), 1909–90. Chairman, Barclays Bank DCO, Chairman, Joseph Rowntree Memorial Trust, Chairman, Seebohm Committee on Local Authority Social Services, 1965–8.

Senior, Nassau William, 1790–1844, economist and barrister. First Professor of Political Economy, University of Oxford, 1825. Worked with Edwin Chadwick (q.v.) on the Poor Law Commission of 1832–4.

Shaftesbury, Lord (Anthony Ashley Cooper, 7th Earl) 1801–85, social reformer. MP (as Lord Ashley) until he succeeded his father in 1851. Involved in ragged schools, reform of the lunacy laws and factory laws, conditions of juveniles (including chimney sweeps and juvenile offenders), lodging houses, housing for the poor, and many other voluntary and statutory movements. Lunacy Commissioner 1828–42, Chairman of Lunacy Commissioners 1842–84, member of the General Board of Health (with Edwin Chadwick) 1848–54. Prominent Evangelical.

Shaw-Lefevre, (Sir) John, 1797–1879, Under-Secretary to Edward Stanley (afterwards Earl of Derby and Prime Minister), FRS, 1820, Poor Law Commissioner, 1834, Vice-Chancellor, University of London, 1842.

Simon, (Sir) John (pronounced 'Simone', he was of Huguenot stock), 1816–1904, sanitary reformer and public health specialist. First Medical Officer of Health for London, 1848, Medical Officer to the General Board of Health and the Medical Department of the Privy Council, 1848–71, retired (under protest) following the setting up of the Local Government Board, 1877.

Smiles, Samuel, 1812–99, medical practitioner and popular writer, lecturer to Mechanics' Institutes etc. Left medical practice 1845, secretary to the Leeds and Thirsk Railway, and then to the South–Eastern

Railway. Author of *Self-Help, Duty, Thrift, Character*, and *The Lives of the Engineers*.

Smith, John, QC, 1938–92, MP for Lanarkshire. Secretary for Trade and Industry in Wilson and Callaghan administrations. Leader of the Parliamentary Labour Party 1992–4.

Smith, (Dr) Thomas Southwood, 1788–1861, sanitary reformer and author of *A Treatise on Fever*. Medical adviser to the Poor Law Commission and the General Board of Health. Grandfather of Octavia Hill (q.v.).

Snow, (Dr) John, medical pioneer, 1813–58. Discovered water was contaminated by cholera (hence the episode of the Broad Street Pump) and introduced the scientific use of ether into English surgical practice.

Temple, William, 1881–1944, Bishop of Manchester and Archbishop of Canterbury, Christian Socialist. Promoted the Life and Liberty Movement in the Church of England, and the Malvern Conference, 1942. Author of *Men without Work* and *Christianity and the Social Order* as well as of theological works.

Thatcher, Margaret (Baroness Thatcher), b. 1925. Secretary of State for Education and Science, 1970–4, Leader of the Opposition, 1975–9, Prime Minister, 1979–94.

Titmuss, Richard Morris, 1907–1973, Professor of Social Administration, London School of Economics. Left school at 14, worked for 16 years for an insurance firm, and never took a degree (though he was awarded eleven honorary degrees). Author of *Problems of Social Policy in War-time* (official history of the Second World War), *Essays on the 'Welfare State'*, *Commitment to Welfare, The Gift Relationship*; described in *DNB* as 'the high priest of the Welfare State'.

Townsend, Peter, b. 1928. Professor of Social Policy, University of Bristol 1982–93, formerly at the London School of Economics and University of Essex. Chairman, Child Poverty Action Group since 1969. Chairman, Disability Alliance since 1974. Author of many works on poverty, disability and old age, member of Government Working Party on Inequalities in Health, joint editor of the *Black Report*.

Tuke, William, 1732–1822, Quaker tea and coffee merchant, founder of the York Retreat for the humane treatment of the insane.

Walter, John, I, 1739–1812, founded *The Times* in 1788.

Walter, John, II, 1776–1847, second son of John Walter I. MP, chief proprietor of *The Times*, High Tory opponent of the New Poor Law.

Walter, John, III, 1818–94, eldest son of John Walter II. MP, chief proprietor of *The Times*, High Tory opponent of the General Board of Health.

Webb, Beatrice (née Potter), 1858–1943, m. *Sidney Webb*, 1859–1947. The Webbs, who worked closely together, were Fabian reformers and social historians. They were involved in the foundation of the *New Statesman and Nation* and the London School of Economics, where they both lectured for many years. Beatrice was a member of the Royal Commission on the Poor Laws, 1905–9, but Sidney is thought to have written the report. He also drafted the original Clause Four of the Labour Party Constitution in 1918. He became Baron Passfield in 1929 (under a Labour Government) but Beatrice refused to use the title. Many of their writings are listed in the Bibliography.

Wilson, Harold (Lord Wilson of Rievaulx), 1916–95. Labour politician. Director of Economics and Statistics, Ministry of Fuel and Power, 1943–5, President, Board of Trade, 1947–51, Leader of the Opposition, 1963–4 and 1970–4. Prime Minister, 1964–70.

Younghusband (Dame) Eileen, 1902–81, social work educator, Lecturer, London School of Economics 1929–39 and 1945–57. Reports on the Assistance Board (1945); Social Work (Carnegie UK Trust 1947); Third International Survey of Social Work (1959); Chairman, Ministry of Health Working Party on Social Workers on the Health and Social Services (report 1959); Gulbenkian Report on Community Work and Social Change (1968); President, International Association of Schools of Social Work, 1959–68.

Notes and Sources

CHAPTER ONE   THE POOR AND THE POOR LAW

1. Sidney and Beatrice Webb, *English Poor Law Policy*, p. 1.
2. J. L. and Barbara Hammond, *The Village Labourer*, vol. 1, chapters 2–4.
3. Elizabeth Longford, *Victoria, R. I.*, p. 154.
4. Adam Smith, *The Wealth of Nations*.
5. P. Dunkley, *The Crisis of the Old Poor Law in England*, p. 99, quoting a letter from Nassau Senior to Lord Brougham, 14 September 1832.
6. T. R. Malthus, *An Essay on the Principle of Population*, especially chapters 1 and 2.
7. D. Ricardo, *The Principles of Political Economy and Taxation*, p. 52.
8. Mary P. Mack, *Jeremy Bentham, An Odyssey of Ideas, 1748–1792*, vol. 1 p. 103.
9. Jeremy Bentham, 'Leading principles of a constitutional code for any state', *The Pamphleteer*, no 44, reprinted in J. Bowring (ed.) *The Works of Jeremy Bentham*.
10. E. J. Hobsbawm and George Rudé, *Captain Swing*.
11. William Cobbett, *Rural Rides*, p. 559.
12. Anthony Brundage, *The Making of the New Poor Law*, pp. 22–4.
13. David Cecil, *Melbourne*, p. 305.
14. S. E. Finer, *The Life and Times of Sir Edwin Chadwick*, pp. 43–114.
15. *Bradford Argus*, 27 June 1837.
16. Anthony Brundage, op. cit., p. 153.
17. *Report of the Select Committee of the House of Commons to enquire into the Andover Union*, Parliamentary Papers, (1846), 11, 22620.

Sources

The best account of the operation of the Old Poor Law is Nassau Senior's in the 1834 Report (*Report of H.M. Commission for enquiring into the Administration and Practical Operation of the Poor Laws*, vol.1). The description in chapter 1 is largely drawn from this source. The Report also describes in considerable detail the Commission's mode of operation and the rationale for its conclusions.

The Webbs' *English Poor Law History* has an exhaustive account of Poor Law practice from mediaeval times, but is perhaps more appropriate for consultation than for solid reading. Their *English Poor Law Policy* begins with the New Poor Law.

Good secondary texts for this subject are Peter Dunkley's *The Crisis of the Old Poor Law in England* and Anthony Brundage's *The Making of the New Poor Law*.

Malthus and Ricardo should be read in the original: both write concisely, and with some passion, and their works are available in a number of different editions. Readers will find many overlaps in their ideas.

Malthus originally published his *Essay on Population* as a pamphlet, but he revised it and added to it on a number of occasions. The Pelican Classics edition (ed. Anthony Flew) has a useful introduction.

Mary Mack's *Jeremy Bentham*, vol. I: *An Odyssey of Ideas* is an interesting account of a complex personality, and her symposium *A Bentham Reader* is probably the best introduction to the many Bentham texts which have been published.

Most people have read *Oliver Twist*. It is worth re-reading the first chapter in the knowledge that it was written in the early days of the implementation of the New Poor Law. Dickens was a journalist, and he wrote to deadlines. If the first chapters of *Oliver Twist* were published in February 1837, they were probably written only weeks or even days before.

John Walter II's invective in his leaders in *The Times* is illuminating. *The Times* has an excellent index, which makes referencing easy.

S. E. Finer's *The Life and Times of Sir Edwin Chadwick* is a major contribution to understanding this remarkable man, using many fresh documentary sources.

CHAPTER TWO   DIRT, DISEASE AND DANGER

1. James Kay, *The Moral and Physical Condition of the Working Classes Employed in the Cotton Manufacture in Manchester.*
2. James Kay and Neil Arnott, *Fever in the Metropolis.*
3. M. W. Flinn, Introduction to Edwin Chadwick, *The Sanitary Condition of the Labouring Population of Great Britain*, p. 4.
4. M. W. Flinn, op. cit., p. 8.
5. T. Southwood Smith, *A Treatise on Fever*, p. 204.
6. M. W. Flinn, Introduction to Edwin Chadwick, *The Sanitary Condition of the Labouring Population of Great Britain*, p. 27.
7. S. E. Finer, *Life and Times of Sir Edwin Chadwick*, p. 125.
8. *Tenth Annual Report of the Registrar-General's Office, 1847*, p. xvii.
9. S. E. Finer, *Life and Times of Sir Edwin Chadwick*, p. 221.

10. M. W. Flinn, Introduction to Edwin Chadwick, *The Sanitary Condition of the Labouring Population of Great Britain*, p. 51.
11. Edwin Chadwick, *The Sanitary Condition of the Labouring Population of Great Britain*, p. 246.
12. S. E. Finer, *Life and Times of Sir Edwin Chadwick*, p. 234, private letter from Chadwick to Major Graham 1843.
13 M. W. Flinn, op. cit., p. 13.
14. Edwin Chadwick, *The Sanitary Condition of the Labouring Population of Great Britain*, p. 256.
15. Chadwick, op. cit., p. 92.
16. Chadwick, op. cit., p. 91.
17 Chadwick, op. cit., p. 339.
18 Chadwick, op. cit., p. 423.
19 Chadwick, op. cit., p. 203.
20 Chadwick, op. cit., pp. 421–2.
21. D. Roberts, *Victorian Origins of the British Welfare State*, p. 71.
22. S. E. Finer, *The Life and Times of Sir Edwin Chadwick*, p. 293.
23. Quoted by D. Roberts, *Victorian Origins of the British Welfare State*, p. 96.
24. D. Roberts, op. cit., p. 77
25. *Supplementary Report on the result of a Special Inquiry into the Practice of Interment in Towns*, Parliamentary Papers (1843), XII.
26. R. A. Lewis, *Edwin Chadwick and the Public Health Movement*, p. 201.
27. *Lancet* (1849) 2: 21, 9 July and (1849) 2: 159–60, 11 August.
28. S. E. Finer, *The Life and Times of Sir Edwin Chadwick*, p. 341. *See also* Edwin Chadwick, *The Sanitary Condition of the Labouring Population of Great Britain*, pp. 148–9.
29. T. Southwood Smith, *A Treatise on Fever*, pp. 348–9.
30 S. E. Finer, *The Life and Times of Sir Edwin Chadwick*, p. 298.
31. C. L. Lewes, *Dr Southwood Smith*, p. 77.
32. R. A. Lewis, *Edwin Chadwick and the Public Health Movement*, p. 190.
33. *The Times*, 1 October 1849.
34 S. E. Finer, op. cit., p. 479.
35. A. Newsholme, *Fifty Years in Public Health*, p. 93. *See also* W. M. Frazer, *A History of English Public Health*, pp. 66–7.
36. S. E. Finer, op. cit., p. 509.

Sources

The most important primary source is the *Sanitary Report* of 1842 – a remarkable document in its command of the subject and the thoroughness of its approach. *The Supplementary Report on Interments* completes a grim picture of the problems of over-population and under-regulation in crowded city centres. Contemporary comment on the General Board of Health in 1853–4, particularly from John Walter III in *The Times* and Thomas Wakley in the *Lancet*, makes lively reading.

The echoes of conflict can be perceived even in the secondary accounts. Finer's *Life and Times of Sir Edwin Chadwick* gives an excellent account of Chadwick's own outstanding contribution to the public health services and the work of the sanitary engineers, but perhaps underplays the contribution of the medical profession. For instance, Finer does not mention the incident of the Broad Street Pump, which may be taken as effective proof of the claims of the specific contagionists. Medical histories are mainly written by public health doctors, who tend to stress the achievements of their own profession, to the detriment of Chadwick and the sanitary engineers. Sir Arthur Newsholme's *Fifty Years in Public Health* covers the years roughly from 1860 to 1909, but includes some of the earlier background, such as the contribution of Kay, Arnott and Southwood Smith, and the work of John Snow, William Farr and John Simon. Sir Arthur was sometime Chief Medical Officer to the Local Government Board, but the book, despite its title, is not based on his own professional experiences, as he was born in 1857. Dr William Mowll Frazer's *History of English Public Health* is a more modern account of the same period written by the Medical Officer of Health for Liverpool.

Of the recent sources, M. W. Flinn's introduction to his edition of the *Sanitary Report* is a comparatively brief but concise account of the issues. Margaret Pelling's *Cholera, Fever and English Medicine* and Frances B. Smith's *The People's Health, 1830–1890* are good on the medical issues, but less concerned with administrative and political problems. Anthony S. Wohl's *Endangered Lives: public health in Victorian Britain* is highly descriptive social history.

David Roberts's *Victorian Origins of the British Welfare State* provides some new insights into the ideas of the reformers, and the ways in which they were translated into administrative systems, particularly in respect of the issue of centralization and the powers of the inspectors.

The companion developments in factory reform, in which Chadwick and Ashley (Shaftesbury) again played leading parts, together with Michael Sadler, Richard Oastler and John Fielden, are well worth study. The appointment of the first factory inspectors in 1833, the struggle to end child labour and protect women workers, the Mines Act of 1842, the campaign for the 'Ten Hours Bill' and the successive Factory Acts of 1847, 1853, 1867, 1874 and 1878 are well chronicled by Fraser (*The Evolution of the British Welfare State*, chapter 1), and by Finer and the Hammonds in their biographies of Chadwick and Shaftesbury. As Fraser notes (p. 26), 'the factory movement disappeared in the 1850s, with great success to its credit'.

CHAPTER THREE   VOLUNTARY ACTION

1. W. Beveridge, *Voluntary Action*, p. 9.
2. Derek Fraser, *The Evolution of the British Welfare State*, p. 115.
3. Kathleen Jones, *The Compassionate Society*, pp. 59–62.
4. F. K. Prochaska, *Women and Philanthropy in Nineteenth Century England*, preface.
5. Prochaska, op. cit., pp. 22–5 and 229.
6. Kathleen Heasman, *Evangelicals in Action*. (1962).
7. See Geoffrey Pearson, *The Deviant Imagination* (1975).
8. Lytton Strachey and Roger Fulford (eds), *The Greville Memoirs*, vol. VI, pp. 52–3.
9. J. L. and Barbara Hammond, *Lord Shaftesbury*, p. 233.
10. C. Woodham Smith, *Florence Nightingale, 1820–1910*, p. 149.
11. Derek Fraser, *The Evolution of the British Welfare State*, p. 121.
12. David Owen, *English Philanthropy, 1661–1960*, p. 218.
13. Goschen Minute of 20 November 1869. See S. and B. Webb, *English Poor Law Policy*, pp. 144–6.
14. David Owen, *English Philanthropy, 1661–1960*, p. 221.
15. Owen, op. cit., p. 243.
16. Beveridge, *Voluntary Action*, pp. 21–117, from which this brief account of friendly societies is largely drawn.
17. E. J. Cleary, *The Building Society Movement*, pp. 1–11.
18. Martin Boddy, *The Building Societies*, p. 8.
19. G. D. H. Cole and Raymond Postgate, *The Common People*, pp. 638–9.
20. Henry W. Wolff, *People's Banks*, p. 2.
21. G. J. Holyoake, *The Rochdale Pioneers*, pp. 2, 10.
22. Beveridge, *Voluntary Action*, p. 57
23. Samuel Smiles, *Self-Help*, p. 1.
24. Smiles, *Self-Help*, p. 269.
25. *Dictionary of National Biography*.
26. Samuel Smiles, *Thrift*, p. 37.
27. Smiles, *Thrift*, p. 183.

Sources

In general, Conservative writers tend to stress the importance of the philanthropic movement, while Liberal writers tend to emphasize the friendly societies, and Socialist writers the trade union and co-operative movements. Smiles is rarely mentioned in modern texts, though the views he represents enjoyed a resurgence in the 1980s.

The standard scholarly accounts of philanthropy are B. Kirkman Gray's *History of English Philanthropy* and David Owen's *English Philanthropy, 1661–1960*. Kirkman Gray's book, published in 1905, has a period flavour. Owen's account has a sharper analytical edge, and represents a more modern view of the subject, though a spread of 300 years is rather long for a single volume.

The Dictionary of National Biography (DNB) provides a quick source of reference about individual philanthropists, and there are specialized biographies available in most libraries of those whose work is well-known.

There are two main accounts of the work of the Charity Organisation Society: Charles Loch's *Charity Organisation* and Helen Bosanquet's *Social Work in London*.

Lord Beveridge's *Voluntary Action* is somewhat patchy, and gives the appearance of having been written in a hurry by a busy man. It was written five or six years after the Beveridge Report, when the 'Welfare State' legislation was at last coming into effect, and Beveridge was much involved with the voluntary social services. He deals fairly briefly with philanthropy. 'A chapter of pioneers' gives potted biographies of twenty-seven individuals he considers worthy of note – some well known and some lesser known. As might be expected, his main enthusiasm is reserved for the Friendly Societies, which were the forerunners of the social security system. Beveridge wrote with the advantage of a long practical involvement with the Friendly Societies, and an affection for curious bodies like the Total Abstinence Sons of the Phoenix Society.

Sidney and Beatrice Webb made major studies of the Socialist mutual aid movements – *A History of Trade Unionism* and *The Consumers' Co-operative Movement*. G. D. H. Cole's account of Mutual Aid in the symposium edited by A. F. C. Bourdillon, *The Voluntary Social Services*, also stresses the contribution made by these movements. The symposium, undertaken for the Nuffield College Social Reconstruction Survey in the final years of the Second World War, has many interesting sidelights on the development of the voluntary services.

The most lively account of the Co-operative movement is George Jacob Holyoake's *The Rochdale Pioneers*. According to the Webbs, Holyoake was himself one of the Co-operative pioneers in the Owenite tradition – disappointed when the plans for 'a multiplication of self-governing workshops' failed and only the consumers' movement was left. Holyoake's book attracted international attention, and was translated into several European languages, including Hungarian.

There is a good deal of literature on building societies, including individual histories of some of the major societies. A useful and comparatively recent text is Martin Boddy's *The Building Societies*, published in 1980.

H. J. Hamilton's *Savings and Savings Institutions* and Henry Wolff's *The People's Banks* cover common ground, but Hamilton emphasizes the social effects of the movement, while Wolff is more concerned with its economic success.

The works of Samuel Smiles make fairly repetitive reading, but *Self-Help* at least should be encountered in the original. There are still many copies in circulation. The only full-length biography of Smiles appears to be one written by a relative, Aileen Smiles, entitled *Samuel Smiles and his Surroundings*.

CHAPTER FOUR   DARKEST ENGLAND AND THE
POVERTY SURVEYS

1. H. Mayhew, *London Labour and the London Poor: a cyclopaedia of those that will work, those that cannot work and those that will not work*, no.1, 1851, pp. 2–4, 'Of wandering tribes in general'.
2. H. Mayhew, op. cit., no. 1, 1851, pp. 2–4.
3. William Booth, *In Darkest England, or The Way Out*, pp. 11–12.
4. F. D. Hyndman, *Record of an Adventurous Life*, pp. 330–2.
5. F. D. Hyndman, op. cit., p. 322.
6. F. D. Hyndman, op. cit., p. 330–1.
7. Beatrice Webb, *My Apprenticeship*, p. 219.
8. Charles Booth, *Life and Labour of the People of London*, vol. II, p. 21.
9. Charles Booth, op. cit., vol. XVII, p. 216. The allusion is to the Book of Ezekiel, chapter 37, verses 1–10.
10. T. S. Simey, *Charles Booth, Social Scientist*, Appendix V, p. 278.
11. B. Seebohm Rowntree, *Poverty – A Study of Town Life*, p. 305.
12. Asa Briggs, *Social Thought and Social Action: a study of the work of Seebohm Rowntree*, p. 37.
13. Peter Townsend, *The Social Minority*, pp. 25–32.
14. Robert Holman, *Poverty*, pp. 813.
15. Asa Briggs, *Social Thought and Social Action . . .*, p. 38.
16. Asa Briggs, op. cit., p. 37.
17. J. Veit-Wilson, 'Paradigms of poverty: a rehabilitation of B. S. Rowntree', *Journal of Social Policy*, 15 (1986), 1, pp. 69–9.

Sources

The main sources referred to in the text are readily available. Mayhew's *London Labour and the London Poor* was originally published in penny copies, and achieved book form in 1851. The modern editions unfortunately omit the interesting theories about the 'wandering hordes'. E. P. Thompson and Eileen Yeo, in *The Unknown Mayhew* carried out a rehabilitation exercise on Mayhew, presenting more sober selections of his investigations on various trades, such as the Spitalfields weavers, merchant seamen, dressmakers and milliners. These articles are good journalism, but it is difficult to sustain the view that they show Mayhew as a 'systematic empirical sociologist' and a precursor to Booth and Rowntree. Thompson admits, in a curious phrase (p. 45) that the book may 'redress the balance too far'. General Booth's *In Darkest England* sold 70,000 copies in the first year of publication, but has not been reprinted since 1890.

Charles Booth's *Life and Labour of the People of London* runs to seventeen volumes, of which the first four may be the most rewarding for general readers to consult. His biographer, T. S. Simey (later Lord Simey of Toxteth), was Charles Booth Professor of Social Science in the University of Liverpool.

Seebohm Rowntree's *Poverty – A Study of Town Life* was originally published in 1901, reprinted in 1902, came out in a cheap edition in 1922, and reached a further revised edition in 1922. Asa Briggs (later Lord Briggs) devotes only one chapter of his life of Rowntree to the first Poverty Study, but provides some useful comparisons with Rowntree's later work: *Poverty and Progress* (1936) and *Poverty and the Welfare State* (with G. R. Lavers, 1951), together with a complete bibliography of Rowntree's writings.

A good modern analysis of the argument about absolute and relative poverty can be found in Stein Ringen's *The Possibility of Politics: a study in the political economy of the Welfare State*, chapter 7.

CHAPTER FIVE.   BY-PASSING THE POOR LAW

1. Brian Abel-Smith, *A History of the Nursing Profession*, p. 40. See also W. M. Frazer, *A History of English Public Health*, pp. 68–9.
2. Louisa Twining, *Recollections of Workhouse Management and Visiting*, pp. 69–70.
3. Twining, op. cit., pp. 64, 65.
4. *D N B* (entry for Professor Nassau Senior. His daughter-in-law was not accorded a separate entry).
5. W. M. Frazer, *A History of English Public Health*, pp. 161–87.
6. John Simon, *English Sanitary Institutions*, p. 232.
7. Simon, op. cit., pp. 355–6.
8. Simon, op. cit., p. 389.
9. K. B. Smellie, *A History of Local Government*, p. 60.
10. Smellie, op. cit., p.60.
11. Smellie, op. cit., p. 68.
12. David Owen, *English Philanthropy, 1661–1960*, p. 242.
13. Deborah Dwork, *War is Good for Babies and Other Young Children*, p. 11.
14. A. Newsholme, *Fifty Years in English Public Health*, pp. 55–6.
15. Jean Donnison, *Midwives and Medical Men*.

Sources

The story of the Medical Officers of Health and their departments does not appear to have greatly engaged the interest of recent scholars. Medical Officers of Health ceased to exist in 1975, when most of the public health responsibilities of the local authority were transferred to the Community Medicine Department of the District Health Authority. By that time, the main public health problems had been conquered. This example of a self-eliminating profession would have pleased Jeremy Bentham.

Sir John Simon and Sir Arthur Newsholme were both public health doctors, though their accounts relate more to central government policy than to local government. Dr W. M. Frazer was Medical Officer of Health for Liverpool, and his *History of English Public Health* is a good foundation. F. F. Cartwright's *A Social History of Medicine* and M. W. Flinn's *Public Health Reform in Britain* tell the story from varying approaches.

Roy McLeod, in *Treasury Control and Social Administration*, blames the difficulties of the Local Government Board after 1871 on the 'fiscal frustration' caused by tight Treasury control, but makes it clear that health interests took second place because the Board was 'bound from birth to the ill-starred traditions of its senior partner, the Poor Law Board' (p. 8). Christine Bellamy, in *Administering Central–Local Relations, 1871–1919* notes that 'The Medical Department was assimilated into a ministerial department based on the Poor Law Board' (p. 127).

Brian Abel-Smith's *The Hospitals, 1800–1948* and *A History of the Nursing Profession* provide a well-documented account of the complementary developments in hospital medicine in the same period. Developments in the Mental Health Services have been chronicled elsewhere (Kathleen Jones, *Asylums and After*).

K. B. Smellie's *History of Local Government* is a standard work which puts all the pieces of a somewhat fragmented subject together.

Jean Donnison's *Midwives and Medical Men* is a case-study in gender politics, and in the emergence of the first of the professions 'ancillary to medicine'. Midwives achieved nationally recognized status in 1902, and general nurses (State Registered Nurses) not until 1918.

Deborah Dwork's *War is Good for Babies and Other Young Children*, despite its unwieldy title, provides a much-needed study of maternity and child welfare provision.

CHAPTER SIX   VICTORIAN VALUES OR SOCIALIST VISIONS?

1. David Owen, *English Philanthropy 1661–1960*, p. 218.
2. Owen, op. cit., p. 224.
3. Helen Dendy, in B. Bosanquet (ed.), *Aspects of the Social Problem*, pp. 167–8.
4. C. S. Loch, *Charity Organisation*.
5. Margaret Cole, *The Story of Fabian Socialism*, p. 138.
6. Beatrice Webb, *My Apprenticeship*, p. 195.
7 Margaret Cole, *The Story of Fabian Socialism*, p. 18.
8 Cole, op. cit., p. 69.
9. Beatrice Webb, *Our Partnership*, ed. B. Drake and M. Cole, p. 329.
10. Beatrice Webb, op. cit., p. 377.
11. Beatrice Webb, op. cit., p. 392.
12. *Report of the Royal Commission on the Poor Laws and the Relief of Distress, 1909*, HMSO. Cmd. 4499, 1909, vol. 1, pp. 102–3.
13. Margaret Cole, *The Story of Fabian Socialism*, p. 138.

14. *Poor Law Report, 1909*, evidence, vol. 18, p. 389.
15. op. cit., p. 61.
16. Beatrice Webb, *Our Partnership*, p. 419.
17. Helen Bosanquet, *The Poor Law Report of 1909*, (1912).
18. Margaret Cole, *Beatrice Webb*, p. 109.
19. W. Ivor Jennings, editor's introduction to *The Poor Law Code*, 1930.

Sources

The main sources for the work of the Royal Commission on the Poor Laws of 1905–9 are the Majority and Minority Reports. As indicated in the text of Chapter Seven, these should be read with care, and with some knowledge of the personal and ideological conflicts involved.

Beatrice Webb's *Our Partnership* devotes most of chapter 7 to extracts from her diaries relating to the Commission's work. *The Diaries of Beatrice Webb*, edited by Margaret Cole, are separately published.

Margaret Cole's *The Story of Fabian Socialism* is the standard account of the Fabian movement before 1960. This is always pro-Fabian, but not always pro-Webb. In particular, Mrs Cole contends that the 'real partnership' was 'Sidney and Bernard' (Bernard Shaw), rather than 'Sidney and Beatrice'. Though Sidney Webb and G. B. S. did work together on a number of occasions, the evidence of the Webbs' joint work is really too strong to sustain this view.

The COS view of the debate is given in Helen Bosanquet's *The Poor Law Report of 1909*, which studiously avoids any suggestion of controversy or disagreement, and does not even mention the Fabians. Though all 34 volumes of the appendices are meticulously listed, the Minority Report is ignored.

Maurice Bruce's edited volume of primary source material, *The Rise of the Welfare State*, includes in chapter 7 a comparison of the Majority and Minority Reports, but this is somewhat misleading.

CHAPTER SEVEN   THE LIBERAL ANSWER

1. Derek Fraser, *The Evolution of the British Welfare State*, p. 136.
2. Flora Thompson, *Lark Rise*, p. 100.
3. Beatrice Webb, *Our Partnership*, pp. 417–18.
4. L. Broad, *Winston Churchill 1874–1951*, p. 60.
5. Quoted in Maurice Bruce, *The Rise of the Welfare State*, pp. 127–8.
6. Violet Bonham Carter, *Winston Churchill as I Knew Him*, p. 135.
7. J. Grigg, *Lloyd George, The People's Champion*, p. 163.
8. Derek Fraser, *The Evolution of the British Welfare State*, p. 151.
9. Quoted in L. du Parcq, *Life of David Lloyd George*, pp. 562–3.
10. *Parliamentary Debates (Hansard), House of Commons*, XXV, 644, Rt Hon. David Lloyd George, 4 May 1911.

11. J. Grigg, *Lloyd George, The People's Champion*, p. 347; L. du Parcq, *Life of David Lloyd George*, p. 581.

Sources
The fullest academic accounts are Bentley Gilbert's *The Evolution of National Insurance in Britain* and Peter Rowland's *The Last Liberal Governments*, vol. 1, *The Promised Land* and vol. 2, *Unfinished Business*. Derek Fraser's *The Evolution of the Welfare State* has a good chapter on the Liberal reforms, which includes original, if rather anti-Liberal, comment. Lloyd George's biographies devote a considerable amount of space to the National Insurance Act. Lloyd George's speeches in the House of Commons, particularly on the Old Age Pensions Bill and the National Insurance Bill, are a classic mixture of social conviction and rhetoric.

Maurice Bruce's edited volume of primary source material, *The Rise of The Welfare State*, has some well-chosen extracts on this period in chapter 7, 'Turning away from the Poor Law'.

CHAPTER EIGHT   THE HUNGRY THIRTIES

1. A. J. P. Taylor, *English History 1914–45*, p. 313.
2. Wal Hannington, *Unemployed Struggles 1919–1936*, pp. 80–1.
3. Hannington, op. cit., p. 167.
4. Hannington, op. cit., pp. 276–7.
5. George Orwell, *The Road to Wigan Pier*, p. 16.
6. Orwell, op. cit., pp. 76–7.
7. *Report of the Unemployment Insurance Committee*, chairman, Lord Blanesburgh (*Blanesburgh Report*), HMSO, 1927, para. 16.
8. Beveridge Papers, quoted in Fraser, *The Evolution of the British Welfare State*, p. 177.
9. *Report of the Royal Commission on Unemployment Insurance*, chairman, Judge Holman Gregory (*Holman Gregory Report*), HMSO, Cmd. 4185, 1932, paras 196–7.
10. *Holman Gregory Report*, para. 258.
11. George Orwell, *The Road to Wigan Pier*, pp. 79–80.
12. Wal Hannington, *The Problem of the Distressed Areas*, p. 21.
13. *Parliamentary Debates (Hansard), House of Commons*, vol. 265, col. 1868, Rt. Hon. David Lloyd George, 6 December 1934.
14. Wal Hannington, *The Problem of the Distressed Areas*, p. 24.
15. Derek Fraser, *The Evolution of the British Welfare State*, p.183.
16. Bernard Wickwar, *The Social Services: an historical survey*.
17. B. Seebohm Rowntree, *Poverty and Progress*, p. v.
18. Rowntree, op. cit., pp. 478–92.

19. op. cit., p. 114.
20. Rowntree, op. cit., pp. 468–9.
21. *Report on the British Social Services*, PEP, p. 169.
22. *Report on the British Health Services*, PEP, p. 387.
23. op. cit., p. 393.
24. op. cit., p. 414.

Sources

The PEP reports, published in 1937, give a balanced picture, based on original research, of the services in the mid-1930s. Sharper and briefer is Appendix B to the Beveridge Report (*Social Insurance and Allied Services*, HMSO, Cmd 6404, 1942) which contains Beveridge's own summary of the gaps and anomalies in the insurance system.

Wal Hannington's account of the hunger marches has a remarkable immediacy and simplicity. George Orwell's *The Road to Wigan Pier* and *Down and Out In Paris and London* are more journalistic – the first deals with individual squalor rather than family poverty, and the second is concerned with single homelessness – a situation in which men genuinely seeking work were treated as vagrants.

Among novels of the period, Walter Greenwood's *Love on the Dole*, which describes the impact of unemployment on a working-class family in a small Lancashire town, and A. J. Cronin's *The Stars Look Down*, based on a mining community in Tyneside, are particularly impressive. Cronin's *The Citadel* is a health service classic, describing the contrasts between a 'panel' practice in South Wales and private medical practice in a fashionable area of London. Both the Cronin books were made into films which are fairly faithful to the originals.

Of the secondary accounts, Bentley Gilbert's *British Social Policy 1914–1939* is both full and detailed, with less immediacy but more objectivity than the primary accounts.

CHAPTER NINE   WAR, PEACE AND THE BEVERIDGE PLAN

1. Richard M. Titmuss, *Problems of Social Policy*, Official History of the Second World War, p. 506.
2. Derek Fraser, *The Evolution of the British Welfare State*, p. 195.
3. Arthur Marwick, *Britain in the Century of Total War*, p. 304.
4. Pauline Gregg, *The Welfare State*, p. 31.
5. Derek Fraser, *The Evolution of the British Welfare State*, p. 206.
6. Report of the Inter-Departmental Committee on Social Insurance and Allied Services (*Beveridge Report*) HMSO, 1942, Cmd. 6404, para. 40.
7. *Beveridge Report*, paras 303–9.
8. *Beveridge Report*, para. 310.

9. *Beveridge Report*, para. 311.
10. At this time (before the general introduction of the antibiotics, developed in the early 1940s) the normal period of confinement for childbirth was 2–3 weeks, and most babies were born at home because of shortage of hospital accommodation.
11. *Beveridge Report*, paras. 410–43.
12. See Mary Stocks, *Eleanor Rathbone: a biography*.
13. War Cabinet Papers no. 18 of 1943, quoted in Martin Gilbert, *Winston Churchill*, vol. 7, p. 292.
14. War Cabinet Papers no. 65 of 1943, quoted Martin Gilbert, *Winston Churchill*, vol. 7, p. 293.
15. William Beveridge, *Power and Influence*, p. 332.
16. Beveridge, op. cit., p. 323.
17. op. cit., pp. 329–31.
18. op. cit., p. 325.
19. Derek Fraser, *The Evolution of the British Welfare State*. p. 203.

Sources

There are many sources of information on the Second World War, including autobiographies of the main participants. Contemporary films (many of them made with the support of the Ministry of Information) to raise public morale and assist the war effort) tend to perpetuate the functional myths of wartime rather than representing reality. Arthur Marwick's *Britain in the Century of Total War*, which formed part of an Open University course on war, is detailed and balanced. A. J. P. Taylor's *English History 1914–1945* is good on the general background, but more concerned with military and political events than with their social consequences.

Richard Titmuss's *Problems of Social Policy in Wartime* is a detailed and well-written study of his three chosen subjects: evacuation, care of the homeless and the Emergency Medical Services – but since it is part of the official history it tends, unlike his later works, to be somewhat bland. Sheila Ferguson and Hilda Fitzgerald's *Studies in the Social Services*, another volume in the same series, deals with maternity and child welfare.

The *Beveridge Report* contains much detail about the insurance proposals. General readers may find it useful to start from the principles indicated in the text above, and then to extend their reading by the use of Beveridge's index. The Report is a document to be consulted rather than read from cover to cover. The story of Beveridge's relations with Government after the publication of the report are treated in both his *Power and Influence* and in his wife's account (Janet Beveridge, *Beveridge and his Plan*).

Despite the problems of publishing in wartime (shortage of paper, lack of printers and typesetters, and a disrupted distribution system) many pamphlets were published commenting on the Government proposals from differing political points of view. Unfortunately, the quality of paper and binding was so poor that most of them have not survived, though collections of Army Bureau of Current Affairs (ABCA) pamphlets, which give a very lively picture of the debates, are still to be found in some major libraries.

The Nuffield College Social Reconstruction Survey, *The Voluntary Social Services*, edited by A. F. C. Bourdillon and published in 1945, is a valuable summary of academic opinion on voluntary organizations at the end of the war.

CHAPTER TEN   SETTING UP THE 'WELFARE STATE'

1. Hugh Dalton, *High Tide and After, Memoirs*, vol. 3, p. 3.
2. Cyril Clemens, *The Man from Limehouse: Clement Attlee*, p. 94.
3. Clement Attlee, *As It Happened*, p. 163.
4. *Social Insurance, Part I*, HMSO, Cmd. 6550, September 1944. *Social Insurance Part II (Industrial Injuries)*, HMSO, Cmd. 6551, September 1944.
5. *A National Health Service*, HMSO, Cmd. 6502, February 1944.
6. Michael Foot, *Aneurin Bevan*, vol. 1, p. 16.
7. Aneurin Bevan, *In Place of Fear* (Quartet, 1976), pp. 9–101.
8. *Employment Policy*, HMSO, Cmd. 6527, May 1944.
9. *The Supply, Recruitment and Training of Teachers and Youth Leaders* (*McNair Report*), HMSO, 1944.
10. *Curriculum and Examination: Report of the Committee of the Secondary Schools Examination Council* (*Norwood Report*), HMSO, Cmd. 6502, 1943.
11. *Educational Reconstruction*, HMSO, Cmd. 6458, 1943.
12. The school leaving age was raised to 15 in 1947 and to 16 in 1972.
13. Pauline Gregg, *The Welfare State*, p. 194.
14. *Report of the Royal Commission on the Distribution of the Industrial Population* (*Barlow Report*), HMSO, Cmd. 6513, 1940.
15. *Report of the Committee on Land Utilisation in Rural Areas*, (*Scott Report*), HMSO, Cmd. 6378, 1942.
16. *Report of the Expert Committee on Compensation and Betterment* (*Uthwatt Report*), HMSO, Cmd. 6386, 1942.

Sources

The best sources for this period are the White Papers and Government Reports which have been noted above. House of Commons Debates are a good source for the views of individual politicians, but it was a period of much rhetoric, and the speeches add little to the debates which had already taken place across the country in the preceding years.

Biographies or autobiographies of Labour politicians tend to be disappointing.

There is polemic, on the lines of Aneurin Bevan's *Why Not Trust the Tories?*; there is quiet and reflective autobiography on the lines of Lord Attlee's unassuming *As It Happened*; but the major interest of both participants and commentators is in the nationalization of public utilities, which was still controversial, rather than in the social programme, which it was assumed represented a national consensus, It is also necessary to remember that the Attlee Government of 1945–50 had other things on its mind – the ending of the war with Japan, the changeover from war to peace conditions, the settlement with Germany, the economic situation, the withdrawal from Palestine when the state of Israel was set up, the withdrawal from India and other parts of the Empire. As a result, there is surprisingly little about the new welfare system. The literature comes before and after the legislative changes, not while they were in progress.

The curious title of Cyril Clemens's life of Clement Attlee, *The Man from Limehouse*, results from the fact that Clemens, an American, had already written a life of President Truman entitled The *Man from Missouri*. Limehouse was Clement Attlee's constituency as a member of the House of Commons, but he was not 'from Limehouse' in the sense that Truman was 'from Missouri'.

Paul Addison's *The Road to 1945* is a useful modern summary of developments in the Second World War and the growth of political consensus on social reform.

Pauline Gregg's *The Welfare State* is more concerned with nationalization policies than with the social legislation of the period, though chapters 3 and 4 give lively accounts of the setting up of the social security system and the National Health Service. Derek Fraser's *The Evolution of the British Welfare State* covers the main legislation, but omits Town and Country Planning.

Arthur Willcocks's *The Creation of the National Health Service* is a valuable case-study in social policy, originally written as the author's PhD thesis in the mid-1950s. The subject matter was then considered so controversial that publishers were unwilling to take a risk on it, and it was not published until 1967, when the controversy appeared to have died down.

Sir James Stirling Ross's *The National Health Service in Great Britain*, written soon after the setting up of the NHS, is a factual and fairly unexciting account of its subject, but it has one lyrical passage in which the author compares the events of the Appointed Day for the operation of the National Insurance Act, the National Assistance Act and the National Health Service Act (5 July 1948) to the opening of a gigantic bank vault. All the tumblers, it seemed, were falling into place at last.

CHAPTER ELEVEN   PROBLEMS OF EXPANSION

1. The Rt Hon. Barbara Castle, television interview, BBC1, 28 September 1989.
2. Kathleen Jones, *The Teaching of Social Studies in British Universities*, Occasional Papers in Social Administration, chapter IV.

3. Kenneth O. Morgan, *Labour in Power, 1945–51*, p. 161.

4. *Enquiry into the Cost of the National Health Service – the Report of the Guillebaud Committee*, HMSO, Cmd. 9663, 1956.

5. 'The social services – needs and means': analysis by two Conservative MPs (generally assumed to be Iain MacLeod and Enoch Powell), *The Times*, 17 January 1952, and editorial in the same edition.

6. Iain MacLeod and Enoch Powell, *The Social Services – Needs and Means* (Conservative Political Centre, 1954).

7. John Jewkes and Sylvia Jewkes, *The Genesis of the National Health Service*.

8. D. S. Lees, *Health Through Choice* (Institute of Economic Affairs pamphlet, 1961).

9. R. M. Titmuss, *Commitment to Welfare*, pp. 247–62.

10. R. M. Titmuss, op. cit., pp. 263–8.

11. Brian Abel-Smith, *Value for Money in Health Services: a comparative study*, p. 122.

12. *A Hospital Plan for England and Wales*, HMSO, Cmd. 1604, 1962.

13. R. M. Titmuss, *Commitment to Welfare*, p. 104.

14. *Health and Welfare: the development of community care*, HMSO, Cmd. 1973, 1963.

15. Stuart Lowe, *Housing*, p. 11.

16. P. Dunleavy, *The Politics of Mass Housing in Britain, 1945–75*, p. 39.

17. J. Burnett, *A Social History of Housing 1815–1985*, p. 282.

18. Kenneth O. Morgan, *Labour in Power*, p. 175.

19. *15 to 18, Report of the Central Advisory Council for Education – England (Crowther Report)*, 2 vols, HMSO, 1959.

20. *Half Our Future: Report of the Central Advisory Council for Education – England (Newsom Report)* HMSO, 1963.

21. *Higher Education, Report of the Royal Commission on Higher Education (Robbins Report)*, HMSO, Cmd. 2154, 1963.

22. T. H. Marshall, *Social Policy*, p. 182.

23. See introduction to Barbara Rodgers and June Stevenson, *A New Portrait of Social Work*.

24. Eileen Younghusband, *Report on the Employment and Training of Social Workers* (Carnegie United Kingdom Trust, 1947); Eileen Younghusband, *Second Report on the Employment and Training of Social Workers* (Carnegie United Kingdom Trust, 1951).

25. Kathleen Jones, *Eileen Younghusband: a biography*, chapters 7–9, pp. 49–83.

26. *Report of the Working Party on Social Workers in the Local Authority Health and Welfare Services (Younghusband Report)* HMSO, 1959.

27. T. H. Marshall, *Social Policy*, p. 97.

28. Kenneth Harris, *Thatcher*, pp. 12–13, 23–38, 290–3.

Sources

This was a period in which Government reports on social affairs were of a high standard. The members of Commissions, committees and working parties were experts, and in many cases they were given finance for their own research and enquiries. Major reports have been mentioned in the text and referenced above. The Newsom research (published in volume 2 of the Report) is a classic. The Robbins research involved an extensive statistical analysis of population trends and patterns of higher education.

Richard Titmuss's *The Gift Relationship*, referred to later in Chapter 13, contains the developed version of his philosophy. Throughout the 1960s, the Institute of Economic Affairs produced a series of Hobart Papers under the editorship of Arthur Seldon which advocated a free market approach to the health and social services.

Sources on Housing for this period include John Burnett's *A Social History of Housing, 1815–1985*, P. Dunleavy's *The Politics of Mass Housing in Britain, 1945–75*, J. B. Cullingworth's *Housing Needs and Planning Policy*, Anthony Sutcliffe (ed.), *Multi-Storey Living: the British working-class experience* and Elizabeth Gittus's *Flats, Families and the Under-Fives*. The Parker-Morris Report, *Homes for Today and Tomorrow*, proposed what became known as 'Parker-Morris standards' for house building. The history of Housing can also be studied from life: any large town will provide ample evidence of the mistakes of the post-war period, the adverse features of tower blocks and the constricted life of hastily developed estates.

Eileen Younghusband's *Social Work in Britain, 1950–75* is a meticulous record of the development of social work, though on the dull side. (Dame Eileen, as she became in 1964, often referred to it as 'the Albatross': it was a work of duty rather than pleasure.) The present writer's *Eileen Younghusband: a biography* is an attempt to show the human side of the process.

T. H. Marshall's *Social Policy* sums up the development of the subject in the first half of the twentieth century in less than a hundred pages, with a distinct preference for the quantifiable aspects, such as social insurance. The second half of the book, on 'Social policy at mid-century' is now only of historical interest. Marshall's last book, *Social Welfare and the Citizen* contains a full exposition of his theories of citizenship which may have implications for future development. See John Ferris, 'Citizenship and the crisis in the Welfare State', in Philip Bean, John Ferris and David Whynes, *In Defence of Welfare*, chapter 3.

CHAPTER TWELVE   PROBLEMS OF CONTRACTION

1. R. H. S. Crossman, *The Diaries of a Cabinet Minister*, vol. 2, p. 13.
2. Eric Butterworth, 'Race relations – the next step' (chapter 9) in *The Year Book of Social Policy in Britain, 1973*. Note: this series ended in 1989, to be replaced by the *Social Policy Review*.
3. R. H. S. Crossman, *Diaries*, vol. 2, p. 20n.
4. Crossman, op. cit., pp. 28–9.

5. Alan Little, 'The Race Relations Act, 1976' (chapter 7) in *The Year Book of Social Policy in Britain, 1976.*

6. See Christian Howard, 'Women and the professions' (chapter 7) and Nancy Seear, 'Equal opportunities for men and women' (chapter 8) in *The Year Book of Social Policy in Britain, 1973.*

7. Peter Townsend and Brian Abel-Smith, *The Poor and the Poorest*, Occasional Papers in Social Administration, (1966).

8. Kathleen Jones, John Brown and J. R. Bradshaw, *Issues in Social Policy*, chapter 3, *passim.*

9. Social Services for All? Fabian Tracts 382–5 (1968).

10. *Report of the Committee on Local Authority and Allied Social Services, (Seebohm Report)*, HMSO, Cmd. 3703, 1968.

11. Seebohm Report, paras 581–663.

12. Medical Services Review Committee, *A Review of Medical Services in Great Britain (Porritt Report)*, Social Assay, 1963.

13. The first Green Paper: *Administrative Structure of Medical and Related Services in England and Wales* (1968). The second Green Paper: *The Future Structure of the National Health Service* (1970). The White Paper: *National Health Service Reorganisation: a consultative document* (1971). All these documents were published by DHSS/HMSO.

14. *Management Arrangements for the Reorganised National Health Service* (The 'Grey Book'), (HMSO, 1972).

15. *Report of the Royal Commission on the National Health Service*, HMSO, Cmnd. 7615, 1979 (*the Merrison Report*), para. 3.23, p. 27.

16. White Paper *Patients First*, HMSO, 1979.

17. Hedley Marshall, 'An introduction to reorganisation', in *The Year Book of Social Policy in Britain 1973*, part 1, chapter 1, p. 4.

18. *Report of the Royal Commission on Local Government*, (the *Redcliffe-Maud Report*), 3 vols, HMSO, Cmd. 4040–1, 1969.

19. J. D. Stewart, 'The politics of local government reorganisation', in *The Year Book of Social Policy in Britain, 1973*, part 1, chapter 2.

20. *Children and their Primary Schools: Report of the Central Advisory Council for Education (England) (Plowden Report)*, 2 vols, HMSO, 1966 and 1967.

21. A. H. Halsey (ed.), *Educational Priority: report on a project sponsored by the Department of Education and Science and the Social Science Research Council*, HMSO, 1972, vol. 1, *EPA Problems and Policies.*

22. H. Acland in Martin Bulmer (ed.) *Royal Commissions and Departmental Committees of Inquiry: the lessons of experience.*

23. Brian Cox and A. F. Dyson (eds), *The Black Papers on Education*; Brian Cox and Rhodes Boyson (eds), *Black Paper 1975.*

24. Paul Lodge, 'Education', in Paul Wilding (ed.), *In Defence of the Welfare State*, pp. 22–3.

25. *Parliamentary Debates (Hansard), House of Commons*, vol. 195, col. 776, The Rt Hon. James Callaghan (Prime Minister), 14 July 1977.
26. Quoted by Martin Loney, *Community Against Government*, p. 183.
27. Martin Loney, *Community Against Government*, p. 183.
28. Lewis Corina, 'Community work and local authority decision-making', *Community Development Journal*, 11 (1976), 3, pp. 179–80.
29. Martin Loney, op. cit., p. 145.
30. For comment see Martin Loney, op. cit., pp. 65–7; Kathleen Jones, John Brown and J. R. Bradshaw, *Issues in Social Policy*, pp. 170–3.
31. 'Secretary of State for the Social Services' was the somewhat misleading title given to the minister in charge of the Department of Health and Social Security DHSS) from 1967 to 1988.
32. Jonathan Bradshaw, *The Family Fund: an initiative in social policy.*
33. R. C. O. Matthews' preface to Michael Rutter and Nicola Madge, *Cycles of Transmitted Deprivation.*
34. Michael Rutter and Nicola Madge, *Cycles of Transmitted Deprivation*, pp. 302–28.
35. Muriel Brown and Nicola Madge, *Despite the Welfare State.*
36. Denis Healey, *The Time of My Life*, pp. 378–9.
37. Denis Healey, op. cit., p. 434.

Sources

No period is better supplied with primary material – reports of Royal Commissions and Government Committees, White Papers, Green Papers, research reports and pamphlets were published in profusion.

The journal *New Society* provided a weekly analysis of events. In the 1970s, it was devoted very largely to social policy issues, though it later veered towards the more sensational aspects of sociology.

The Year Book of Social Policy in Britain provides analyses by politicians and academics of current issues during the period covered by this chapter.

Fabian Tracts and other publications of the Fabian Society are an important source of left-wing analysis in the 1960s and 1970s. The Fabian Society has continued to act as the research arm of the Labour Party. Child Poverty Action Group publications include the Poverty Leaflets, Poverty Pamphlets, Rights Guides, Rights Leaflets and the Welfare Rights Bulletin. The Low Pay Unit produced its own series of research reports on families with low incomes.

The Institute of Economic Affairs published over 300 pamphlets between 1964 and 1970, of which the Hobart Papers were probably the most influential. Most of these follow the approach of the New Right. Some are described as representing a Liberal approach – but 'Liberal' is used in a sense which would have been recognized by Lord Melbourne and Nassau Senior rather than the Liberal Party of the 1960s. The IEA has also produced Progress Reports, Occasional Papers and Lectures. *Full Employment at Any Price?* by F. A. von Hayek (no. 45 of the 1975 Occasional Papers series) is of particular significance in analysing the economic basis of monetarist thinking.

Phoebe Hall's *Reforming the Welfare* is a good introduction to the Seebohm reforms. Ronald Walton's *Women in Social Work* describes the changes which took place when men began to take over many of the senior posts which had previously been filled by women.

The research reports of the EPA Projects are summarized in A. H. Halsey's *EPA Problems and Policies*. Five volumes of research material were also published. The CDP Projects are summarized and listed in Martin Loney's *Community Against Government* and the Transmitted Deprivation Projects in Brown and Madge, *Despite the Welfare State*.

The Central Council for Education and Training in Social Work (CCETSW) has issued a number of influential reports on the nature of social work, and recruitment and training issues.

Biographies, autobiographies and memoirs of leading politicians of the period, such as Enoch Powell, James Callaghan, Barbara Castle, Denis Healey, Harold Wilson, R. H. S. Crossman and Edward Heath provide much information on how and why particular policies were followed. But much of the official material, being covered by the 30-year rule, will not be available for study for some years.

The full force of opposition to 'Welfare State' policies comes out most clearly in the *Black Papers on Education* (Cox and Dyson, Cox and Boyson), in Rhodes Boyson's *Down with the Poor*, in which he compares. the British public to battery hens, imprisoned by the bonds of Socialist thinking, and in *Breaking the Spell of the Welfare State*, by Digby Anderson, June Lait and David Marsland, which argues for major cuts in social work and education.

CHAPTER THIRTEEN   BREAKING THE CONSENSUS

1. *Newsweek*, 27 April 1992, pp. 14–15.
2. Andrew Gamble, 'Politics 2000', in P. Dunleavy, A. Gamble *et al.*, *Developments in British Politics*, 5, p. 259.
3. John Peterson, 'Britain, Europe and the World', in P. Dunleavy, A. Gamble *et al.*, *Developments in British Politics*.
4. Milton Friedman, b. Brooklyn, 1912. Author of *A Programme for Maintaining Stability*, 1960; *Free To Choose*, 1980; *The Tyranny of the Status Quo*.
5. Friedrich August von Hayek, b. Vienna, 1899. Author of *The Pure Theory of Capital*, 1941; *The Road to Serfdom*, 1944; *The Constitution of Liberty*, 1960.
6. This phrase is attributed to Samuel Brittan, brother of Sir Leon Brittan and author of *The Role and Limits of Government*, 1983.
7. Raymond Plant, 'The very idea of a Welfare State' in Philip Bean, John

Ferris and David Whynes (eds), *In Defence of Welfare*, 1985, pp. 5–6, quoting von Hayek, *The Constitution of Liberty*.

8 Raymond Plant, 'The very idea of a welfare state', pp. 14–15.

9. *Parliamentary Debates (Hansard)* 12 June 1979, vol. 968, c. 246.

10. *The Economist*, 18–24 September 1982, pp. 25–6.

11. *Annual Abstract of Statistics, 1988*, p. 116, table 6.8.

12. Kenneth Harris, *Thatcher*, pp. 215–17 and 224–36.

13. Jonathan Bradshaw, 'A defence of social security', in Philip Bean, John Ferris and David Whynes, *In Defence of Welfare*, pp. 231–2.

14. Jonathan Bradshaw, 'A defence of social security', pp. 231–2.

15. Ken Livingstone, *If Voting Changed Anything, They'd Abolish It*, 1988, pp. 146–307.

16. Stuart Lowe, 'Home ownership and capital accumulation' in Maria Brenton and Clare Ungerson (eds) *The Social Policy Review 1990*.

17. Sarah Monk and Mark Kleinman, 'Housing', in Philip Brown and Richard Sparks (eds) *Beyond Thatcherism*, 1989, p. 127.

18. Monk and Kleinman, op. cit., p. 128.

19. Roger Jowell *et al.*, *British Social Attitudes 1987*, p. 3 and *1998/9*, p. 96.

20. Margaret Thatcher, *The Revival of Britain: speeches on Home and European Affairs, 1985–8*, compiled by Alistair B. Cooke, 1989.

21. 'What happened to democracy?' *The Independent on Sunday*, 28 March 1993.

22. Hugo Young, *One of Us: a biography of Margaret Thatcher*, p. 413.

23. *Government Statistical Services* (the Rayner Report), HMSO, Cmnd. 8236, 1981, annexe 2, para. 21.

24. Report in *The Independent*, 9 October 1989.

25. DHSS, *Inequalities in Health: The Report of a Working Group, chairman, Sir Douglas Black*, 1980 [Photocopy only]. Peter Townsend and Nick Davidson (eds), *Inequalities in Health: the Black Report*.

26. Home Office, *The Brixton Disorders, 10–12 April 1981; report of an inquiry by Lord Scarman*, HMSO, Cmnd. 8427, 1981.

27. Lord Scarman, *The Brixton Disorders*, preface.

28. *Faith in the City: a call for action by the Church and the nation*, report of the Bishops' Commission on Urban Priority Areas, para. 1.34, p. 18.

29. *Faith in the City*, para 1.44, p. 22.

Sources

This chapter deals with a period of acute ideological conflict, which makes dispassionate analysis difficult. Source-material is very scattered. As the text suggests, official sources, so plentiful in the 1970s, became less than adequate. The two principal biographies of Margaret Thatcher, while necessarily focused on one personality, do contain helpful references to such major events as 'The Winter of Discontent', the abrupt ending of consensus politics, the battle with the trade unions and the miners' strike, and the conflict with the left-wing local authorities. The pamphlet publications of the Institute of Economic Affairs and the Fabian Society, so plentiful in the 1970s, became relatively sparse.

Nicholas Bosanquet's *After the New Right*, Brown and Sparks' *Beyond Thatcherism*, Paul Wilding's *In Defence of the Welfare State* and Bean, Ferris and Whynes's *In Defence of Welfare* are useful collections of papers by academic writers in social policy, containing contemporary analyses of policies in the 1980s, and speculations on the possible directions of change in the 1990s.

CHAPTER FOURTEEN   DISMANTLING THE FRAMEWORK

1. *Newsweek*, 27 April 1992, pp. 14–15.
2. L. Challis, P. Day, R. Klein and E. Scrivens, 'Managing quasi-markets' in W. Bartlett, C. Proper *et al.*, *Quasi-Markets in the Welfare State*, pp. 10–32.
3. The standard analysis is Stuart Maclure's *Education Re-Formed. See also* S. J. Bull, *Education Reform: a critical and non-structural approach*; D. M. Hart, *A Guide to the Education Reform Act 1988.*
4. Hugo Young, *One of Us: a biography of Margaret Thatcher*, p. 414.
5. *The Times*, 4 January 1985; 25 January 1985; Article, 'Does Oxford speak for the nation?, 1 February 1985.
6. K. Harris, *Thatcher*, p. 208.
7. DHSS. *Report of the Royal Commission on the National Health Service* (the *Merrison Report*), HMSO, Cmnd. 7615, 1979.
8. Personal information. See also N. Timmins, *The Five Giants*, pp. 417, 472–7.
9. Department of Health and Social Security, *Report of the National Health Service Management Committee* (the first Griffiths report), HMSO, 1983.
10. *See* Kathleen Jones, *Asylums and After* (1993), chapter 12 *passim*.
11. *Sunday Times*, 12 August, 1990.
12. W. Bartlett and J. LeGrand, introduction to *Quasi-Markets and Social Policy*, pp. 1, 4–5.
13. These were largely contributed by Colin Brewer and June Lait, and are summarized in their book, *Can Social Work Survive?*
14. *Social Work Today*, pp. 6–7.
15. Borough of Brent, *A Child in Trust: report of the panel of inquiry into the circumstances surrounding the death of Jasmine Beckford*, 1985; Borough of Lambeth, *Whose Child? Report of the panel appointed to inquire into the death of Tyra Henry*, 1987; Dame Elizabeth Butler-Sloss, *Report of the Inquiry into Child Abuse in Cleveland*, HMSO, Cm. 412, 1988.
16. House of Commons, second report of the Social Services Committee, *Community Care with special reference to adult mentally ill and mentally handicapped people*, vol. 1, HMSO, 1985.

17. Audit Commission for Local Authorities in England and Wales, *Making a Reality of Community Care*, HMSO, 1986.
18. DHSS, *Community Care: agenda for action* (the second Griffiths Report), HMSO, 1988.
19. Sarah Monk and Mark Kleinman, 'Housing', in Philip Brown and Richard Sparks (eds) *Beyond Thatcherism*, pp. 127–8.
20. Council of Mortgage Lenders, reported in *The Independent*, 15 September 1990.
21. *The Times*, 20 March 1991.
22. See Bruce Anderson, *John Major: the making of a Prime Minister*, Edward Pearse, *The Quiet Rise of John Major*, John Major, *John Major: The Autobiography*.
23. *See*, for example, D. Kavanagh, 'A Major agenda?' in D. Kavanagh and A. Seldon, *The Major Effect*; P. Alcock, 'Consolidation or stagnation?' in *Social Policy Review 9*, 1997, pp. 17–33.
24. Kenneth Clarke, Chancellor of the Exchequer, *Hansard*, vol. 233, cc. 924–5, 30 November 1993.
25. See, for example, *The Guardian*, 21 March 1998.
26. *Statistics: a matter of trust*, Cm. 3882, 1988, pp. 4–5.
27. *The Times*, 30 March 1991 and 1 December 1993.
28. Cabinet Office, *The Citizen's Charter Unit*, HMSO, Cm. 2970, 1992.
29. Cabinet Office, *The Citizen's Charter Unit: the facts and figures* HMSO, Cm. 3370, 1996.
30. *The Times*, 9 October 1993.
31. *The Times*, 11 October 1993 and 13 October 1993.

Sources

There are not many general sources on the Major Governments, apart from the rather poorly referenced lives of John Major and Part IV of Nicholas Timmins's excellent (though journalistic) *The Five Giants*. For the rest, one is dependent on primary sources – newspapers, journals, television interviews. *New Society*, an excellent source for material in the 1960s and 1970s, declined, and joined the *New Statesman* in 1988, to be finally dropped from the title of that journal in 1996. The annual *British Journal of Social Policy* became the intermittent *Social Policy Review*, with frequent changes of editor. There are at least three reasons for the lack of literature: the catastrophic decline in the amount and the quality of Government documents; their inordinate expense; and the fact that the social science community was so stunned by the loss of subject-matter and the growing burdens of university teaching that they no longer had the resources or the time to write books covering the whole field. With their numbers reduced, their teaching loads increased, and their library resources cut, it was all they could do to tackle it piece by piece. Perhaps for these reasons, the theory arose that history and general studies of the field were no longer important, and post-modernist theories (which derive from Existentialism as well as from a profound Nietzschean depression) took hold.

CHAPTER FIFTEEN   NEW LABOUR – NEW SOCIAL POLICY?

1. John Rentoul, *Tony Blair*, pp. 307–44.
2. *Report of the Commission on Social Justice*, pp. 3 and 64–77.
3. op. cit., pp. 3 and 88–94.
4. op. cit., pp. 3 and 84–90.
5. op. cit., p. 90.
6. John Hills, *The Future of Welfare: a guide to the debate*.
7. *Report of the Commission on Social Justice*, p. 187.
8. op. cit., p. 234.
9. op. cit., p. 249.
10. Editorial, *New Statesman and Society*, 28 October 1994.
11. John Sopel, *Tony Blair: the Moderniser*, p. 3.
12. Foreword by Tony Blair to *The Personal World: John Macmurray on self and society*, ed. Philip Cornford.
13. John Sopel, *Tony Blair: the Moderniser*, p. 145.
14. A. Etzioni, *The Spirit of Community: rights, responsibilities and the communitarian agenda*, p. x.
15. A. Giddens with C. Pierson, *Conversations with Anthony Giddens*, p. 168.
16. A. Giddens, *The Constitution of Society*; *The Consequences of Modernity*; *Modernity and Self-Identity*; *The Transformation of Intimacy*; *Beyond Left and Right*; *Reflexive Modernisation: politics, tradition and aesthetics in the modern social order* (with L. Beck and S. Lash).
17. *Conversations with Anthony Giddens*, p. 152.
18. *Conversations with Anthony Giddens*, p. 154.
19. See, for example, D. Held and J. B. Thompson (eds), *Anthony Giddens and his critics*; Ian Craib, *Anthony Giddens*; Kenneth Tucker, *Anthony Giddens and Modern Social Theory*.
20. The full text of the old Clause Four and the new Clause Four, with an illustration in Tony Blair's handwriting, is given in the biographies by Rentoul and Sopel.
21. Tony Blair, *The Third Way*, Fabian pamphlet no. 588.
22. John Sopel, *Tony Blair: the Moderniser*, p. 145.
23. *The Times*, 11 August 1999.
24. Tony Blair, *The Third Way*, p. 3.
25. *The Third Way*, p. 6.
26. *The Third Way*, p. 7.
27. Except in the case of the Law Lords, the highest Court of Appeal, who have traditionally had regard to natural justice in making their decisions.

28. Convention for the Protection of Human Rights and Fundamental Freedoms, Rome, 4 November 1950. The United Kingdom ratified the Convention on 8 March 1951, Cmd. 8689.
29. *The Times*, 14 December 1998.
30. Budget speech by the Chancellor of the Exchequer, Gordon Brown, *Hansard*, 9 March 1999.
31. Speech by Gordon Brown to a seminar of Poverty specialists, 14 July 1999.
32. *The government's annual report 98/99*, pp. 20–1.
33. *The Times*, 28 July 1998.
34. TSO, Cm. 3805.
35. *Hansard*, 1 June 1999.
36. John Rentoul, *Tony Blair*, p. 396.
37. *The government's annual report 98/99*, pp. 8–9.
38. *The government's annual report 98/99*, p. 74.
39. *The Times*, 2 December 1998.
40. *The Times*, 19 July 1999.
41. DEE Press release, 18 January 1988.
42. 'Why heads cannot rate staff', *The Times*, 4 December 1998.
43. *Hansard*, 13 June 1999.
44. J. Cousins, *Listening to Four-Year-Olds*, Early Learning Network.
45. BBC 1, *On the Record*, 10 November 1998. Frank Dobson interviewed by John Humphreys.
46. *The government's annual report 98/99*, pp. 32–3.
47. Frank Dobson to John Humphreys. See note 45.
48. *The government's annual report 98/99*, pp. 32–5 and 76.
49. *The Times*, 12 August 1999.
50. *The Times*, 18 October 1999.
51. Statement by the Home Secretary, Jack Straw, *The Times*, 12 Jan. 1999.
52. Paul Boateng, Home Office minister, on BBC 2 TV, 12 January 1999.
53. ITV, *Newsnight*, 12 January 1999. *Hansard*, Third Reading of the Access to Justice Bill, 22 June 1999.
54. *RADAR Bulletin* no. 282, July 1998.
55. *Disability Now*, June 1999, p. 1.
56. For example, on *Kilroy*, BBC 1 TV, 12 January 1999.
57. *With Respect to Old Age*, Report of the Royal Commission on the Elderly, chairman, Sir Stuart Sutherland, Cm. 4192, 1999.
58. Anthony Giddens, *The Third Way*, p. 112.
59. Anthony Giddens, *The Third Way*, p. 117.
60. A. Giddens with C. Pierson, *Conversations with Anthony Giddens*, pp. 218–26.
61. *The Times*, 22 June 1999 carries statements on this subject from John Monk, Secretary of the Trade Union Congress, and Lord Hattersley, former Deputy Leader of the Labour Party.

Sources

New Labour has promised in *A Matter of Trust* to overhaul the Government documentary and statistical service. This is no longer listed as HMSO, Her Majesty's Stationery Office, but as TSO, The Stationery Office: these initials now appear on Command papers and other official publications from central Government; but much of the material coming from the Departments of Health, Education and Employment and Social Security is no longer available from this source. It is only available from the individual departments, which sometimes have difficulty in locating paper documents, and are apt to reply to enquirers, 'You *may* find it on the Internet'. This can be a lengthy process if they do not provide references, and it is a fairly expensive one.

Hansard and *The Times* publish very detailed annual indexes, which are useful for locating people and events. Most academic libraries keep House of Commons Sessional Papers, though increasingly they are only kept on microfiche, and delivery is rather slow.

A new problem is that much social policy discussion takes place on radio or television. Ministers may make announcements during interviews before matters have reached Parliament, and sometimes they do not reach Parliament at all. Much material on the Internet is unattributed, and some of dubious validity: there is no quality control of the kind which good publishers and their referees exert on the academic authors of books.

APPENDIX I.   QUASI-MARKETS, QUALITY AND MEASUREMENT

1. See, for example, Julian LeGrand and Will Bartlett (eds), *Quasi-Markets and the Welfare State*; Will Bartlett, Carol Propper, Deborah Wilson and Julian LeGrand (eds) *Quasi-Markets in the Welfare State*; Ian Kendall, Martin Blackmore, Yvonne Bradshaw, Sandra Jenkinson and Norman Johnson, 'Quality services in quasi-markets', *Social Policy Review*, 9, pp. 184–202; R. Flynn and G. Williams (eds) *Contracting for Health: Quasi-Markets and the National Health Service*.
2. Will Bartlett and Julian LeGrand, *Quasi-Markets and Social Policy*, Introduction, p. 1.
3. R. M. Titmuss *The Gift Relationship*, p. 145.
4. Entropy is the inevitable loss of energy by randomly scattered molecules: the principle of the second law of thermodynamics, which, in a celebrated analysis, Ludwig van Bertalanffy applied to open systems in physics and biology. His seminal paper is reproduced in *Systems Thinking*, ed. F. E. Emery. It was much quoted by management theorists in the 1970s as applying to human organizations (and indeed to the entire universe).
5. *The government's annual report 98/99*, pp. 3 and 76. Manifesto pledge no. 53.
6. Simon Jenkins, *The Times*, 2 December 1998.

Bibliography

All books published in or near London unless otherwise indicated.

Abel-Smith, Brian, *A History of the Nursing Profession*, Heinemann, 1960.
— *The Hospitals, 1800–1948*, Heinemann, 1964.
— *Value for Money in Health Services: a comparative study*, Heinemann 1976.
— and Peter Townsend, *The Poor and the Poorest*, Occasional Papers in Social Administration, Bell, 1966.
Addison, Paul, *The Road to 1945: British Politics and the Second World War*, Jonathan Cape, 1977.
Anderson, Bruce, *John Major: the making of a Prime Minister*, Fourth Estate, 1991.
Anderson, Digby C., June Lait and David Marsland, *Breaking the Spell of the Welfare State*, Social Affairs Unit, 1981.
Andover Union: Report of Select Committee of the Andover Union 1846. Parliamentary Papers 11, 22620.
Annual Abstract of Statistics, HMSO.
Archbishop's Commission on Urban Priority Areas; *Faith in the City: a call for action by the Church and the nation*, Church Publishing House, Westminster, 1985.
Attlee, Clement, *As It Happened*, Heinemann, 1954.
Audit Commission for Local Authorities in England and Wales, *Making a Reality of Community Care*, HMSO, 1986.

Baldwin, Sally, Gillian Parker and Robert Walker (eds), *Social Security and Community Care*, Avebury, Gower, 1988.
[Barlow Report], *Report of the Royal Commission on the Distribution of the Industrial Population*, HMSO, Cmd. 6513, 1940.
Bartlett, Will, Carol Propper, Deborah Wilson and Julian LeGrand, (eds), *Quasi-Markets in the Welfare State: the emerging findings*, Bristol, SAUS, 1995.
Baxter, O. Wythen, *The Book of the Bastiles, or, The History of the Working of the New Poor Law*, Stephens, 1841.

Bean, Philip, John Ferris and David Whynes (eds), *In Defence of Welfare*, Tavistock Publications, 1985.

Beckford, Jasmine, *see* Brent.

Bellamy, Christine, *Administering Central–Local Relations, 1871–1919*, Manchester University Press, 1988.

Bentham, Jeremy, *The Works of Jeremy Bentham*, edited by J. Bowring, Edinburgh, Tait, 1843.

Bevan, Aneurin, *In Place of Fear*, McGibbon and Kee, 1952, reprinted by Quartet, 1976.

— (as 'Celticus'), *Why Not Trust the Tories?*, Gollancz, 1944.

Beveridge, Janet, *Beveridge and his Plan*, Hodder and Stoughton, 1954.

[Beveridge Report] *Report of the Committee on Social Insurance and Allied Services*, HMSO, Cmd. 6404, 1942.

Beveridge, William, *Full Employment in a Free Society*, Allen and Unwin, 1944.

— *Voluntary Action: a Report on methods of social advance*, Allen and Unwin, 1948.

— *Power and Influence*, Hodder and Stoughton, 1953.

[Black Report], *Inequalities in Health, Report of a Research Working Group*, DHSS, 1980 (photocopy only, see Townsend).

Blair, Tony, *The Third Way*, Fabian pamphlet no. 588, 1988. Obtainable from the Fabian Society, 11 Dartmouth Street, London SW1H 9BN.

— Foreword to *The Personal World: John Macmurray on self and society*, ed. Philip Cornford, 1996. See Macmurray.

[Blanesburgh Report], *Report of the Unemployment Insurance Committee*, 2 vols. HMSO, 1927.

Boddy, Martin, *The Building Societies*, Macmillan, 1980.

Bonham Carter, Violet, *Winston Churchill as I Knew Him*, Eyre and Spottiswoode, 1965.

Booth, Charles, *Life and Labour of the People of London*, Macmillan, 17 vols, 1889–1903.

Booth, William, *In Darkest England, or, The Way Out*, Salvation Army, 1890.

Bosanquet, Bernard (ed.) *Aspects of the Social Problem*, Macmillan, 1895.

Bosanquet, Helen, *Social Work in London*, Murray, 1914.

— *The Poor Law Report of 1909*, Macmillan, 1912.

Bosanquet, Nicholas, *After the New Right*, Heinemann, 1983.

Bourdillon, A. F. C. (ed.), *The Voluntary Social Services: their place in the modern state*, Methuen, 1965.

Bowley, Marion, *Housing and the State*, Allen and Unwin, 1944.

Boyson, Rhodes, *Down with the Poor*, Churchill Press, 1971.

Bradshaw, Jonathan, *The Family Fund*, Routledge and Kegan Paul, 1980.

— 'A defence of social security', in Philip Bean, John Ferris and David Whynes (eds.), *A Defence of Welfare*, Tavistock Publications, 1985.

Brent, Borough of, *A Child in Trust*, 1985.

Brewer, Colin and June Lait, *Can Social Work Survive?*, Temple Smith, 1980.

Briggs, Asa, *Social Thought and Social Action: a study of the work of Seebohm Rowntree, 1871–1954*, Longmans, 1961.

Bristol Corporation of the Poor, *Selected Records 1696–1834*, Bristol Records Society Publications, 1932.

Brittan, Samuel, *The Role and Limits of Government: essays in political economy*, Temple Smith, 1983.

Broad, L., *Winston Churchill, 1874–1951*, Hutchinson, 1951.

Brown, Muriel and Nicola Madge, *Despite the Welfare State*, Heinemann, 1982.

Brown, Philip and Richard Sparks (eds), *Beyond Thatcherism: social policy, politics and society*, Open University Press, 1989.

Bruce, Maurice, *The Coming of the Welfare State*, Batsford, 1961.

— (ed.), *The Rise of the Welfare State*, Weidenfeld and Nicolson, 1973.

Brundage, Anthony, *The Making of the New Poor Law*, Hutchinson, 1978.

Bryant, C. G. and David Jury, *Anthony Giddens: critical assessment*, Routledge, 1996.

Bull, S. J., *Education Reform: a critical and non-structural approach*, Milton Keynes, Open University, 1994.

Bulmer, Martin, (ed.) *Royal Commissions and Departmental Committees of Inquiry: the lessons of experience*, Royal Institute of Public Administration, 1983.

Burnett, John, *A Social History of Housing, 1815–1985*, Methuen, 1978.

Butler-Sloss, Elizabeth, *Report . . . on Child Abuse in Cleveland*, HMSO, 1988.

Butterworth, Eric, 'Race Relations – the next step', chapter 9 in *The Year Book of Social Policy, 1973*, Routledge and Kegan Paul, 1974.

Cartwright, Frederick F., *A Social History of Medicine*, Longmans, 1977.

Castle, Barbara, *The Castle Diaries*, Weidenfeld and Nicolson, 1980.

Cecil, David, *Lord M*, Constable 1954, reprinted in David Cecil, *Melbourne*, Book Club, 1972.

Chadwick, Edwin, *The Sanitary Condition of the Labouring Population of Great Britain*, with an introduction by M. W. Flinn, Edinburgh University Press, 1965.

Child Poverty Action Group: Poverty Leaflets, Research Leaflets, Rights Leaflets.

Citizen's Charter Unit, The, Cabinet Office, HMSO Cm. 2970, 1997.

Citizen's Charters: the facts and figures, HMSO Cm. 3370, 1996.

Cleary, E. J., *The Building Society Movement*, Elek Books, 1965.

Clemens, Cyril, *The Man from Limehouse: Clement Attlee*, New York, Didier, 1946.

Cobbett, William, *Rural Rides*, 1830, repr. A. Cobbett, 1853.

Cohen, Percy, *The British System of Social Insurance*, Allan, 1932.

— *Unemployment Insurance and Assistance in Britain*, Harrap, 1938.

Cole, G. D. H. and Raymond Postgate, *The Common People*, Methuen, 1948.

Cole, Margaret, *The Story of Fabian Socialism*, Heinemann, 1961, repr. Mercury, 1963.

Cole, Margaret (ed.), *The Diaries of Beatrice Webb, 1924–1932*, Gollancz, 1945.

Cooney, E. W., 'High flats in local authority housing in England and Wales since 1945', in Anthony Sutcliffe (ed.), *Multi-Storey Housing: the British working class experience*, Croom Helm, 1974.

Cooper, M. and A. J. Culyer, *The Price of Blood*, Hobart Papers 48, 1968.

Corina, Lewis, 'Community work and local authority decision-making', *Community Development Journal*, 11 (1976), 3.

Cousins, J., *Listening to Four-Year-Olds*, Early Learning Network, 1999.

Cox, Brian and A. E. Dyson (eds.), *The Black Papers On Education*, Davis Poynter, 1971.

Cox, Brian and Rhodes Boyson, *Black Paper 1975*, Dent, 1975.

Cronin, A. J., *The Stars Look Down*, Gollancz, 1935.

— *The Citadel*, Gollancz, 1937.

Crossman, R. H. S., *The Diaries of a Cabinet Minister*, 3 vols. Hamish Hamilton and Jonathan Cape, 1976, vol. 2.

[Crowther Report], *15 to 18: Report of the Central Advisory Council for Education – England*, 2 vols, HMSO, 1959.

Cullingworth, J. B., *Housing Needs and Planning Policy*, Routledge and Kegan Paul, 1960.

Dalton, Hugh, *High Tide and After: Memoirs*, 3 vols, Frederick Muller, 1962, vol. 3.

Dant, Tim, 'Old, poor and at home: social security and elderly people in the community', in Sally Baldwin, Gillian Parker and Robert Walker (eds), *Social Security and Community Care*, Avebury, Gower, 1988.

Department of Health; Department of Health and Social Security; see Health.

Dickens, Charles, *Oliver Twist*, many editions, inc. Chapman and Hall, 1901.

Donnison, Jean, *Midwives and Medical Men*, Heinemann, 1977.

Dunkley, Peter, *The Crisis of the Old Poor Law in England, 1795–1834* New York, Garland, 1982.

Dunleavy, P., *The Politics of Mass Housing in Britain 1945–75*, Oxford University Press, 1981.

Dunleavy, P., A. Gamble, A. Holliday and G. Peck (eds.), *Developments in British Politics*, 5, Basingstoke, Macmillan, 1997.

du Parcq, L., *Life of David Lloyd George*, Canon, 1912.

Dwork, Deborah, *War is Good for Babies and Other Young Children: a history of the infant and child welfare movement*, Tavistock, 1987.

Eden, Frederick, *The State of the Poor*, 3 vols., 1797.

Education: for reports by the Ministry of Education and the Department of

Education and Science: see under McNair, Norwood, Crowther, Newsom, Plowden, Robbins.

Educational Reconstruction, HMSO, Cmd. 6458, 1943.

Elderly: *Report of Royal Commission on the Elderly*, TSO, Cm. 4192, 1999.

Employment Policy, HMSO, Cmd. 6527, 1944.

Engels, F., *The Condition of the Working Class in England*, 1842. Many editions available.

Etzioni, Amitai, *The Spirit of Community: rights, responsibilities and the communitarian agenda*, Fontana, 1995.

Fabian Society publications:

    Bosanquet, Nicholas, *A New Deal for the Elderly*, Fabian Tracts 435, 1975.

    Brooke, Rosalind, *Advice Centres in Welfare Rights*, Fabian Research Series 329, 1972.

    Bull, David, *Action for Welfare Rights*, Fabian Research Series 288, 1970.

    Castle, Barbara, *The NHS Revisited*, Fabian Tracts 440, 1976.

    Crossman, R. H. S., *Paying for the Social Services*, Fabian Tracts 399, 1969.

    Draper, Peter *et al.*, *The National Health Service: three views*, Fabian Research Series 287, 1970.

    Lynes, Tony, *Welfare Rights*, Fabian Tracts 395, 1969.

    Rendel, Margherita *et al.*, *Equality for Women*, Fabian Research Series 268, 1968.

    Sinfield, Adrian, *Which Way for Social Work?*, Fabian Tracts 393, 1969.

    Townsend, Peter, *et al.*, *Social Services for All*, Fabian Tracts 382–5, 1968.

    Townsend, Peter, *Why are the Many Poor?* Fabian Tracts 500, 1984.

Ferguson, Sheila, and Hilda Fitzgerald, *Studies in the Social Services, History of the Second World War*, United Kingdom Civil Series, HMSO, 1954.

Finer, S. E., *The Life and Times of Sir Edwin Chadwick*, Methuen, 1952.

Flinn, M. W., ed. and intro. to Edwin Chadwick's *The Sanitary Condition of the Labouring Population of Great Britain*, (1842), Edinburgh University Press, 1965.

Flinn, M. W., *Public Health Reform in Britain*, Macmillan, 1968.

Flynn, Robert and Gareth H. Williams, *Contracting for Health: Quasi-Markets and the National Health Service*, Oxford University Press, 1997.

Foot, Michael, *Aneurin Bevan*, McGibbon and Kee, 1962.

Fraser, Derek, *The Evolution of the British Welfare State*, Macmillan, 1973.

Frazer, William Mowll, *A History of English Public Health*, Baillière, Tindall and Cox, 1950.

Galton, Francis, *Hereditary Genius: an inquiry into its laws and con-sequences*, 1869, 2nd edition 1892.

Giddens, Anthony, *The Constitution of Society*, Polity Press, 1984.

Giddens, Anthony, *The Consequences of Modernity*, Polity Press, 1990.
— *The Third Way: the renewal of social democracy*, Polity Press, 1990.
— *The Transformation of Intimacy*, Polity Press, 1992.
— *Beyond Left and Right*, Polity Press, 1994.
— *Modernity and Self-Identity*, Polity Press, 1995.
— with L. Beck and S. Lash, *Reflexive Modernisation: politics, tradition and aesthetics in the modern social order*, Polity Press, 1994.
— with Christopher Pierson, *Conversations with Anthony Giddens*, Polity Press, 1998.
Gilbert, Bentley B., *The Evolution of National Insurance in Britain: the origins of the welfare state*, Michael Joseph, 1966.
— *British Social Policy, 1914–1939*, Batsford, 1970.
Gilbert, Martin, *Winston Churchill*, Heinemann, vol. 7, 1986.
Gittus, Elizabeth, *Flats, Families and the Under-Fives*, Routledge and Kegan Paul, 1960.
government's annual report 98/99, the, TSO Cm. 4401, 1999.
Gray, B. Kirkman, *A History of English Philanthropy*, King, 1905.
Green Papers on the National Health Service, 1968 and 1970, see Health.
Greenwood, Walter, *Love on the Dole*, Jonathan Cape, 1933.
Gregg, Pauline, *The Welfare State*, Harrap, 1967.
[Gregory], *Holman Gregory Report, Final Report of Royal Commission on Unemployment Insurance*, HMSO Cmd. 4185, 1932.
Griffiths, Sir Roy, see Health.
Grigg, John, *Lloyd George, The People's Champion*, Eyre Methuen, 1978.

Hall, Phoebe, *Reforming the Welfare*, Heinemann, 1976.
Halsey, A. H., *Educational Priority: report on a project sponsored by the Department of Education and Science and the Social Science Research Council*, HMSO, 1972, vol. 1, *EPA Problems and Policies*.
Hamilton, H. J., *Savings and Savings Institutions*, New York, Macmillan, 1902.
Hammond, J. L. and Barbara Hammond, *Lord Shaftesbury*, Constable, 1923.
— *The Age of the Chartists*, Longmans Green, 1930.
— *The Village Labourer*, 2 vols., Longmans Green, 1911, and Guild Books, 1948.
— *The Town Labourer 1760–1832*, 2 vols., Longmans Green, 1917, and Guild Books, 1949.
Hannington, Wal, *The Problem of the Distressed Areas*, Gollancz, 1937.
— *Ten Lean Years*, Gollancz, 1940.
— *Unemployed Struggles 1919–1936: My Life and Struggles*, Lawrence and Wishart, 1936, reprinted 1979.
Harris, Jose, *William Beveridge*, Oxford University Press, 1977.
Harris, Kenneth, *Thatcher*, Weidenfeld and Nicolson, 1988, and Fontana, 1989.

Hart, D. M. (ed.), *A Guide to the Education Reform Act 1988*, National Association of Head Teachers.

Hayek, F. A. von, *The Constitution of Liberty*, Routledge and Kegan Paul, 1960. See Institute of Economic Affairs for other Hayek titles.

Healey, Denis, *The Time of My Life*, Michael Joseph, 1989.

Health (National Health Service): Ministry of Health (1918–67), Department of Health and Social Security (DHSS) (1967–88), Department of Health from 1988:

   Ministry of Health: A National Health Service, HMSO, Cmd. 6502, 1944.

   Enquiry into the Cost of the National Health Service (The Guillebaud Report), HMSO, Cmd. 9663, 1956.

   A Hospital Plan for England and Wales, HMSO, Cmd. 1604, 1962.

   Health and Welfare: the development of community care, HMSO, Cmnd. 1973, 1963.

   Department of Health and Social Services:

   Administrative Structure of Medical and Related Services in England and Wales (First Green Paper), HMSO, 1968.

   The Future Structure of the National Health Service (Second Green Paper), HMSO, 1970.

   National Health Service Reorganisation: consultative document (White Paper), HMSO, 1971.

   Management Arrangements for the Reorganised National Health Service, (the 'Grey Book'), HMSO , 1972.

   Report of Royal Commission on the National Health Service, (the Merrison Report), HMSO Cmnd. 7615, 1979.

   Patients First (White Paper), HMSO, 1979.

   Report of the National Health Service Management Committee, chairman, Sir Roy Griffiths (the first *Griffiths Report*, HMSO, 1983).

   Department of Health:

   Community Care: agenda for action (the second *Griffiths Report*), HMSO, 1988.

   Caring for People: community care in the next decade and beyond, HMSO, Cm. 849, 1989.

Heasman, Kathleen, *Evangelicals in Action*, Bles, 1962.

Henry, Tyra, see Lambeth.

Hills, John, *The Future of Welfare: a guide to the debate*, Joseph Rowntree Foundation, 1993.

Hobart Papers, see Institute of Economic Affairs.

Hobsbawm, E. J. and George Rudé, *Captain Swing*, New York, Pantheon Books, 1968.

Hodder, Edwin, *The Life and Work of the Seventh Earl of Shaftesbury*, 3 vols, Cassell, 1886.

Holman Gregory, see Gregory.

Holman, Robert A., *Poverty*, Robertson, 1978.

Holyoake, George Jacob, *The Rochdale Pioneers*, Allen and Unwin, 10th edition, 1983.

House of Commons, *Second Report of the Social Services Committee, Session 1985, Community Care* vol I (HMSO, 1985).

Housing: The Government's Proposals, HMSO, Cmd. 214, 1987.

Howard, Christian, 'Women and the professions' (chapter 7) in *The Year Book of Social Policy, 1973*, Routledge and Kegan Paul, 1974.

Hutton, John, Sandra Hutton, Trevor Pinch and Alan Shiel, *Dependency to Enterprise*, Routledge, 1991.

Hyndman, F. D., *Record of an Adventurous Life*, Macmillan, 1911.

Institute of Economic Affairs:

> Burton, John, *et al.*, *Keynes' General Theory 50 Years On*, Hobart Papers 26, 1986.

> Cooper, Michael and A. J. Culyer, *The Price of Blood*, Hobart Papers 8, 1968.

> Ferns, Henry Stanley, *Towards an Independent University*, Occasional Papers 25, 1969.

> Friedman, Milton, *Unemployment versus Inflation? An Evaluation of the Phillips Curve*, Occasional Papers 44, 1975.

> Hanson, C. G., *Trade Unions: a century of privilege*, Occasional Papers, 38, 1973.

> Harris, Ralph (Lord Harris), *Beyond the Welfare State: an economic, political and moral critique of indiscriminate state welfare*, Occasional Papers 77, 1988.

> Hayek, F. A. von, *Economic Freedom and Representative Government*, Occasional Papers 39, 1973.

> — *Full Employment at Any Price?* Occasional Papers 45, 1975.

> Houghton, Douglas, *Paying for the Social Services*, Occasional Papers 16, 1967.

> Jewkes, John, *et al.*, *Economics, Business and Government*, Occasional Papers 8, 1966.

> Lees, D. S., *Health Through Choice*, Hobart Papers 14, 1961.

> Lees, D. S., *et al.*, *Monopoly or Choice in Health Services?* Occasional Papers 3, 1964.

> Prest, A. R., *Financing University Education: a study of university fees and loans to students in Great Britain*, Occasional Papers 12, 1966.

> Seldon, Arthur, *After the NHS*, Occasional Papers 21, 1968.

> *Whither the Welfare State*, Occasional Papers 69, 1981.

> — and Hamish Gray, *Universal or Selective Social Benefits?* Research Monographs 8, 1967.

[Interment], *Supplementary Report on the result of a Special Inquiry into the Practice of Interment in Towns*, Parliamentary Papers, 1843, 12.

Jennings, Ivor (ed.), *The Poor Law Code*, Knight, 1930.

Jewkes, John and Sylvia Jewkes, *The Genesis of the National Health Service*, Oxford, Blackwell, 1961.

Jones, Kathleen, *The Teaching of Social Studies in British Universities*, Occasional Papers in Social Administration no.12, Bell, 1965.

— *The Compassionate Society*, SPCK, 1966.

— *Eileen Younghusband: a biography*, Bedford Square Press, 1984.

— *Asylums and After: A revised history of the mental health services*, Athlone, 1993.

Jones, Kathleen, John Brown and Jonathan Bradshaw, *Issues in Social Policy*, Routledge and Kegan Paul, 1978, revised edn 1984.

Jordan, Bill, *Poor Parents*, Routledge and Kegan Paul, 1974.

Joseph, (Sir) Keith, 'A summary of some Conservative strategies', in *The Year Book of Social Policy in Britain*, Routledge and Kegan Paul, 1972.

Jowell, Roger, *et al.*, *British Social Attitudes*, Ashgate, Aldershot, Gower and Dartmouth, (annual) 1984–97.

Kavanagh, Dennis and Anthony Seldon, *The Major Effect*, Basingstoke, Macmillan, 1994.

Kay, James (Sir James Kay-Shuttleworth), *The Moral and Physical Condition of the Working Classes Employed in the Cotton Manufacture in Manchester*, Ridgway, 1832.

Keynes, J. Maynard, *A General Theory of Unemployment, Interest and Money*, Macmillan, 1936.

Klein, Rudolph and Michael O'Higgins, *The Future of Welfare*, Oxford, Blackwell, 1985.

Lambeth Borough Council, *Whose Child?*, 1987. (The Tyra Henry case).

Lambert, Royston, *Sir John Simon, 1816–904 and English Social Administration*, McGibbon and Kee, 1963.

LeGrand, Julian and Will Bartlett, *Quasi-Markets and the Welfare States*, Basingstoke, Macmillan, 1993.

Lewes, C. L., *Dr Southwood Smith: a retrospect*, Edinburgh, 1899.

Lewis, Peter, *George Orwell: the road to 1984*, Heinemann, 1981.

Lewis, R. A., *Edwin Chadwick and the Public Health Movement*, Longmans Green, 1952.

Lister, Ruth, *Welfare Benefits*, Sweet and Maxwell, 1981.

Little, Alan, 'The Race Relations Act, 1976, chapter 7 in *The Year Book of Social Policy, 1976*, Routledge and Kegan Paul, 1977.

Livingstone, Ken, *If Voting Changed Anything, They'd Abolish It*, Collins, 1988.

Local Government, Report of Royal Commission, 1969; *see Redcliffe-Maud Report*.

Loch, C. S., *Charity Organisation*, Swan Sonnenschein, 1905.

Lodge, Paul, 'Education', chapter 1 in Paul Wilding (ed.), *In Defence of the Welfare State*, Manchester University Press, 1986.

Loney, Martin, *Community Against Government*, Heinemann, 1983.

Longford, Elizabeth, *Victoria, R. I.*, Weidenfeld and Nicolson, 1964.

Lowe, Stuart, 'Home ownership and capital accumulation', in Maria Brenton and Clare Ungerson, (eds) *Social Policy Review 1990*, Longmans, 1990.

— *Housing*, Longmans Social Policy Today Series, 1985.

Lynes, Tony, *The Penguin Guide to Supplementary Benefits*, Penguin Books, 1972.

MacCleary, G. F., *The Maternity and Child Welfare Movement*, King, 1935.

Mack, Mary P., *A Bentham Reader*, New York, Pegasus, 1969.

— *Jeremy Bentham*, vol I, *An Odyssey of Ideas, 1748–1792*, Heinemann, 1962.

MacLeod, Iain and Enoch Powell, *The Social Services – Needs and Means*, Conservative Political Centre, 1954.

McLeod, Roy M., *Treasury Control and Social Administration*, Occasional papers in Social Administration no.23, Bell, 1968.

Maclure, J. Stuart, *Education Re-Formed*, Hodder and Stoughton, 1988, repr. 1993.

Macmurray, John, *The Personal World: John Macmurray on self and society*, ed. Philip Cornford, 1996.

[McNair Report],, *The Supply, Recruitment and Training of Teachers and Youth Leaders*, HMSO, 1944.

Major, John, *John Major: the Autobiography*, HarperCollins, 1999.

Malthus, T. R., *An Essay on the Principle of Population*, 1st edition 1798, edited by Anthony Flew, Penguin, 1970.

Marshall, Hedley, 'An introduction to reorganisation' chapter 1 in *The Year Book of Social Policy in Britain, 1973*, Routledge and Kegan Paul, 1974.

Marshall, T. H., *Social Policy*, Hutchinson, 1965, revised edition 1967.

— *The Right to Welfare*, Heinemann, 1981.

Martineau, Harriet, *Harriet Martineau's Autobiography*, 2 vols, Smith, Elder, 1877.

Marwick, Arthur, *Britain in the Century of Total War*, 1968, Penguin, 1970.

Mayhew, Henry, *London Labour and the London Poor*, 1851. Originally issued in weekly parts in the *Morning Chronicle*. Peter Quennell's edited versions are *Mayhew's London*, Pilot Press, 1949; *London's Underworld*, Kimber, 1950; and *Mayhew's* Characters, Kimber, 1951.

Mearns, Andrew, *The Bitter Cry of Outcast London*, 1883, reprint edited by Anthony S. Wohl, Victorian Library, Leicester University Press, 1970.

Medical Services Review Committee, see Porritt.

Merrison Report, see Health (Department of Health and Social Services), Report of the Royal Commission.

Ministry of Health, see Health.

Monk, Sarah and Mark Kleinman, 'Housing', in Philip Brown and Richard Sparks (eds), *Beyond Thatcherism*, Open University Press, 1989.

Morgan, Kenneth O., *Labour in Power, 1945–51*, Oxford, Clarendon Press, 1984.

National Health Service: see Health.

Newsholme, Arthur, *Fifty Years in Public Health*, Allen and Unwin, 1935.

[Newsom Report] *Half Our Future: Report of the Central Advisory Council for Education – England*, HMSO, 1963.

[Norwood Report] *Curriculum and examination: Report of the Committee of the Secondary Schools Examination Council*, HMSO, Cmd. 6502, 1943.

Orwell, George, *Down and Out in Paris and London*, Gollancz, 1933, Penguin, 1940.

— *The Road to Wigan Pier*, Gollancz, 1937, Penguin, 1962.

Owen, David, *English Philanthropy, 1661–1960*, Oxford University Press, 1965.

Owen, Robert, *The Life of Robert Owen, by himself*, with an introduction by John Butt, Knight, 1971.

Pakenham, Elizabeth, see Longford.

[Parker-Morris Report] Central Housing Advisory Committee, *Homes for Today and Tomorrow*, HMSO, 1961.

Pearse, Edward, *The Quiet Rise of John Major*, Weidenfeld and Nicolson, 1991.

Pearson, Geoffrey, *The Deviant Imagination*, Macmillan, 1975.

Peden, G. C., *British Economic and Social Policy: Lloyd George to Margaret Thatcher*, Philip Allen, 1985.

Pelling, Margaret, *Cholera, Fever and English Medicine*, Oxford University Press, 1978.

PEP (Political and Economic Planning), *Report on the British Social Services*, June 1937.

— *Report on the British Health Services*, December 1937.

Pinker, Robert A., *The Idea of Welfare*, Heineman, 1979.

Plant, Raymond, 'The very idea of a welfare state', in Philip Bean, John Ferris and David Whynes (eds) *in Defence of Welfare*, Tavistock Publications, 1985.

[Plowden Report], *Children and their Primary Schools: Report of the Central Advisory Council for Education (England)*, HMSO, vol. 1, 1966, vol. 2, 1967.

[Poor Laws] *Report of H. M. Commission for enquiring into the administration and practical operation of the Poor Laws, 1834*, 1 vol. plus 11 vols of evidence.

Report of Royal Commission on the Poor Laws and the Relief of Distress, one vol. plus 37 vols of evidence; HMSO, Cmd. 4499,1909. Majority Report. *Break Up the Poor Law and Abolish the Workhouse*, Minority Report published separately by the Fabian Society, 1909.

[Porritt Report] *A Review of Medical Services in Great Britain*, Medical Services Review Committee, Social Assay, 1963.

Prochaska, F. K., *Women and Philanthropy in Nineteenth Century England*, Oxford, Clarendon Press, 1980.

[Redcliffe-Maud Report], *Report of the Royal Commission on Local Government*, 3 vols., HMSO, Cmnd. 4040–1, 1969.

Rentoul, John, *Tony Blair*, Warner, 1996.

Ricardo, David, *The Principles of Political Economy and Taxation*, 1817 ed. W. Fellner, Homewood, Illinois, Irwin, 1963.

Ringen, Stein, *The Possibility of Politics*, Oxford University Press, 1987.

[Robbins Report], *Higher Education*, HMSO, Cmnd. 2154, 1963.

Roberts, David, *Victorian Origins of the British Welfare State*, New Haven, Connecticut, Yale University Press, 1960.

Rodgers, Barbara, and June Stevenson, *A New Portrait of Social Work*, Heinemann, 1973.

Ross, J. Stirling, *The National Health Service in Great Britain*, Oxford University Press, 1956.

Rowland, Peter, *The Last Liberal Governments*: vol. 1, *The Promised Land 1905–10*, Barrie and Cresset, 1965; vol. 2, *Unfinished Business 1911–18* Barrie and Jenkins, 1971.

Rowntree, B. Seebohm, *Poverty: A Study of Town Life*, Macmillan, 1901.

— *Poverty and Progress*, Longmans Green, 1941.

Rowntree, B. S. and G. R. Lavers, *Poverty and the Welfare State: a third social survey of York*, Longmans, 1951.

Rutter, Michael and Nicola Madge, *Cycles of Transmitted Deprivation*, Heinemann, 1976.

Scarman, Leslie (Lord), *The Brixton Disorders, 10–12 April 1981, report of an inquiry by Lord Scarman*, HMSO, Cmd. 8427, 1981.

[Scott Report], *Report of the Committee on Land Utilisation in Rural Areas*, HMSO, Cmd. 6378, 1942.

Seear, Nancy, 'Equal opportunities for men and women', chapter 8 in *The Year Book of Social Policy in Britain, 1973*, Routledge and Kegan Paul, 1974.

[Seebohm Report], *Report of the Committee on Local Authority and Allied Social Services*, HMSO, Cmd. 3703, 1968.

Simey, T. S., *Charles Booth, Social* Scientist, Oxford University Press, 1960.

Simon, John, *English Sanitary Institutions*, Cassell, 1890.

Sinfield, Adrian, *What Unemployment Means*, Robertson, 1981.

Smellie, K. B,, *A History of Local Government*, Unwin, 1968.

Smiles, Aileen, *Samuel Smiles and his Surroundings*, Hale, 1956.

Smiles, Samuel, *Self-Help*, Murray, 1859.

— *Character*, Murray, 1871.

— *Thrift*, Murray, 1875.

— *Duty*, Murray, 1880.

Smith, Adam, *The Wealth of Nations*, 1776. Available in modern editions.

Smith, Cecil Woodham, see Woodham Smith.

Smith, Francis Barrymore, *The People's Health, 1830–1890*, Croom Helm, 1979.
— *Florence Nightingale: reputation and power*, Croom Helm, 1982.
Smith, Jef, 'Top jobs in the Social Services', in *The Year Book of Social Policy in Britain, 1971*, Routledge and Kegan Paul, 1972.
Smith, Thomas Southwood, *A Treatise on Fever*, London, 1830.
Social Affairs Unit:
    Anderson, Digby, (ed.), *Full Circle? Bringing up children in the post-permissive society*, 1988.
    — *Breaking the Spell of the Welfare State: strategies for reducing public expenditure*, 1981.
    O'Keefe, Dennis, *The Wayward Curriculum: a cause for parents' concern?* 1986.
Social Insurance, Part I, HMSO, Cmd. 6550, 1944.
Social Insurance, Part II: Industrial Injuries, HMSO, Cmd. 6551, 1944.
Social Justice: *Report of the Commission on Social Justice*, Vintage, 1994.
Social Policy Review (formerly *The Year Book of Social Policy*), various editors, intermittent. Social Policy Association.
Sopel, John, *Tony Blair: the Moderniser*, Bantam, 1995.
Statistics: a matter of trust, TSO, Cm. 3882, 1998.
Stocks, Mary D., *Eleanor Rathbone: a biography*, Gollancz, 1949.
Strachey, Lytton, and Roger Fulford (eds), *The Greville Memoirs*, Macmillan, 1938.
Sutcliffe, Anthony (ed.), *Multi-Storey Housing: the British working-class experience*, Croom Helm, 1974.

Taylor, A. J. P., *English History 1914–1945*, Oxford University Press, 1965, Pelican Books, 1970, repr. 1987.
Tebbit, Norman, *Upwardly Mobile*, Futura, 1989.
Thane, Pat, *The Foundations of the Welfare State*, Longmans, 1982.
Thompson, E. P. and Eileen Yeo, *The Unknown Mayhew: Selections from the Morning Chronicle*, Merlin Press, 1971.
Thompson, Flora, *Lark Rise*, Oxford University Press, 1939.
Timmins, Nicholas, *The Five Giants: a biography of the Welfare State*, Fontana, 1996.
Titmuss, R. M., *Problems of Social Policy in Wartime*, Official History of the Second World War, United Kingdom Civil Series, HMSO, 1950.
Essays on 'The Welfare State', Allen and Unwin, 1958.
— *Commitment to Welfare*, Allen and Unwin, 1968.
— *The Gift Relationship*, Allen and Unwin, 1970.
Tivey, Leonard and Anthony Wright, *Party Ideology in Britain*, Routledge, 1989.
Townsend, Peter, *The Last Refuge*, Routledge and Kegan Paul, 1963.
— *The Social Minority*, Allen Lane, 1972.
— and Brian Abel-Smith, *The Poor and the Poorest*, Occasional Papers in Social Administration, Bedford Square Press, 1966.
— and Nick Davidson (eds.), *Inequalities in Health: the Black Report*, Penguin, 1982.

Tucker, Kenneth, *Anthony Giddens and Modern Social* Theory, Sage, 1995.
Twining, Louisa, *Recollections of Workhouse Management and Visiting*, Kegan Paul, 1880.

[Uthwatt Report], *Report of the Expert Committee on Compensation and Betterment*, HMSO, Cmd. 6386, 1942.

Veit-Wilson, John, 'Paradigms of Poverty: a rehabilitation of B. S. Rowntree', *Journal of Social Policy*, 15 (1986), 1, pp. 6–9.

Walton, Ronald, *Women in Social Work*, Routledge and Kegan Paul, 1975.
Webb, Beatrice, *My Apprenticeship*, Longmans Green, 1929.
— *Our Partnership*, ed. B. Drake and M. Cole, Longmans Green, 1948.
Webb, Sidney and Beatrice Webb, *The Consumers' Co-operative Movement*, Longmans Green, 1921, revised edition, 1930.
— *English Poor Law History*, Longmans Green, vol. 1, 1910, vol. 2, 1929.
— *English Poor Law Policy*, Longmans Green, 1910.
— *A History of Trade Unionism*, Longmans Green, 1894.
Wickwar, Bernard, *The Social Services: an historical survey*, Cobden Sanderson, 1936.
Wilding, Paul (ed.), *In Defence of the Welfare State*, Manchester University Press 1986.
Willcocks, A. J., *The Creation of the National Health Service*, Routledge and Kegan Paul, 1967.
Wohl, Anthony S., *Endangered Lives: public health in Victorian Britain*, Methuen, 1984.
Wolff, Henry W., *People's Banks: a record of social and economic success*, King, 3rd edition, 1910.
Woodlham Smith, Cecil, *Florence Nightingale, 1821–1910*, Constable 1950.

Year Book of Social Policy in Britain, Routledge and Kegan Paul (annual, 1971–9, various editors). *See Social Policy Review.*
Young, Hugo, *One of Us: a biography of Margaret Thatcher*, Macmillan, 1989.
Younghusband, Eileen, *Report on the Employment and Training of Social Workers*, Carnegie United Kingdom Trust, 1947.
— *Second Report on the Employment and Training of Social Workers, Carnegie United Kingdom Trust, 1951.*
— *Social Work in Britain, 1950–1975*, 2 vols, Allen and Unwin, 1978.
[Younghusband Report], *Report of Working Party on Social Workers in the Local Authority Health and Welfare Services*, HMSO, 1959.

Index

Lightning Source UK Ltd.
Milton Keynes UK
26 November 2010

163453UK00002B/25/P